The New Official LSAT
TriplePrep
Volume 8™

T0282931

A Publication of the Law School Admission Council,
Newtown, PA

From the Editor

Although these PrepTests are presented to you in paper form, the LSAT® is now delivered electronically. Please visit LSAC.org for the most up-to-date information about these tests.

ISBN-13: 979-8-9902338-0-5

Print number
5 4 3 2 1

Table of Contents

Introduction to the LSAT

The Law School Admission Test (LSAT) is designed to measure skills considered essential for success in law school: the reading and comprehension of complex texts with accuracy and insight; the ability to think critically; and the analysis and evaluation of the reasoning and arguments of others.

The LSAT provides a standard measure of acquired reading and verbal reasoning skills that law schools can use as one of several factors in assessing applicants.

For up-to-date information about LSAC's services, go to our website, LSAC.org.

Scoring

Your LSAT score is based on the number of questions you answered correctly. This is called your "raw score." All test questions are weighted exactly the same. The total number of questions you get right, not which particular questions you get right or wrong, is what matters for your score. There is no deduction for incorrect answers.

To make it easier to compare scores earned across different LSAT administrations, your raw score is converted to an LSAT scale. The LSAT scale ranges from 120 to 180, with 120 being the lowest possible score and 180 being the highest possible score.

The LSAT Multiple-Choice Question Types

The multiple-choice questions on the LSAT reflect a broad range of academic disciplines and are intended to give no advantage to candidates from a particular academic background.

The following material presents a general discussion of the nature of each question type and some strategies that can be used in answering them.

Logical Reasoning Questions

Arguments are a fundamental part of the law, and analyzing arguments is a key element of legal analysis. Training in the law builds on a foundation of basic reasoning skills. Law students must draw on the skills of analyzing, evaluating, constructing, and refuting arguments. They need to be able to identify what information is relevant to an issue or argument and what impact further evidence might have. They need to be able to reconcile opposing positions and use arguments to persuade others.

Logical Reasoning questions evaluate the ability to analyze, critically evaluate, and complete arguments as they occur in ordinary language. The questions are based on short arguments drawn from a wide variety of sources, including newspapers, general interest magazines, scholarly publications, advertisements, and informal discourse. These arguments mirror legal reasoning in the types of arguments presented and in their complexity, though few of the arguments actually have law as a subject matter.

Each Logical Reasoning question requires you to read and comprehend a short passage, then answer one question (or, rarely, two questions) about it. The questions are designed to assess a wide range of skills involved in thinking critically, with an emphasis on skills that are central to legal reasoning.

These skills include:

- Recognizing the parts of an argument and their relationships

- Recognizing similarities and differences between patterns of reasoning

- Drawing well-supported conclusions

- Reasoning by analogy

- Recognizing misunderstandings or points of disagreement

- Determining how additional evidence affects an argument

- Detecting assumptions made by particular arguments

- Identifying and applying principles or rules

- Identifying flaws in arguments

- Identifying explanations

The questions do not presuppose specialized knowledge of logical terminology. For example, you will not be expected to know the meaning of specialized terms such as "ad hominem" or "syllogism." On the other hand, you will be expected to understand and critique the reasoning contained in arguments. This requires that you possess a university-level understanding of widely used concepts such as argument, premise, assumption, and conclusion.

Suggested Approach

Read each question carefully. Make sure that you understand the meaning of each part of the question. Make sure that you understand the meaning of each answer choice and the ways in which it may or may not relate to the question posed.

Do not pick a response simply because it is a true statement. Although true, it may not answer the question posed.

Answer each question on the basis of the information that is given, even if you do not agree with it. Work within the context provided by the passage. LSAT questions do not involve any tricks or hidden meanings.

Reading Comprehension Questions

Both law school and the practice of law revolve around extensive reading of highly varied, dense, argumentative, and expository texts (for example, cases, codes, contracts, briefs, decisions, evidence). This reading must be exacting, distinguishing precisely what is said from what is not said. It involves comparison, analysis, synthesis, and application (for example, of principles and rules). It involves drawing appropriate inferences and applying ideas and arguments to new contexts. Law school reading also requires the ability to grasp unfamiliar subject matter and the ability to penetrate difficult and challenging material.

The purpose of LSAT Reading Comprehension questions is to measure the ability to read, with understanding and insight, examples of lengthy and complex materials similar to those commonly encountered in law school. The Reading Comprehension section of the LSAT contains four sets of reading questions, each set consisting of a selection of reading material followed by five to eight questions. The reading selection in three of the four sets consists of a single reading passage; the other set contains two related shorter passages. Sets with two passages are a variant of Reading Comprehension called Comparative Reading, which was introduced in June 2007.

Comparative Reading questions concern the relationships between the two passages, such as those of generalization/instance, principle/application, or point/counterpoint. Law school work often requires reading two or more texts in conjunction with each other and understanding their relationships. For example, a law student may read a trial court decision together with an appellate court decision that overturns it, or identify the fact pattern from a hypothetical suit together with the potentially controlling case law.

Reading selections for LSAT Reading Comprehension questions are drawn from a wide range of subjects in the humanities, the social sciences, the biological and physical sciences, and areas related to the law. Generally, the selections are densely written, use high-level vocabulary, and contain sophisticated argument or complex rhetorical structure (for example, multiple points of view). Reading Comprehension questions require you to read carefully and accurately, to determine the relationships among the various parts of the reading selection, and to draw reasonable inferences from the material in the selection. The questions may ask about the following characteristics of a passage or pair of passages:

- The main idea or primary purpose

- Information that is explicitly stated

- Information or ideas that can be inferred

- The meaning or purpose of words or phrases as used in context

- The organization or structure

- The application of information in the selection to a new context

- Principles that function in the selection

- Analogies to claims or arguments in the selection

- An author's attitude as revealed in the tone of a passage or the language used

- The impact of new information on claims or arguments in the selection

Suggested Approach

Since reading selections are drawn from many different disciplines and sources, you should not be discouraged if you encounter material with which you are not familiar. It is important to remember that questions are to be answered exclusively on the basis of the information provided in the selection. There is no particular knowledge that you are expected to bring to the test, and you should not make inferences based on any prior knowledge of a subject that you may have. You may, however, wish to defer working on a set of questions that seems particularly difficult or unfamiliar until after you have dealt with sets you find easier.

Strategies. One question that often arises in connection with Reading Comprehension has to do with the most effective and efficient order in which to read the selections and questions. Possible approaches include:

- reading the selection very closely and then answering the questions;

- reading the questions first, reading the selection closely, and then returning to the questions; or

- skimming the selection and questions very quickly, then rereading the selection closely and answering the questions.

Test takers are different, and the best strategy for one might not be the best strategy for another. In preparing for the test, therefore, you might want to experiment with the different strategies and decide what works most effectively for you. Remember that your strategy must be effective under timed conditions. For this reason, the first strategy—reading the selection very closely and then answering the questions—may be the most effective for you. Nonetheless, if you believe that one of the other strategies might be more effective for you, you should try it out and assess your performance using it.

Reading the selection. Whatever strategy you choose, you should give the passage or pair of passages at least one careful reading before answering the questions. Try to distinguish main ideas from supporting ideas, and opinions or attitudes from factual, objective information. Note transitions from one idea to the next and identify the relationships among the different ideas or parts of a passage, or between the two passages in Comparative Reading sets. Consider how and why an author makes points and draws conclusions. Be sensitive to implications of what the passages say.

You may find it helpful to mark key parts of passages. For example, you might underline main ideas or important arguments, and you might circle transitional words—"although," "nevertheless," "correspondingly," and the like—that will help you map the structure of a passage. Also, you might note descriptive words that will help you identify an author's attitude toward a particular idea or person.

Answering the Questions

- Always read all the answer choices before selecting the best answer. The best answer choice is the one that most accurately and completely answers the question being posed.

- Respond to the specific question being asked. Do not pick an answer choice simply because it is a true statement. For example, picking a true statement might yield an incorrect answer to a question in which you are asked to identify an author's position on an issue, since you are not being asked to evaluate the truth of the author's position but only to correctly identify what that position is.

- Answer the questions only on the basis of the information provided in the selection. Your own views, interpretations, or opinions, and those you have heard from others, may sometimes conflict with those expressed in a reading selection; however, you are expected to work within the context provided by the reading selection. You should not expect to agree with everything you encounter in Reading Comprehension passages.

Taking the PrepTests Under Simulated LSAT Conditions

One important way to prepare for the LSAT is to simulate the day of the test by taking a practice test under actual time constraints. Taking a practice test under timed conditions helps you to estimate the amount of time you can afford to spend on each question in a section and to determine the question types on which you may need additional practice.

Since the LSAT is a timed test, it is important to use your allotted time wisely. During the test, you may work only on the section designated by the test supervisor. You cannot devote extra time to a difficult section and make up that time on a section you find easier. In pacing yourself, and checking your answers, you should think of each section of the test as a separate minitest.

Be sure that you answer every question on the test. When you do not know the correct answer to a question, first eliminate the responses that you know are incorrect, then make your best guess among the remaining choices. Do not be afraid to guess as there is no penalty for incorrect answers.

When you take a practice test, abide by all the requirements specified in the directions and keep strictly within the specified time limits. Work without a rest period. When you take an actual test, you will have a short break between two of the sections.

When taken under conditions as much like actual testing conditions as possible, a practice test provides very useful preparation for taking the LSAT.

Official directions for the four multiple-choice sections are included in these PrepTests so that you can approximate actual testing conditions as you practice.

To take the test:

- Set a timer for 35 minutes. Answer all the questions in Section I. Stop working on that section when the 35 minutes have elapsed.

- Repeat, allowing yourself 35 minutes each for Sections II, III, and IV.

- Refer to the "Computing Your Score" section at the end of each PrepTest for instruction on evaluating your performance. An answer key is provided for that purpose.

PrepTest 137

SECTION I
Time—35 minutes
27 Questions

Directions: Each set of questions in this section is based on a single passage or a pair of passages. The questions are to be answered on the basis of what is **stated** or **implied** in the passage or pair of passages. For some questions, more than one of the choices could conceivably answer the question. However, you are to choose the **best** answer; that is, choose the response that most accurately and completely answers the question and mark that response on your answer sheet.

Until my present study, African American entertainer Lorenzo Tucker had not been extensively discussed in histories of United States theater and film. Yet during a span of 60 years, from 1926 to 1986, he acted in 20 films and performed hundreds of times on stage as a dancer, vaudeville straight man, singer, actor, and master of ceremonies. Behind the scenes he worked as a producer, company manager, publicity person, lighting designer, photographer, and actors' union administrator. In addition, Tucker was a firsthand witness to the history of African American theater and film from the late 1920s until his death in 1986. During his later years, he amassed a large collection of African American theater and film memorabilia, and these artifacts, along with his personal memories, help shed new light on a part of U.S. entertainment history about which, so far, there has been insufficient scholarship.

I gathered much of the background material for my study of Tucker's life through research in special collections of the New York and Los Angeles public libraries, including microfilmed correspondence, photographs, programs, and newspapers. Also examined—as primary source material for an analysis of Tucker's acting technique—were the ten still available films in which Tucker appeared. Additional information was acquired through interviews with some of Tucker's contemporaries and fellow performers. The primary source of information for this study, however, was a group of personal, in-depth interviews I conducted with Tucker himself in 1985 and 1986.

There are both advantages and disadvantages in undertaking a biographical study of a living person. The greatest advantage is that the contemporary biographer has access to that person's oral testimony. Yet this testimony must be approached with caution, since each person recounting his or her version of events for the historical record has a vested interest in the project, and no matter how fair-minded and objective one intends to be, the fact is that people often remember the events they want to remember in the version they prefer. It is the duty of the biographer, therefore, to verify as much of the oral narrative as possible.

Information from Tucker has undergone careful scrutiny and has been placed up against the known facts for verification, and for the most part, information that could not be verified was not included in this study. But Tucker's recollections of his personal life could not always be independently verified, of course, since most of the daily events in the life of any individual go unrecorded. So only those elements of Tucker's personal life that had a bearing on his career have been recorded here. At the same time, however, it is important to note that the majority of these recollections tend to corroborate, while illuminating and providing a valuable perspective on, other relevant historical evidence that is available. This study, therefore, will weave together oral and other evidence to create the career biography of Lorenzo Tucker.

1. Which one of the following most accurately summarizes the passage?

    (A) The career biography of Tucker constitutes an important addition to the history of U.S. theater and film mainly because of the innovative methods used in researching this subject, which correct previous misinterpretations of an aspect of U.S. film and theater history.

    (B) Evidence from a variety of sources, including information from Tucker's own oral accounts, has been scrutinized and combined to create a career biography of Tucker that fills certain gaps in the historical record of U.S. theater and film.

    (C) Tucker's interest in preserving a record of the development of African American film and theater and his initiative in making that record public have led to the filling of a gap in the published histories of performing arts.

    (D) The research methods used in creating the biography of Tucker exemplify some of the problems inherent in the quest for objectivity in recording the history of recent or contemporary events and persons.

    (E) Previous theater and film historians have been mistaken in paying too little attention to the extensive nonperforming contributions that Tucker made to the development of African American film and theater.

GO ON TO THE NEXT PAGE.

2. The author's main purpose in mentioning Tucker's collection of memorabilia (final sentence of the first paragraph) is to

(A) indicate a source from which the author drew information about Tucker's life and times

(B) provide a counterexample to a general claim about typical scholarly approaches to gathering historical data

(C) justify reliance on Tucker's personal memories

(D) give evidence of the range and diversity of Tucker's nonprofessional interests and accomplishments

(E) indicate the nature of the data that are typically available to scholars who chronicle the lives of entertainers

3. Suppose that a well-known nuclear physicist has written and published a book consisting of that physicist's own recollections of the events surrounding some important scientific discoveries. It can be inferred that the author of the passage would be most likely to view the physicist's book as

(A) being at considerable risk of misrepresenting some historical facts

(B) a source of information that merely duplicates what is available in the public record

(C) a type of source that is rarely used for scholarly history writing

(D) a type of source that is appropriate for biographies of entertainers but generally not for histories of scientific discovery

(E) an authoritative account that does not require objective verification

4. The passage most strongly supports the inference that the author would agree with which one of the following statements about the text that this passage introduces?

(A) Its subject matter and methodology make it appropriate for publication by a publisher of popular books but not for publication by an academic press.

(B) It should be valuable to scholars not only because of the research-based information it contains, but also because of the innovative research methods developed and implemented by the author.

(C) It should be interesting not only because of its account of Tucker's career, but also because of the significant information it provides regarding U.S. entertainment history.

(D) It should not be taken mainly as an attempt to report an objectively accurate historical record of events in Tucker's career.

(E) It should be accepted as a useful and reliable methodological guide for use in verifying the authenticity of U.S. entertainment memorabilia.

5. The author of the passage is primarily concerned with

(A) criticizing and correcting certain political and intellectual traditions with regard to history

(B) proposing an alternative method of historical investigation

(C) summarizing the main points, and assessing the value, of the historical study that will follow this introduction to a text

(D) reexamining a previously held historical point of view, identifying its weaknesses, and outlining the correction that will follow this introduction to a text

(E) explaining the author's choice of subject matter and methods used in researching a particular subject

6. Which one of the following does the author mention as a source that was used in gathering information for the text that this passage introduces?

(A) critics' reviews of productions in which Tucker performed

(B) memorabilia concerning Tucker collected by some of his fellow performers

(C) scripts of some of the plays and films that Tucker produced

(D) interviews with people who performed with Tucker

(E) union records of Tucker's activities as a performers' advocate

7. Information in the passage most strongly supports which one of the following inferences regarding the text that this passage introduces?

(A) It assesses well-known African American films in ways that have little in common with the assessments of previous critics and historians.

(B) It was written by a person who participated with Tucker in at least some of the theatrical ventures that Tucker undertook.

(C) It was written by a person who does not expect to be recognized as a mainstream participant in scholarship concerning U.S. film and theater history.

(D) Its analysis of Tucker's acting technique is not based on a close examination of a preponderance of the films in which Tucker performed.

(E) Its rhetorical structure is not closely analogous to the structures of a majority of previous scholarly biographies of African American performers.

GO ON TO THE NEXT PAGE.

Taking the explication of experience as its object as well as its method, Marjorie Shostak's *Nisa: The Life and Words of a !Kung Woman* weaves together three narrative strands, and in doing so challenges the ethnographer's penchant for the general and the anonymous. The first strand, the autobiographical details of a 50-year-old woman's life among the seminomadic !Kung hunter-gatherers of Botswana, adds to the ethnographical literature on the !Kung. The second presents Nisa's story as a metaphor for woman's experience, a story that reflects many of the experiences and dilemmas addressed in recent feminist writing. The third tells the story of an intercultural encounter in which the distinction between ethnographer and subject becomes blurred.

Nisa explains Nisa's personality in terms of !Kung ways and, for the general reader, corrects and qualifies a number of received attitudes about "simple" societies. Michel Leiris' warning that "We are all too inclined to consider a people happy if considering them makes us happy" applies particularly to the !Kung, whose seemingly uncomplicated way of life, enlightened attitudes toward child rearing, and undeniable charm make them prime candidates for Western appreciation. But Nisa's answer to Shostak's question, "What is it to be a !Kung woman?" makes us feel the force of ugly facts we might otherwise skim over. Only 54 percent of !Kung children live to marry; Nisa loses all four of her children and a cherished husband. Nisa's memories of sibling rivalries, of her terrible rages when denied her mother, of nasty fights over food undermine the idyllic vision Westerners cherish of childhoods lived in such "simple" circumstances.

Woven into Nisa's autobiography are allusions to Shostak's personal engagement with issues of gender. Nisa's response to "What is it to be a !Kung woman?" also seems to answer another question, "What is it to be a woman?" In fact, Nisa's answers illuminate not just one woman's experience, but women's experience in general. It is a salutary shock to realize how much ethnographic literature omits the perspective of women about women.

Nisa's story is interwoven with Shostak's presentation of their encounter; at times each seems to exist primarily in response to the other. Nisa's autobiography is a distinct narrative in a particular voice, but it is manifestly the product of a collaboration. Indeed, by casting *Nisa* in the shape of a "life," Shostak employs a potent Western literary convention. Real lives, in fact, do not easily arrange themselves as stories that have recognizable shapes: Nisa, for example, often says "We lived in that place, eating things. Then we left and went somewhere else." It is in the process of the dialogue between Nisa and Shostak that a shaped story emerges from this seemingly featureless background.

8. Shostak's approach to ethnography differs from the approach of most ethnographers in which one of the following ways?

(A) She observes the culture of one group in order to infer the cultural characteristics of other, similar groups.

(B) She studies the life experiences of individuals apart from the cultural practices of a group.

(C) She contrasts individuals' personal histories with information about the individuals' culture.

(D) She exemplifies her general hypotheses about a culture by accumulating illustrative empirical data.

(E) She emphasizes the importance of the personal and the individual.

9. Which one of the following best expresses the author's opinion of the way most ethnographic literature deals with women's views of women?

(A) It is admirable that many ethnographic studies avoid the narrow focus of some recent feminist thought as it deals with women's views of women.

(B) It is encouraging that most women ethnographers have begun to study and report the views of women in the groups they study.

(C) It is unfortunate that most ethnographic literature does not deal with women's views of women at all.

(D) It is surprising that more ethnographic studies of women do not use the information available through individual interviews of women about women.

(E) It is disappointing that most ethnographic studies of women's views about women fail to connect individual experiences with larger women's issues.

GO ON TO THE NEXT PAGE.

10. It can be inferred that which one of the following best exemplifies the "received attitudes" mentioned in the first sentence of the second paragraph?

(A) The !Kung are people of undeniable charm.
(B) Considering the !Kung makes Western observers happy.
(C) People who live seminomadic lives have few serious problems.
(D) A large percentage of !Kung children die before reaching adulthood.
(E) The experience of seminomadic women is much like that of other women.

11. Which one of the following would most clearly support the author's contention that Nisa's experience as a !Kung woman illuminates women's experience in general?

(A) A systematic survey of a representative sample of Western women indicates that these women sympathize with Nisa's tragedies.
(B) The use of the explication of experience as both a subject and a method becomes an extremely fruitful technique for ethnographers studying issues facing both men and women in non-Western cultures.
(C) Critics of feminist writers applaud the use of Shostak's dialogue technique in the study of women's issues.
(D) Another ethnographer explores the experiences of individual women in a culture quite different from that of the !Kung and finds many issues that are common to both cultures.
(E) Ethnographers studying the !Kung interview !Kung women other than Nisa and find that most of them report experiences similar to those of Nisa.

12. It can be inferred that the "potent Western literary convention" mentioned in the middle of the final paragraph is most probably which one of the following?

(A) personal revelation
(B) dramatic emphasis
(C) expository comparison
(D) poetic metaphor
(E) novelistic storytelling

13. The approach of which one of the following is most similar to Shostak's approach as her approach is described in the passage?

(A) The producer of a documentary film interacts on film with the film's subject to reveal insights about the subject's life.
(B) A work presented as an athlete's autobiography is actually ghostwritten by a famous biographer.
(C) An ethnographer describes the day-to-day life of an individual in order to exemplify the way of life of a group of desert dwellers.
(D) A writer illustrates her views of women's experience by recounting stories from her own childhood.
(E) The developer of a series of textbooks uses anecdotes based on the experiences of people of many cultures to highlight important points in the text.

14. It can be inferred that the author of the passage believes that the quotation near the end of the final paragraph best exemplifies which one of the following?

(A) the cultural values of seminomadic peoples such as the !Kung
(B) the amorphous nature of the accounts people give of their lives
(C) the less-than-idyllic nature of the lives of nomadic people
(D) an autobiographical account that has a recognizable story
(E) a distinction between ethnographer and subject

GO ON TO THE NEXT PAGE.

Passage A

Until recently, conservationists were often complacent about the effect of nonindigenous plant and animal species on the ecosystems they invade. Many shared Charles Elton's view, introduced in his 1958 book on invasive species, that disturbed habitats are most vulnerable to new arrivals because they contain fewer or less vigorous native species. Now, however, ecologists realize that when humans introduce new species into existing ecosystems, even pristine, species-rich habitats are threatened. The rapidly increasing conservation problems and high damage and control costs generated by these invasions merit serious concern.

Invasive plants profoundly affect ecosystems and threaten biodiversity throughout the world. For example, to the untrained eye, the Everglades National Park in Florida appears wild and natural. Yet this and other unique ecosystems are being degraded as surely as if by chemical pollution. In Florida, forests are growing where none existed before. Traditionally, saw grass dominated large regions of Florida's marshes, providing habitat for unique Everglades wildlife. Although saw grass grows over 9 feet tall, introduced Australian melaleuca trees, typically 70 feet tall, now outcompete marsh plants for sunlight. As melaleuca trees grow and form dense stands, their leaf litter increases soil elevations, inhibiting normal water flow. Wildlife associated with saw grass marshes declines. Similarly, in Australia, the introduction of Scotch broom plants led to the disappearance of a diverse set of native reptiles.

Passage B

The real threat posed by so-called invasive species isn't against nature but against humans' ideas of what nature is supposed to be. Species invasion is not a zero-sum game, with new species replacing old ones at a one-to-one ratio. Rather, and with critical exceptions, it is a positive-sum game, in which ecosystems can accept more and more species. Indeed, in both marine and terrestrial ecosystems, ecologists have found that invasions often increase biodiversity at the local level: if you add many new species and lose few or no native species, the overall species count goes up.

Invasions don't cause ecosystems to collapse. Invasions may radically alter the components of an ecosystem, perhaps to a point at which the ecosystem becomes less valuable or engaging to humans. But 50 years of study has failed to identify a clear ecological difference between an ecosystem rich in native species and one chock-full of introduced species. Unlike ecosystem destruction—clear cutting of forests, for example—invasions don't make ecosystems shrink or disappear. They simply transform them into different ecosystems.

When the issue is phrased as one of ecosystem destruction, the stakes are stark: we choose between nature's life and nature's death. In actuality, introduced species present a continuum. A few species do cause costly damage and tragic extinctions. But most plant

and animal species simply blend in harmlessly. The issue they present for humans is not whether we will be surrounded by nature but rather what kind of nature we will have around us.

15. Both passages are concerned with answering which one of the following questions?

(A) Why are some ecosystems more vulnerable to introduced species than others?

(B) What distinguishes introduced species that are harmful from those that are harmless?

(C) What approach should be taken to protect ecosystems from introduced species?

(D) How are ecosystems affected by the introduction of new species?

(E) How are species able to spread beyond their native ecosystems?

16. Passage A, but not passage B, asserts which one of the following regarding ecologists who study introduced species?

(A) Their research has been limited to studying the economic impact of introduced species.

(B) They are inconsistent in their use of criteria for determining what defines an ecosystem.

(C) Most agree that introduced species can cause extinctions.

(D) Before Elton, most of them were concerned only with preserving biodiversity at the local level.

(E) They do not share Elton's view that introduced species primarily threaten disturbed habitats.

GO ON TO THE NEXT PAGE.

17. The author of passage B would be most likely to agree with which one of the following statements about the term "natural" as it is used in passage A (second sentence of the second paragraph)?

(A) It correctly characterizes a difference between pristine and disturbed environments.

(B) It contradicts a concept of nature put forth elsewhere in passage A.

(C) It helps to clarify a difference between the "wild" and the "natural."

(D) It introduces an unconventional definition of nature.

(E) It conflates physical nature with an arbitrary ideal of nature.

18. Which one of the following is most analogous to the main point of passage B?

(A) The loss of a favorite piece of clothing when it starts to fray after many years is not necessarily a meaningful loss.

(B) The alteration of a culture's folk music by the influence of music from other cultures is not always lamentable.

(C) The expansion of urban development into previously rural areas is a necessary consequence of progress.

(D) Cultures can only benefit when they absorb and adapt ideas that originated in other cultures.

(E) While horticulturalists can create new plant species through hybridization, hybridization also occurs in the wild.

19. Which one of the following most accurately characterizes the relationship between the two passages?

(A) Passage A presents a hypothesis about the causes of a particular phenomenon, while passage B presents an alternative hypothesis about the causes of that phenomenon.

(B) Passage A questions a common assumption about a particular phenomenon, while passage B shows why that assumption is well-founded.

(C) Passage A presents evidence that a particular phenomenon is widely considered to be undesirable, while passage B presents evidence that the same phenomenon is usually considered to be beneficial.

(D) Passage A warns about the dangers of a particular phenomenon, while passage B argues that the phenomenon should not generally be considered dangerous.

(E) Passage A proposes a particular course of action, while passage B raises questions about the advisability of that approach.

GO ON TO THE NEXT PAGE.

Can a sovereign have unlimited legal power? If a sovereign does have unlimited legal power, then the sovereign presumably has the legal power to limit or even completely abdicate its own legal power. But doing so would mean that the sovereign no longer has unlimited legal power, thereby contradicting the initial supposition. This theoretical conundrum is traditionally known as the paradox of omnipotence.

Social scientists have recognized that sovereign omnipotence can be a source of considerable practical difficulty for sovereigns themselves. Douglass North and Barry Weingast show that English and French monarchies in the seventeenth and eighteenth centuries confronted a practical challenge created by the paradox of their own omnipotence.

North and Weingast point out that it is often in a sovereign's best interest to make a credible commitment not to perform certain acts. For example, a sovereign with absolute power can refuse to honor its financial commitments. Yet creditors will not voluntarily lend generous amounts at favorable terms to an absolute monarch who can renege upon debts at will.

In the struggle to expand their empires, the English and French monarchies required vast amounts of capital. At the outset of the seventeenth century, however, neither regime could credibly commit itself to repay debts or to honor property rights. The absence of limitations upon the legal power of monarchs meant that there was no law or commitment monarchs could make that they could not also unmake or disregard. Consequently, these monarchs earned a reputation for expropriating wealth, repudiating debts, and reneging upon commitments. Not surprisingly, creditors took such behavior into account and demanded higher interest rates from monarchs than from the monarchs' wealthy subjects.

North and Weingast argue that the constitutional settlement imposed in England by the Glorious Revolution of 1688 halted such faithless conduct. Henceforth, Parliament controlled the Crown's purse strings. Parliament, in turn, represented commercial interests that would not tolerate governmental disregard for property rights. The Crown's newfound inability to dishonor its commitments translated into a newfound ability to borrow: the Crown's borrowing increased and interest rates fell, because lenders concluded that the Crown would honor its debts.

Thanks to North, Weingast, and others writing in the same vein, it is now conventional to hold that constitutional arrangements benefit sovereigns by limiting their power. But such scholars neglect the extent to which constitutions can fail in this regard. For example, the constitutional settlement imposed by the Glorious Revolution did not solve the paradox of omnipotence but just relocated the problem from one branch of government to another: whereas it was once the Crown that lacked the power to bind itself, it is now Parliament that lacks this power. The doctrine of parliamentary sovereignty is a pillar of England's unwritten constitution, and it provides that Parliament lacks legal power over the extent of its own legal power.

20. Which one of the following most accurately expresses the main point of the passage?

(A) The paradox of omnipotence poses a practical problem for governments, which is not necessarily solved by constitutional arrangements.
(B) Abstract theoretical paradoxes often have practical analogues in the political sphere.
(C) The paradox of omnipotence ceased to be an acute practical problem for English monarchs after the Glorious Revolution.
(D) Contrary to what many social scientists believe, the Glorious Revolution did not solve the practical problem of sovereign omnipotence faced by English monarchs.
(E) The supposition that a sovereign has unlimited legal power leads to a logical contradiction.

21. The passage most strongly supports the claim that creditors in England and France in the years before 1688 held which one of the following views about wealthy subjects in those countries?

(A) They did not contribute their fair share to the cost of expanding the empires.
(B) They focused on short-term gains at the expense of their own credibility.
(C) They were trying to establish a government that would respect property rights.
(D) They clearly understood the paradox of sovereign omnipotence.
(E) They were more likely than their monarchs to honor financial commitments.

GO ON TO THE NEXT PAGE.

22. Based on the passage, which one of the following considerations would be most important for an English creditor after the Glorious Revolution who is deciding whether to lend money to the Crown at a relatively low interest rate?

(A) whether most members of Parliament are aware of the paradox of sovereign omnipotence
(B) whether Parliament can be depended on to adequately represent commercial interests
(C) when the most recent Parliamentary elections were held
(D) how many new laws Parliament has enacted in the past year
(E) whether the Crown's borrowing has increased in recent years

23. Which one of the following principles underlies the author's argument in the last paragraph of the passage?

(A) The adequacy of a solution to a political problem should be judged in terms of practical consequences rather than theoretical considerations.
(B) A genuine solution to a political problem must eliminate the problem's fundamental cause rather than just its effects.
(C) A problem inherent in a certain form of government can be solved only if that form of government is completely abandoned.
(D) In terms of practical consequences, it is preferable for unlimited legal power to rest with an elected body rather than an unelected monarch.
(E) A country's constitution should explicitly specify the powers of each branch of government.

24. According to the passage, which one of the following was a consequence of the absence of limitations on the legal power of English and French monarchs in the seventeenth and eighteenth centuries?

(A) It was difficult for those monarchs to finance the expansion of their empires.
(B) Those monarchs enacted new laws to specify the obligations of creditors.
(C) It became increasingly easy for wealthy subjects in England and France to borrow money.
(D) Those monarchs borrowed more money than they would have if their power had been restricted.
(E) Those monarchs were forced to demonstrate a willingness to respect property rights.

25. The author mentions the English and French monarchies' need for capital (first sentence of the fourth paragraph) primarily in order to

(A) cast doubt on the claim that it is in a sovereign's interest to make a commitment not to perform certain acts
(B) illustrate the low opinion that creditors had of monarchs
(C) emphasize the unlimited nature of the legal power of monarchs
(D) help explain why the paradox of omnipotence was an acute practical problem for those monarchies
(E) reinforce the claim that sovereigns have historically broken their commitments for short-term gain

26. Suppose the Parliament in England makes a commitment to become a permanent member of a multinational body. It can be inferred from the passage that

(A) the commitment will undermine Parliament's ability to obtain credit on favorable terms
(B) lenders will become more confident that Parliament will honor its debts
(C) Parliament has the legal authority to end the commitment at any time
(D) the commercial interests represented by Parliament will disapprove of the commitment
(E) the commitment will increase Parliament's legal power

27. Which one of the following claims would be accepted by North and Weingast but not by the author of the passage?

(A) After 1688, commercial interests in England trusted Parliament to protect their property rights.
(B) The paradox of omnipotence is no longer a practical problem for any actual government.
(C) In England, the Crown was able to borrow money at lower interest rates after the Glorious Revolution than before.
(D) In the seventeenth century, English and French monarchs had a reputation for failing to uphold financial commitments.
(E) The constitutional settlement imposed by the Glorious Revolution solved the problem of sovereign omnipotence.

S T O P

IF YOU FINISH BEFORE TIME IS CALLED, YOU MAY CHECK YOUR WORK ON THIS SECTION ONLY.
DO NOT WORK ON ANY OTHER SECTION IN THE TEST.

SECTION II
Time—35 minutes

25 Questions

Directions: Each question in this section is based on the reasoning presented in a brief passage. In answering the questions, you should not make assumptions that are by commonsense standards implausible, superfluous, or incompatible with the passage. For some questions, more than one of the choices could conceivably answer the question. However, you are to choose the **best** answer; that is, choose the response that most accurately and completely answers the question and mark that response on your answer sheet.

1. Planting peach trees on their farm makes more sense for the Johnsons than planting apricot trees. Although fresh, locally grown apricots are very popular in this area, the same is true of peaches. However, individual peach trees cost much less to purchase and plant than do apricot trees, and peach trees also begin bearing fruit at a much younger age.

   Which one of the following, if true, would most seriously weaken the argument?

   (A) Fresh, locally grown apricots sell at a much higher price than do fresh, locally grown peaches.
   (B) Apricot trees tend to stop being productive at a younger age than do peach trees.
   (C) It costs as much to water and fertilize peach trees as it does to water and fertilize apricot trees.
   (D) The market for fresh, locally grown apricots has grown in recent years as awareness of the health benefits of eating fresh fruit has increased.
   (E) Peach production has decreased dramatically over the last several years.

2. For years, a rare variety of camel was endangered because much of its habitat was used as a weapons testing range. After the testing range closed, however, the population of these camels began falling even more quickly.

   Which one of the following, if true, most helps to explain the increased rate of population loss?

   (A) The weapons tests had kept wildlife poachers out of the testing range.
   (B) Weapons testing in the range did more harm to the camels in the first years of the testing than in later years.
   (C) Because of unexploded bombs, the land within the testing range was still somewhat dangerous after the range closed down.
   (D) The camels had to overcome two different outbreaks of disease during the time the testing range was in operation.
   (E) The weapons tests were most harmful to the camels in years when food was scarce.

3. A person reading a new book for pleasure is like a tourist traveling to a new place. The reader reads, just as the tourist travels, to enlarge understanding rather than simply to acquire information. Thus, it is better to read fewer books and spend more time on each rather than to quickly read as many as one can, just as it is better to travel to fewer places and spend more time in each rather than to spend a small amount of time in many different places.

   Which one of the following, if true, most strengthens the argument?

   (A) Tourists typically learn something about the places they visit even when they are there only to relax.
   (B) Tourists gain much more understanding of a place once they have spent several days at that place than they do in their first few days there.
   (C) Many people report that they can learn far more about a place by visiting it than they can by reading about it.
   (D) Tourists who have read about a place beforehand tend to stay longer in that place.
   (E) Some tourists are unconcerned about gaining information about a place other than what is necessary for their immediate enjoyment.

GO ON TO THE NEXT PAGE.

4. One way to furnish a living room is with modular furniture. Instead of buying a standard sofa, for example, one can buy a left end, a right end, and a middle piece that can be combined to create an L-shaped sofa. Modular furniture, however, is far more expensive than standard furniture. On average, a three-piece modular sofa costs almost twice as much as a standard sofa of comparable size and quality.

Each of the following, if true, helps to account for the greater cost of modular furniture **except**:

(A) Modular furniture, unlike standard furniture, is not mass-produced.

(B) The consumer demand for sofas sometimes increases more quickly than the supply.

(C) The most fashionable designers tend to use modular furniture designs.

(D) Because modular furniture pieces are custom ordered, they are never put on sale.

(E) Modular sofas, on average, have a greater area of upholstered surfaces than do standard sofas.

5. The hormone testosterone protects brain cells from injury and reduces levels of the protein beta-amyloid in the brain. Beta-amyloid causally contributes to Alzheimer's disease, and people whose brain cells are susceptible to injury are probably more susceptible to Alzheimer's disease. So there is reason to think that _____.

Which one of the following most logically completes the argument?

(A) anyone whose brain cells are susceptible to injury will eventually develop Alzheimer's disease

(B) whether a person develops Alzheimer's disease is dependent entirely on the level of beta-amyloid in his or her brain

(C) Alzheimer's disease leads to a reduction in testosterone level

(D) only people with Alzheimer's disease are at risk for injury to brain cells

(E) a decline in testosterone level puts one at increased risk for Alzheimer's disease

6. The profitability of a business is reduced by anything that undermines employee morale. This is why paying senior staff with stock options, which allows them to earn more when the enterprise prospers, is not a wise policy because it increases dramatically the difference in income between senior staff and employees who are paid only a fixed salary.

Which one of the following is an assumption on which the argument depends?

(A) Large income differences between fixed-salary employees and senior staff tend to undermine employee morale.

(B) Reductions in the profitability of a company are usually due to low employee morale.

(C) Business firms that pay senior staff with stock options are less profitable than other firms.

(D) Reducing the difference in income between senior staff and employees paid only a fixed salary invariably increases a company's profitability.

(E) Employees whose incomes rise as the profits of their employers rise are more productive than those paid only a fixed salary.

7. Antibiotics are standard ingredients in animal feed because they keep animals healthy and increase meat yields. However, scientists have recommended phasing out this practice, believing it may make antibiotics less effective in humans. If meat yields are reduced, however, some farmers will go out of business.

Which one of the following is most strongly supported by the information above?

(A) If scientists are correct that antibiotic use in animal feed makes antibiotics less effective in humans, then some farmers will go out of business.

(B) If antibiotic use in animal feed is not phased out, some antibiotics will become ineffective in humans.

(C) If the scientists' recommendation is not heeded, no farmers will go out of business due to reduced meat yields.

(D) If the health of their animals declines, most farmers will not be able to stay in business.

(E) If antibiotic use in animal feed is phased out, some farmers will go out of business unless they use other means of increasing meat yields.

GO ON TO THE NEXT PAGE.

8. Guideline: It is improper for public officials to influence the award of contracts or to perform other acts related to their office in a way that benefits themselves. Even the appearance of such impropriety should be avoided.

   Application: Greenville's mayor acted improperly in urging the award of the city's street maintenance contract to a company owned and operated by one of the mayor's relatives, whose business would have been in serious financial trouble had it not been awarded the contract.

   Which one of the following principles most helps in justifying the application of the guideline?

   (A) Public officials, when fulfilling their duties, should be held to higher standards than private individuals.
   (B) Publicly funded contracts should be awarded based primarily on cost and the reliability of the contractor.
   (C) Creating the appearance of impropriety is as blameworthy as acting improperly.
   (D) Awarding a contract to a financially troubled business should be regarded as taking excessive risk.
   (E) Benefiting one's family or friends should be regarded as benefiting oneself.

9. To use the pool at City Gym, one must have a membership there. Sarah has a membership at City Gym. She must therefore use the pool there at least occasionally.

   The reasoning in the argument is flawed in that the argument

   (A) mistakes a policy that is strictly enforced for a policy to which exceptions are made
   (B) treats a statement whose truth is required for the conclusion to be true as though it were a statement whose truth ensures that the conclusion is true
   (C) presumes that one or the other of two alternatives must be the case without establishing that no other alternative is possible
   (D) concludes that a person has a certain attribute simply because that person belongs to a group most of whose members have that attribute
   (E) draws a conclusion that merely restates a claim presented in support of that conclusion

10. Annie: Our university libraries have been sadly neglected. Few new books have been purchased during the last decade, and most of the older books are damaged. The university's administrators should admit that their library policies have been in error and should remedy this situation in the fastest way possible, which is to charge students a library fee and use the funds for library improvements.

    Matilda: The current poor condition of the university libraries is the fault of the library officials, not the students. Students should not have to pay for the mistakes of careless library administrators.

    Annie and Matilda disagree about whether

    (A) library administrators are to blame for the poor condition of the university libraries
    (B) library improvements could be most quickly effected through charging students additional fees
    (C) students will ultimately benefit from the library improvements that could be funded by additional student fees
    (D) those not responsible for the current condition of the libraries should bear the cost for remedying it
    (E) funds for library improvements could be raised without additional student fees

11. Scientists examined diamonds that were formed on Earth about 2.9 billion years ago. These diamonds had a higher-than-normal concentration of sulfur-33. This concentration can be explained only by certain chemical reactions that are stimulated by ultraviolet light. If there had been more than a trace of oxygen in Earth's atmosphere 2.9 billion years ago, then not enough ultraviolet light would have reached Earth's surface to stimulate the chemical reactions.

    The information above most strongly supports which one of the following?

    (A) Most diamonds with higher-than-normal concentrations of sulfur-33 were formed at least 2.9 billion years ago.
    (B) Ultraviolet light causes the oxygen in Earth's atmosphere to react chemically with sulfur-33.
    (C) Earth's atmosphere contained very little, if any, oxygen 2.9 billion years ago.
    (D) Sulfur-33 is rarely found in diamonds that were formed more recently than 2.9 billion years ago.
    (E) The formation of diamonds occurs only in the presence of ultraviolet light.

GO ON TO THE NEXT PAGE.

12. When a patient failed to respond to prescribed medication, the doctor hypothesized that the dosage was insufficient. The doctor first advised doubling the dosage, but the patient's symptoms remained. It was then learned that the patient regularly drank an herbal beverage that often inhibits the medication's effect. The doctor then advised the patient to resume the initial dosage and stop drinking the beverage. The patient complied, but still showed no change. Finally, the doctor advised the patient to double the dosage and not drink the beverage. The patient's symptoms disappeared. Hence, the doctor's initial hypothesis was correct.

Which one of the following most accurately describes the manner in which the doctor's second set of recommendations and the results of its application support the doctor's initial hypothesis?

(A)   They establish that the doctor's concerns about the healthfulness of the beverage were well founded.
(B)   They make it less plausible that the beverage actually contributed to the ineffectiveness of the prescribed medication.
(C)   They give evidence that the beverage was responsible for the ineffectiveness of the prescribed medication.
(D)   They suggest that the beverage was not the only cause of the ineffectiveness of the prescribed dosage.
(E)   They rule out the possibility that the doctor had initially prescribed the wrong medication for the patient's ailments.

13. Although most builders do not consider the experimental building material papercrete to be a promising material for large-scale construction, those who regularly work with it, primarily on small-scale projects, think otherwise. Since those who regularly use papercrete are familiar with the properties of the material, it is likely that papercrete is indeed promising for large-scale construction.

The argument is most vulnerable to criticism on the grounds that it

(A)   confuses what is promising for small-scale construction with what is promising for large-scale construction
(B)   presumes that what the majority of builders thinks is promising must in fact be promising
(C)   equivocates between two different meanings of the term "promising"
(D)   does not consider the views of the builders who have the most experience working with the material
(E)   fails to consider that most builders might not regularly use papercrete precisely because they are familiar with its properties

14. Drama critic: There were many interesting plays written last year. Surely some will gain widespread popularity for at least a few years, and some will even receive high critical acclaim, but none will be popular several centuries from now. The only plays that continue to be performed regularly over many decades and centuries are those that skillfully explore human nature, and none of the plays written last year examine human nature in a particularly skillful way.

The argument relies on assuming which one of the following?

(A)   No play will be popular several centuries from now unless it continues to be performed regularly during the intervening time.
(B)   For a play to deserve high critical acclaim it must be popular for more than just a few years.
(C)   There were no plays written last year that the drama critic has neither read nor seen performed.
(D)   If a play does not skillfully explore human nature, it will not receive critical acclaim.
(E)   Any play that skillfully examines human nature will be performed regularly over the centuries.

GO ON TO THE NEXT PAGE.

15. Doctor: It is wrong for medical researchers to keep their research confidential, even if the companies for which they work would rather that they do so. If research results are not shared, the development of effective medical treatments may be delayed, and thus humans may suffer unnecessarily.

Which one of the following principles, if valid, most helps to justify the doctor's argument?

(A) Medical researchers should never engage in any behavior that they know will cause humans to suffer.

(B) If the most important moral principle is to prevent human suffering, then it is wrong for medical researchers to keep their research confidential.

(C) Medical researchers should not keep information confidential if it is possible that sharing that information would prevent some unnecessary human suffering.

(D) Medical researchers should always attempt to develop effective medical treatments as rapidly as they can while fulfilling their other moral obligations.

(E) It is wrong for any company to ask its medical researchers to keep their research confidential, if failure to share the research might delay development of effective medical treatments.

16. Marife: That was a bad movie because, by not providing viewers with all the information necessary for solving the murder, it violated a requirement of murder mysteries.

Nguyen: But the filmmaker wanted viewers to focus on the complex relationship between the chief detective and her assistant. The murder just provided the context in which the relationship developed, and should not be taken as a defining characteristic of the film.

Marife's and Nguyen's comments indicate that they disagree about

(A) whether the movie was a bad one
(B) whether the relationship between the chief detective and her assistant was an important part of the movie
(C) whether the movie should be classified as a murder mystery
(D) the appropriateness of trying to find criteria that all mystery movies must meet
(E) whether the filmmaker wanted viewers to be able to solve the murder

17. Educator: Some experimental educational programs, based on the principle that children's first education should take place at home, instruct parents in how to be their child's "first teacher." The school performance of the children in these programs is better than average. This shows that these programs are successful and should be expanded.

Which one of the following, if true, most weakens the educator's argument?

(A) Not all small children enjoy being taught by their parents.

(B) Most of the parents participating in the programs have prior experience as educators.

(C) Surveys show that most parents would approve expanding the programs.

(D) The cost of expanding the programs has not been precisely determined.

(E) Some children who did not participate in the programs performed exceptionally well in school.

GO ON TO THE NEXT PAGE.

18. Censor: All anarchist novels have two objectionable characteristics: a subversive outlook and the depiction of wholesale violence. Therefore, it is permissible to ban any anarchist novel that would do more harm than good to society.

Which one of the following principles, if valid, most helps to justify the censor's reasoning?

(A)   If a novel has a subversive outlook but does not depict wholesale violence, it is impermissible to ban it.

(B)   If a novel depicts wholesale violence, then it is permissible to ban it if doing so would do more good than harm to society.

(C)   It is permissible to ban a novel only if the novel has a subversive outlook and would do more harm than good to society.

(D)   It is permissible to ban a novel that would cause society more harm than good if the novel has two or more objectionable characteristics.

(E)   It is permissible to ban a novel that depicts wholesale violence only if that novel has at least one other objectionable characteristic.

19. In 1996, all ResearchTech projects were funded either by the government or by private corporations. The Gilman Survey, a ResearchTech project, was not funded by the government but was conducted in 1996. It must therefore have been funded by private corporations.

Which one of the following is most similar in its reasoning to the argument above?

(A)   Legal restrictions on consumer purchases have a variety of aims; for example, some are paternalistic, and others are designed to protect civil liberties. Ordinance 304, a legal restriction on alcohol sales, does not protect civil liberties. It must therefore be paternalistic.

(B)   Legal restrictions on consumer purchases, such as Ordinance 304, are either paternalistic or protect civil liberties. Ordinance 304 is not paternalistic, so it must protect civil liberties.

(C)   Ordinance 304 is not paternalistic. Since all legal restrictions on consumer purchases are either paternalistic or designed to protect the environment, the purpose of Ordinance 304 must not be to protect the environment.

(D)   Legal restrictions on consumer purchases are either paternalistic or designed to protect civil liberties. All ordinances passed in 1993 are paternalistic. Since Ordinance 304 was passed in 1993, it must be a legal restriction on consumer purchases.

(E)   Ordinance 304 should be exercised only in order to protect civil liberties or to protect consumers from self-harm. The mayor's last exercise of Ordinance 304 does not protect civil liberties, so it must have been intended to protect consumers from self-harm.

GO ON TO THE NEXT PAGE.

20. Astronomer: Earth was bombarded repeatedly by comets and asteroids early in its history. This bombardment probably sterilized the surface and prevented life from originating during this early period in Earth's geological history. Meanwhile, Mars escaped severe bombardment, and so there could have been microbial life on Mars prior to there being such life on Earth. Because many meteorites originating from Mars have landed on Earth, life on Earth may have started when living microbes were carried here from Mars on a meteorite.

Which one of the following most accurately describes the role played in the astronomer's argument by the statement that there could have been microbial life on Mars prior to there being such life on Earth?

(A) It is a claim for which no justification is provided but that is required in order to establish the argument's main conclusion.

(B) It is a claim for which no justification is provided and that, if true, ensures the truth of the argument's main conclusion.

(C) It is a claim for which some justification is provided and that is required in order to establish the argument's main conclusion.

(D) It is a claim for which justification is provided and that, if true, establishes the truth of the argument's main conclusion.

(E) It is a claim that provides some support for the argument's conclusion but that neither ensures the truth of that conclusion nor is required in order to establish that conclusion.

21. The presence of bees is necessary for excellent pollination, which, in turn, usually results in abundant fruits and vegetables. Establishing a beehive or two near one's garden ensures the presence of bees. Keeping bees is economical, however, only if the gardener has a use for homegrown honey. Thus, gardeners who have no use for homegrown honey will tend not to have beehives, so their gardens will fail to have excellent pollination.

Which one of the following most accurately describes a flaw in the reasoning of the argument?

(A) The argument fails to consider the possibility that obtaining homegrown honey is only one of several advantages of beehives.

(B) The argument confuses what is necessary for pollination to take place with what would guarantee that it takes place.

(C) The argument confuses what is necessary for an abundance of fruits and vegetables with what is usually conducive to it.

(D) The argument fails to consider that bees might be present even in the absence of a particular condition that would ensure their presence.

(E) The argument bases a claim that there is a causal connection between beehives and excellent pollination on a mere association between them.

22. People often praise poems for their truth. But to argue that expressing true propositions contributes to the aesthetic merit of a poem is misguided. Most of the commonplace beliefs of most people are true. Whatever the basis of poetic excellence is, it must certainly be rare rather than common.

Which one of the following most accurately describes the role played in the argument by the claim that whatever the basis of poetic excellence is, it must certainly be rare rather than common?

(A) It is the overall conclusion drawn by the argument.

(B) It is a premise that, in conjunction with another premise, is intended to support the argument's conclusion.

(C) It is a premise offered as the sole support for the argument's conclusion.

(D) It is background information that, in itself, does not provide support for the argument's conclusion.

(E) It is a proposition for which the argument seeks to advance an explanation.

GO ON TO THE NEXT PAGE.

23. Three million dollars was recently stolen from the City Treasurer's Office, and, from what we know so far, we can conclude that some members of the mayor's staff are suspects. The suspects are all former employees of the City Treasurer's Office, and the mayor's staff includes former employees of that office.

The flawed nature of the argument above can most effectively be demonstrated by noting that, by parallel reasoning, we could conclude that

(A)   some painters are sculptors since some sculptors are famous and some painters are famous
(B)   some cabins are skyscrapers since all skyscrapers are buildings and some buildings are cabins
(C)   some tables are chairs since all tables are furniture and all chairs are furniture
(D)   all supermarkets sell asparagus since all supermarkets sell food and asparagus is a food
(E)   all animals are dogs since some dogs are pets and some animals are pets

24. Why are violins made by Stradivarius in the early 1700s far superior to most other violins? Some experts suggest secret varnishes, but there is no evidence for this. However, climatologists have found that in the 1600s and early 1700s weather patterns in the region of Italy where Stradivarius worked affected tree growth to produce wood with special acoustic properties. Therefore, it is likely that _____.

Which one of the following most logically completes the argument?

(A)   some other Italian violin makers in the early 1700s produced violins that equaled the quality of Stradivarius violins
(B)   Stradivarius was the only violin maker in the early 1700s to use the wood produced in that part of Italy
(C)   no violin made from present-day materials could rival a Stradivarius violin for sound quality
(D)   the special qualities of Stradivarius violins are due in part to the wood used to make them
(E)   Stradivarius did not employ any secret techniques in making his violins

25. Principle: Only if a professor believes a student knowingly presented someone else's ideas without attribution should the professor make an official determination that the student has committed plagiarism.

Application: It is not the case that Professor Serfin should make an official determination that Walters committed plagiarism in the term paper about Willa Cather that Walters wrote for Serfin's class.

Which one of the following, if true, justifies the above application of the principle?

(A)   Professor Serfin does not have completely compelling evidence to conclude that Walters presented someone else's ideas as if they were his own in the term paper about Willa Cather.
(B)   If Walters had realized that the main thesis of his term paper is identical to the main thesis of a book he had read, Walters would have attributed the idea to the book.
(C)   Although the main thesis of Walters's term paper is identical to that of a book that he did not cite, Professor Serfin is convinced that Walters did not knowingly try to pass anyone else's ideas off as his own.
(D)   Walters does not believe that Professor Serfin should make an official determination that he plagiarized.
(E)   Professor Serfin has no intention of making an official determination that Walters plagiarized in the class.

S T O P

IF YOU FINISH BEFORE TIME IS CALLED, YOU MAY CHECK YOUR WORK ON THIS SECTION ONLY.
DO NOT WORK ON ANY OTHER SECTION IN THE TEST.

SECTION III
Time—35 minutes
25 Questions

Directions: Each question in this section is based on the reasoning presented in a brief passage. In answering the questions, you should not make assumptions that are by commonsense standards implausible, superfluous, or incompatible with the passage. For some questions, more than one of the choices could conceivably answer the question. However, you are to choose the **best** answer; that is, choose the response that most accurately and completely answers the question and mark that response on your answer sheet.

1. A research study revealed that, in most cases, once existing highways near urban areas are widened and extended in an attempt to reduce traffic congestion and resulting delays for motorists, these problems actually increase rather than decrease.

    Which one of the following, if true, most helps to explain the discrepancy between the intended results of the highway improvements and the results revealed in the study?

    (A) Widened and extended roads tend to attract many more motorists than used them before their improvement.

    (B) Typically, road widening or extension projects are undertaken only after the population near the road in question has increased and then leveled off, leaving a higher average population level.

    (C) As a general rule, the greater the number of lanes on a given length of highway, the lower the rate of accidents per 100,000 vehicles traveling on it.

    (D) Rural, as compared to urban, traffic usually includes a larger proportion of trucks and vehicles used by farmers.

    (E) Urban traffic generally moves at a slower pace and involves more congestion and delays than rural and suburban traffic.

2. A study found that consumers reaching supermarket checkout lines within 40 minutes after the airing of an advertisement for a given product over the store's audio system were significantly more likely to purchase the product advertised than were consumers who checked out prior to the airing. Apparently, these advertisements are effective.

    Which one of the following, if true, most strengthens the argument?

    (A) During the study, for most of the advertisements more people went through the checkout lines after they were aired than before they were aired.

    (B) A large proportion of the consumers who bought a product shortly after the airing of an advertisement for it reported that they had not gone to the store intending to buy that product.

    (C) Many of the consumers reported that they typically bought at least one of the advertised products every time they shopped at the store.

    (D) Many of the consumers who bought an advertised product and who reached the checkout line within 40 minutes of the advertisement's airing reported that they could not remember hearing the advertisement.

    (E) Many of the consumers who bought an advertised product reported that they buy that product only occasionally.

GO ON TO THE NEXT PAGE.

3. Unless the building permit is obtained by February 1 of this year or some of the other activities necessary for construction of the new library can be completed in less time than originally planned, the new library will not be completed on schedule. It is now clear that the building permit cannot be obtained by February 1, so the new library will not be completed on schedule.

The conclusion drawn follows logically from the premises if which one of the following is assumed?

(A) All of the other activities necessary for construction of the library will take at least as much time as originally planned.

(B) The officials in charge of construction of the new library have admitted that it probably will not be completed on schedule.

(C) The application for a building permit was submitted on January 2 of this year, and processing building permits always takes at least two months.

(D) The application for a building permit was rejected the first time it was submitted, and it had to be resubmitted with a revised building plan.

(E) It is not possible to convince authorities to allow construction of the library to begin before the building permit is obtained.

4. In a study of patients who enrolled at a sleep clinic because of insomnia, those who inhaled the scent of peppermint before going to bed were more likely to have difficulty falling asleep than were patients who inhaled the scent of bitter orange. Since it is known that inhaling bitter orange does not help people fall asleep more easily, this study shows that inhaling the scent of peppermint makes insomnia worse.

Which one of the following, if true, most seriously weakens the argument above?

(A) Several studies have shown that inhaling the scent of peppermint tends to have a relaxing effect on people who do not suffer from insomnia.

(B) The patients who inhaled the scent of bitter orange were, on average, suffering from milder cases of insomnia than were the patients who inhaled the scent of peppermint.

(C) Because the scents of peppermint and bitter orange are each very distinctive, it was not possible to prevent the patients from knowing that they were undergoing some sort of study of the effects of inhaling various scents.

(D) Some of the patients who enrolled in the sleep clinic also had difficulty staying asleep once they fell asleep.

(E) Several studies have revealed that in many cases inhaling certain pleasant scents can dramatically affect the degree to which a patient suffers from insomnia.

5. Dogs learn best when they are trained using both voice commands and hand signals. After all, a recent study shows that dogs who were trained using both voice commands and hand signals were twice as likely to obey as were dogs who were trained using only voice commands.

The claim that dogs learn best when they are trained using both voice commands and hand signals figures in the argument in which one of the following ways?

(A) It is an explicit premise of the argument.

(B) It is an implicit assumption of the argument.

(C) It is a statement of background information offered to help facilitate understanding the issue in the argument.

(D) It is a statement that the argument claims is supported by the study.

(E) It is an intermediate conclusion that is offered as direct support for the argument's main conclusion.

6. Of the many test pilots who have flown the new plane, none has found it difficult to operate. So it is unlikely that the test pilot flying the plane tomorrow will find it difficult to operate.

The reasoning in which one of the following arguments is most similar to the reasoning in the argument above?

(A) All of the many book reviewers who read Rachel Nguyen's new novel thought that it was particularly well written. So it is likely that the average reader will enjoy the book.

(B) Many of the book reviewers who read Wim Jashka's new novel before it was published found it very entertaining. So it is unlikely that most people who buy the book will find it boring.

(C) Neither of the two reviewers who enjoyed Sharlene Lo's new novel hoped that Lo would write a sequel. So it is unlikely that the review of the book in next Sunday's newspaper will express hope that Lo will write a sequel.

(D) Many reviewers have read Kip Landau's new novel, but none of them enjoyed it. So it is unlikely that the reviewer for the local newspaper will enjoy the book when she reads it.

(E) None of the reviewers who have read Gray Ornsby's new novel were offended by it. So it is unlikely that the book will offend anyone in the general public who reads it.

GO ON TO THE NEXT PAGE.

7. Scientist: Any theory that is to be taken seriously must affect our perception of the world. Of course, this is not, in itself, enough for a theory to be taken seriously. To see this, one need only consider astrology.

The point of the scientist's mentioning astrology in the argument is to present

(A) an example of a theory that should not be taken seriously because it does not affect our perception of the world

(B) an example of something that should not be considered a theory

(C) an example of a theory that should not be taken seriously despite its affecting our perception of the world

(D) an example of a theory that affects our perception of the world, and thus should be taken seriously

(E) an example of a theory that should be taken seriously, even though it does not affect our perception of the world

8. Clark: Our local community theater often produces plays by critically acclaimed playwrights. In fact, the production director says that critical acclaim is one of the main factors considered in the selection of plays to perform. So, since my neighbor Michaela's new play will be performed by the theater this season, she must be a critically acclaimed playwright.

The reasoning in Clark's argument is most vulnerable to criticism on the grounds that the argument

(A) takes a condition necessary for a playwright's being critically acclaimed to be a condition sufficient for a playwright's being critically acclaimed

(B) fails to consider that several different effects may be produced by a single cause

(C) treats one main factor considered in the selection of plays to perform as though it were a condition that must be met in order for a play to be selected

(D) uses as evidence a source that there is reason to believe is unreliable

(E) provides no evidence that a playwright's being critically acclaimed is the result rather than the cause of his or her plays being selected for production

9. Legal theorist: Governments should not be allowed to use the personal diaries of an individual who is the subject of a criminal prosecution as evidence against that individual. A diary is a silent conversation with oneself and there is no relevant difference between speaking to oneself, writing one's thoughts down, and keeping one's thoughts to oneself.

Which one of the following principles, if valid, provides the most support for the legal theorist's argument?

(A) Governments should not be allowed to compel corporate officials to surrender interoffice memos to government investigators.

(B) When crime is a serious problem, governments should be given increased power to investigate and prosecute suspected wrongdoers, and some restrictions on admissible evidence should be relaxed.

(C) Governments should not be allowed to use an individual's remarks to prosecute the individual for criminal activity unless the remarks were intended for other people.

(D) Governments should not have the power to confiscate an individual's personal correspondence to use as evidence against the individual in a criminal trial.

(E) Governments should do everything in their power to investigate and prosecute suspected wrongdoers.

GO ON TO THE NEXT PAGE.

10. A ring of gas emitting X-rays flickering 450 times per second has been observed in a stable orbit around a black hole. In light of certain widely accepted physical theories, that rate of flickering can best be explained if the ring of gas has a radius of 49 kilometers. But the gas ring could not maintain an orbit so close to a black hole unless the black hole was spinning.

The statements above, if true, most strongly support which one of the following, assuming that the widely accepted physical theories referred to above are correct?

(A) Black holes that have orbiting rings of gas with radii greater than 49 kilometers are usually stationary.

(B) Only rings of gas that are in stable orbits around black holes emit flickering X-rays.

(C) The black hole that is within the ring of gas observed by the astronomers is spinning.

(D) X-rays emitted by rings of gas orbiting black holes cause those black holes to spin.

(E) A black hole is stationary only if it is orbited by a ring of gas with a radius of more than 49 kilometers.

11. A mass of "black water" containing noxious organic material swept through Laurel Bay last year. Some scientists believe that this event was a naturally occurring but infrequent phenomenon. The black water completely wiped out five species of coral in the bay, including mounds of coral that were more than two centuries old. Therefore, even if this black water phenomenon has struck the bay before, it did not reach last year's intensity at any time in the past two centuries.

Which one of the following is an assumption required by the argument?

(A) Masses of black water such as that observed last summer come into the bay more frequently than just once every two centuries.

(B) Every species of coral in the bay was seriously harmed by the mass of black water that swept in last year.

(C) The mass of black water that swept through the bay last year did not decimate any plant or animal species that makes use of coral.

(D) The mounds of centuries-old coral that were destroyed were not in especially fragile condition just before the black water swept in last year.

(E) Older specimens of coral in the bay were more vulnerable to damage from the influx of black water than were young specimens.

12. Many nurseries sell fruit trees that they label "miniature." Not all nurseries, however, use this term in the same way. While some nurseries label any nectarine trees of the Stark Sweet Melody variety as "miniature," for example, others do not. One thing that is clear is that if a variety of fruit tree is not suitable for growing in a tub or a pot, no tree of that variety can be correctly labeled "miniature."

Which one of the following can be properly inferred from the information above?

(A) Most nurseries mislabel at least some of their fruit trees.

(B) Some of the nurseries have correctly labeled nectarine trees of the Stark Sweet Melody variety only if the variety is unsuitable for growing in a tub or a pot.

(C) Any nectarine tree of the Stark Sweet Melody variety that a nursery labels "miniature" is labeled incorrectly.

(D) Some nectarine trees that are not labeled "miniature" are labeled incorrectly.

(E) Unless the Stark Sweet Melody variety of nectarine tree is suitable for growing in a tub or a pot, some nurseries mislabel this variety of tree.

GO ON TO THE NEXT PAGE.

13. Psychologist: Identical twins are virtually the same genetically. Moreover, according to some studies, identical twins separated at birth and brought up in vastly different environments show a strong tendency to report similar ethical beliefs, dress in the same way, and have similar careers. Thus, many of our inclinations must be genetic in origin, and not subject to environmental influences.

Which one of the following, if true, would most weaken the psychologist's argument?

(A) Many people, including identical twins, undergo radical changes in their lifestyles at some point in their lives.

(B) While some studies of identical twins separated at birth reveal a high percentage of similar personality traits, they also show a few differences.

(C) Scientists are far from being able to link any specific genes to specific inclinations.

(D) Identical twins who grow up together tend to develop different beliefs, tastes, and careers in order to differentiate themselves from each other.

(E) Twins who are not identical tend to develop different beliefs, tastes, and careers.

14. Human beings can live happily only in a society where love and friendship are the primary motives for actions. Yet economic needs can be satisfied in the absence of this condition, as, for example, in a merchant society where only economic utility motivates action. It is obvious then that human beings _____.

Which one of the following most logically completes the argument?

(A) can live happily only when economic utility is not a motivator in their society

(B) cannot achieve happiness unless their economic needs have already been satisfied

(C) cannot satisfy economic needs by means of interactions with family members and close friends

(D) can satisfy their basic economic needs without obtaining happiness

(E) cannot really be said to have satisfied their economic needs unless they are happy

15. Technologically, it is already possible to produce nonpolluting cars that burn hydrogen rather than gasoline. But the national system of fuel stations that would be needed to provide the hydrogen fuel for such cars does not yet exist. However, this infrastructure is likely to appear and grow rapidly. A century ago no fuel-distribution infrastructure existed for gasoline-powered vehicles, yet it quickly developed in response to consumer demand.

Which one of the following most accurately expresses the conclusion drawn in the argument?

(A) It is already technologically possible to produce nonpolluting cars that burn hydrogen rather than gasoline.

(B) The fuel-distribution infrastructure for hydrogen-powered cars still needs to be created.

(C) If a new kind of technology is developed, the infrastructure needed to support that technology is likely to quickly develop in response to consumer demands.

(D) The fuel-distribution infrastructure for hydrogen-powered cars is likely to appear and grow rapidly.

(E) Hydrogen-powered vehicles will be similar to gasoline-powered vehicles with regard to the amount of consumer demand for their fuel-distribution infrastructure.

16. Wildlife management experts should not interfere with the natural habitats of creatures in the wild, because manipulating the environment to make it easier for an endangered species to survive in a habitat invariably makes it harder for nonendangered species to survive in that habitat.

The argument is most vulnerable to criticism on the grounds that it

(A) fails to consider that wildlife management experts probably know best how to facilitate the survival of an endangered species in a habitat

(B) fails to recognize that a nonendangered species can easily become an endangered species

(C) overlooks the possibility that saving an endangered species in a habitat is incompatible with preserving the overall diversity of species in that habitat

(D) presumes, without providing justification, that the survival of each endangered species is equally important to the health of the environment

(E) takes for granted that preserving a currently endangered species in a habitat does not have higher priority than preserving species in that habitat that are not endangered

GO ON TO THE NEXT PAGE.

17. Any food that is not sterilized and sealed can contain disease-causing bacteria. Once sterilized and properly sealed, however, it contains no bacteria. There are many different acceptable food-preservation techniques; each involves either sterilizing and sealing food or else at least slowing the growth of disease-causing bacteria. Some of the techniques may also destroy natural food enzymes that cause food to spoil or discolor quickly.

If the statements above are true, which one of the following must be true?

(A) All food preserved by an acceptable method is free of disease-causing bacteria.

(B) Preservation methods that destroy enzymes that cause food to spoil do not sterilize the food.

(C) Food preserved by a sterilization method is less likely to discolor quickly than food preserved with other methods.

(D) Any nonsterilized food preserved by an acceptable method can contain disease-causing bacteria.

(E) If a food contains no bacteria, then it has been preserved by an acceptable method.

18. Activities that pose risks to life are acceptable if and only if each person who bears the risks either gains some net benefit that cannot be had without such risks, or bears the risks voluntarily.

Which one of the following judgments most closely conforms to the principle above?

(A) A door-to-door salesperson declines to replace his older car with a new model with more safety features; this is acceptable because the decision not to replace the car is voluntary.

(B) A smoker subjects people to secondhand smoke at an outdoor public meeting; the resulting risks are acceptable because the danger from secondhand smoke is minimal outdoors, where smoke dissipates quickly.

(C) A motorcyclist rides without a helmet; the risk of fatal injury to the motorcyclist thus incurred is acceptable because the motorcyclist incurs this risk willingly.

(D) Motor vehicles are allowed to emit certain low levels of pollution; the resulting health risks are acceptable because all users of motor vehicles share the resulting benefit of inexpensive, convenient travel.

(E) A nation requires all citizens to spend two years in national service; since such service involves no risk to life, the policy is acceptable.

19. Ecologist: One theory attributes the ability of sea butterflies to avoid predation to their appearance, while another attributes this ability to various chemical compounds they produce. Recently we added each of the compounds to food pellets, one compound per pellet. Predators ate the pellets no matter which one of the compounds was present. Thus the compounds the sea butterflies produce are not responsible for their ability to avoid predation.

The reasoning in the ecologist's argument is flawed in that the argument

(A) presumes, without providing justification, that the two theories are incompatible with each other

(B) draws a conclusion about a cause on the basis of nothing more than a statistical correlation

(C) treats a condition sufficient for sea butterflies' ability to avoid predators as a condition required for this ability

(D) infers, from the claim that no individual member of a set has a certain effect, that the set as a whole does not have that effect

(E) draws a conclusion that merely restates material present in one or more of its premises

20. Principle: One should criticize the works or actions of another person only if the criticism will not seriously harm the person criticized and one does so in the hope or expectation of benefiting someone other than oneself.

Application: Jarrett should not have criticized Ostertag's essay in front of the class, since the defects in it were so obvious that pointing them out benefited no one.

Which one of the following, if true, justifies the above application of the principle?

(A) Jarrett knew that the defects in the essay were so obvious that pointing them out would benefit no one.

(B) Jarrett's criticism of the essay would have been to Ostertag's benefit only if Ostertag had been unaware of the defects in the essay at the time.

(C) Jarrett knew that the criticism might antagonize Ostertag.

(D) Jarrett hoped to gain prestige by criticizing Ostertag.

(E) Jarrett did not expect the criticism to be to Ostertag's benefit.

GO ON TO THE NEXT PAGE.

21. Safety consultant: Judged by the number of injuries per licensed vehicle, minivans are the safest vehicles on the road. However, in carefully designed crash tests, minivans show no greater ability to protect their occupants than other vehicles of similar size do. Thus, the reason minivans have such a good safety record is probably not that they are inherently safer than other vehicles, but rather that they are driven primarily by low-risk drivers.

Which one of the following, if true, most strengthens the safety consultant's argument?

(A) When choosing what kind of vehicle to drive, low-risk drivers often select a kind that they know to perform particularly well in crash tests.

(B) Judged by the number of accidents per licensed vehicle, minivans are no safer than most other kinds of vehicles are.

(C) Minivans tend to carry more passengers at any given time than do most other vehicles.

(D) In general, the larger a vehicle is, the greater its ability to protect its occupants.

(E) Minivans generally have worse braking and emergency handling capabilities than other vehicles of similar size.

22. Consumer advocate: There is no doubt that the government is responsible for the increased cost of gasoline, because the government's policies have significantly increased consumer demand for fuel, and as a result of increasing demand, the price of gasoline has risen steadily.

Which one of the following is an assumption required by the consumer advocate's argument?

(A) The government can bear responsibility for that which it indirectly causes.

(B) The government is responsible for some unforeseen consequences of its policies.

(C) Consumer demand for gasoline cannot increase without causing gasoline prices to increase.

(D) The government has an obligation to ensure that demand for fuel does not increase excessively.

(E) If the government pursues policies that do not increase the demand for fuel, gasoline prices tend to remain stable.

23. A species in which mutations frequently occur will develop new evolutionary adaptations in each generation. Since species survive dramatic environmental changes only if they develop new evolutionary adaptations in each generation, a species in which mutations frequently occur will survive dramatic environmental changes.

The flawed pattern of reasoning in which one of the following is most closely parallel to that in the argument above?

(A) In a stone wall that is properly built, every stone supports another stone. Since a wall's being sturdy depends upon its being properly built, only walls that are composed entirely of stones supporting other stones are sturdy.

(B) A play that is performed before a different audience every time will never get the same reaction from any two audiences. Since no plays are performed before the same audience every time, no play ever gets the same reaction from any two audiences.

(C) A person who is perfectly honest will tell the truth in every situation. Since in order to be a morally upright person one must tell the truth at all times, a perfectly honest person will also be a morally upright person.

(D) An herb garden is productive only if the soil that it is planted in is well drained. Since soil that is well drained is good soil, an herb garden is not productive unless it is planted in good soil.

(E) A diet that is healthful is well balanced. Since a well-balanced diet includes fruits and vegetables, one will not be healthy unless one eats fruits and vegetables.

GO ON TO THE NEXT PAGE.

24. Music critic: How well an underground rock group's recordings sell is no mark of that group's success as an underground group. After all, if a recording sells well, it may be because some of the music on the recording is too trendy to be authentically underground; accordingly, many underground musicians consider it desirable for a recording not to sell well. But weak sales may simply be the result of the group's incompetence.

Which one of the following principles, if valid, most helps to justify the music critic's argument?

(A) If an underground rock group is successful as an underground group, its recordings will sell neither especially well nor especially poorly.

(B) An underground rock group is unsuccessful as an underground group if it is incompetent or if any of its music is too trendy to be authentically underground, or both.

(C) Whether an underground group's recordings meet criteria that many underground musicians consider desirable is not a mark of that group's success.

(D) An underground rock group is successful as an underground group if the group is competent but its recordings nonetheless do not sell well.

(E) For an underground rock group, competence and the creation of authentically underground music are not in themselves marks of success.

25. Graham: The defeat of the world's chess champion by a computer shows that any type of human intellectual activity governed by fixed principles can be mastered by machines and thus that a truly intelligent machine will inevitably be devised.

Adelaide: But you are overlooking the fact that the computer in the case you cite was simply an extension of the people who programmed it. It was their successful distillation of the principles of chess that enabled them to defeat a chess champion using a computer.

The statements above provide the most support for holding that Graham and Adelaide disagree about whether

(A) chess is the best example of a human intellectual activity that is governed by fixed principles

(B) chess is a typical example of the sorts of intellectual activities in which human beings characteristically engage

(C) a computer's defeat of a human chess player is an accomplishment that should be attributed to the computer

(D) intelligence can be demonstrated by the performance of an activity in accord with fixed principles

(E) tools can be designed to aid in any human activity that is governed by fixed principles

S T O P

IF YOU FINISH BEFORE TIME IS CALLED, YOU MAY CHECK YOUR WORK ON THIS SECTION ONLY.
DO NOT WORK ON ANY OTHER SECTION IN THE TEST.

SECTION IV
Time—35 minutes
25 Questions

Directions: Each question in this section is based on the reasoning presented in a brief passage. In answering the questions, you should not make assumptions that are by commonsense standards implausible, superfluous, or incompatible with the passage. For some questions, more than one of the choices could conceivably answer the question. However, you are to choose the **best** answer; that is, choose the response that most accurately and completely answers the question and mark that response on your answer sheet.

1. Economist: Prosperity is a driving force behind increases in the release of carbon dioxide, the main cause of global warming. As incomes rise, more people spend money on energy-consuming devices such as cars, thereby producing more carbon dioxide. Also, in countries that experienced deep economic recessions, there were steep drops in carbon dioxide emissions.

    Which one of the following most accurately states the overall conclusion drawn in the economist's argument?

    (A) Carbon dioxide is the main cause of global warming.
    (B) Prosperity is an important cause of increases in the release of carbon dioxide.
    (C) When incomes rise, more people spend money on energy-consuming devices.
    (D) Countries that experienced deep economic recessions also experienced steep drops in carbon dioxide emissions.
    (E) When people spend money on energy-consuming devices, more carbon dioxide is produced as a result.

2. Spokesperson: Contrary to what some have claimed, our group's "Clean City" campaign has been a rousing success. After all, the amount of trash on the city's streets today is significantly lower than when the campaign began.

    Which one of the following is an assumption required by the spokesperson's argument?

    (A) The amount of trash on the city's streets was not declining at the same rate or faster before the campaign began than it did during the campaign.
    (B) Those who claim that the campaign has not been a rousing success are unaware of the degree of the decline in the amount of trash since the campaign began.
    (C) The campaign has been more successful in reducing the amount of trash on the city's streets than has any other campaign in the past.
    (D) The spokesperson's group did not receive any special funding to support the planning or execution of the campaign.
    (E) The amount of trash on the city's streets has declined steadily throughout the course of the campaign.

3. Consumption of sugar affects the level of unmetabolized sugar in the blood; the level rises following consumption of sugar. Yet people who consume large amounts of sugar tend to have below-average levels of unmetabolized sugar in their blood.

    Which one of the following, if true, helps most to resolve the apparent paradox described above?

    (A) Persons who are overweight tend to have below-average levels of unmetabolized sugar in their blood.
    (B) Fruits, vegetables, meats, and dairy products often contain as much sugar as sweets.
    (C) Consuming large amounts of sugar causes the body to secrete abnormally high amounts of insulin, a sugar-metabolizing enzyme.
    (D) Consuming large amounts of sugar can lead eventually to the failure of the body to produce enough insulin, a sugar-metabolizing enzyme.
    (E) Sugar passes into the bloodstream before it can be metabolized.

GO ON TO THE NEXT PAGE.

4. An economist has argued that consumers often benefit when government permits a corporation to obtain a monopoly. Without competition, a corporation can raise prices without spending nearly as much on advertising. The corporation can then invest the extra money in expensive research or industrial infrastructure that it could not otherwise afford, passing the fruits of these investments on to consumers.

Which one of the following, if true, most strengthens the economist's argument?

(A) The benefits to consumers are typically greater if a corporation invests in expensive research or industrial infrastructure than if that corporation spends the same amount of money in any other way.

(B) The government's permitting a corporation to obtain a monopoly is advantageous for consumers only if that corporation passes the fruits of at least some of its investments on to consumers.

(C) If a corporation obtains a monopoly, the disadvantage to consumers of any higher prices will be outweighed by the advantages from extra investments in expensive research or industrial infrastructure made by that corporation.

(D) Even if a corporation is not permitted to obtain a monopoly, it typically invests some money in expensive research or industrial infrastructure.

(E) If obtaining a monopoly enables a corporation to raise its prices and invest less money in advertising, that corporation will almost inevitably do so.

5. A natural history museum contains several displays of wild animals. These displays are created by drying and mounting animal skins. In some of the older displays, the animals' skins have started to deteriorate because of low humidity and the heat of the lights. The older displays are lit by tungsten lamps but the newer ones are lit by compact fluorescent lamps designed for use in museums. These lamps give off as much light as the tungsten lamps but less heat.

The statements above, if true, most strongly support which one of the following?

(A) Some of the older displays will last longer if the tungsten lamps that illuminate them are replaced by compact fluorescent lamps.

(B) The displays that are lit by many compact fluorescent lamps are more prone to deterioration than the displays that are lit by a few tungsten lamps.

(C) More of the displays are lit by compact fluorescent lamps than are lit by tungsten lamps.

(D) The newer displays will not be subject to deterioration because of low humidity.

(E) The humidity in the museum is lower today than it was when the older displays were first put in place.

6. Columnist: Contrary to what many people believe, the number of species on Earth is probably not dwindling. Extinction is a natural process, and about as many species are likely to go extinct this year as went extinct in 1970. But the emergence of new species is also a natural process; there is no reason to doubt that new species are emerging at about the same rate as they have been for the last several centuries.

Which one of the following, if true, most weakens the columnist's argument?

(A) In 1970 fewer new species emerged than went extinct.

(B) The regions of the world where new species tend to emerge at the highest rate are also where species tend to go extinct at the highest rate.

(C) The vast majority of the species that have ever existed are now extinct.

(D) There is no more concern now about extinction of species than there was in 1970.

(E) Scientists are now better able to identify species facing serious risk of extinction than they were in 1970.

7. Even though MacArthur's diet book helped many people lose weight, MacArthur should not have published it. It recommended such small portions of fruits and vegetables that it undoubtedly damaged the health of many who followed the diet. MacArthur is a physician, so MacArthur either knew or should have known that diets low in fruits and vegetables are unhealthful.

Which one of the following principles, if valid, most helps to justify the argument's reasoning?

(A) One should not undertake an action if one knows that doing so would seriously damage the health of many people.

(B) One should not follow a particular method for achieving some end if doing so has the potential to damage one's health.

(C) One should publish a book recommending certain health-related measures if doing so is likely to improve many people's lives without also causing harm.

(D) One should not publish a book recommending a particular means of attaining a goal unless one knows that the particular means can bring about that goal.

(E) One should not publish a book recommending a particular course of action if one either knows or ought to know that taking that course of action would be unhealthful.

GO ON TO THE NEXT PAGE.

8. Principle: If the burden of a proposed policy change would fall disproportionately on people with low incomes, that policy change should not be made.

Application: The city of Centerburgh plans to reintroduce rock salt as a road de-icing agent, after having stopped its use several years ago on the grounds that it accelerated the corrosion of automobiles. Although the city claims that cars are now better protected from salt's corrosive properties than they were even as recently as five years ago, the city's plan should be halted.

Which one of the following, if true of Centerburgh, most justifies the above application of the principle?

(A) Individuals with low incomes are more likely to use public transportation and are less likely to drive cars than are individuals with higher incomes.

(B) Road maintenance is primarily funded by local sales taxes, which disproportionately burden people with low incomes.

(C) Cars now cost twice what they did when rock salt was last used as a road de-icing agent.

(D) People with low incomes are more likely to purchase older vehicles than are people with higher incomes.

(E) Among drivers, those with low incomes are less likely than those with higher incomes to use roads that have been treated with de-icing agents.

9. In a medical study of all of the residents of Groverhill, 35 people reported consulting their physician last year seeking relief from severe headaches. Those same physicians' records, however, indicate that 105 consultations occurred last year with Groverhill patients seeking relief from severe headaches. Obviously, then, many residents who consulted physicians for this condition did not remember doing so.

The reasoning in the argument is most vulnerable to criticism on the grounds that the argument

(A) generalizes inappropriately from an unrepresentative sample of residents of Groverhill

(B) fails to consider whether any residents of Groverhill visit physicians who are not located in Groverhill

(C) overlooks the possibility that residents of Groverhill visited their physicians more than once during the year for the same condition

(D) fails to provide any evidence to support the claim that the residents of Groverhill have an unusually high occurrence of severe headaches

(E) takes for granted that every resident of Groverhill who suffers from severe headaches would consult a physician about this condition

10. Economist: In free market systems, the primary responsibility of corporate executives is to determine a nation's industrial technology, the pattern of work organization, location of industry, and resource allocation. They also are the decision makers, though subject to significant consumer control, on what is to be produced and in what quantities. In short, a large category of major decisions is turned over to business executives. Thus, business executives have become public officials.

Which one of the following, if true, most weakens the economist's argument?

(A) Most of the decisions made by business executives in free market systems are made by the government in countries with centrally planned economies.

(B) Making decisions about patterns of work organization, resource allocation, and location of industry is not the core of a public official's job.

(C) The salaries of business executives are commensurate with the salaries of high-ranking public officials.

(D) What a country produces and in what quantities is not always completely controlled by corporate executives.

(E) Public officials and business executives often cooperate in making decisions of national importance.

GO ON TO THE NEXT PAGE.

11. Science fiction creates an appetite for interstellar space exploration among certain people. Unfortunately, this appetite cannot be satisfied with any technology humanity will soon possess. Since gaps between expectations and reality spur discontent, no doubt one effect of science fiction has been to create an unproductive dissatisfaction with the way the world actually is.

Which one of the following is an assumption the argument requires?

(A) The fact that the appetite for interstellar space exploration cannot be satisfied with any technology humanity will soon possess has created a gap between reality and some people's expectations.

(B) If science fiction has created an unproductive dissatisfaction with the way the world actually is, it has done so only by creating an appetite for interstellar space exploration among certain people.

(C) Few if any of the appetites that science fiction has created in people could be satisfied with any technology humanity will soon possess.

(D) Most people unrealistically expect that technology that humanity will soon possess could satisfy the appetite for interstellar space exploration.

(E) If the appetites science fiction has created in people could all be satisfied with technologies that humanity will soon possess, then science fiction could not create an unproductive dissatisfaction with the way the world is.

12. Tamika: Many people have been duped by the claims of those who market certain questionable medical products. Their susceptibility is easy to explain: most people yearn for easy solutions to complex medical problems but don't have the medical knowledge necessary to see through the sellers' fraudulent claims. However, the same explanation cannot be given for a recent trend among medical professionals toward a susceptibility to fraudulent claims. They, of course, have no lack of medical knowledge.

Tamika's argument proceeds by

(A) showing by analogy that medical professionals should not be susceptible to the fraudulent claims of those who market certain medical products

(B) arguing against a hypothesis by showing that the hypothesis cannot account for the behavior of everyone

(C) explaining the susceptibility of medical professionals to the fraudulent claims of those marketing certain medical products by casting doubt on the expertise of the professionals

(D) arguing that since two groups are disanalogous in important respects, there must be different explanations for their similar behavior

(E) arguing that an explanation should be accepted in spite of apparent evidence against it

13. Business ethicist: Managers of corporations have an obligation to serve shareholders as the shareholders would want to be served. Therefore, corporate managers have an obligation to act in the shareholders' best interest.

The business ethicist's conclusion follows logically if which one of the following is assumed?

(A) Corporate managers are always able to discern what is in the best interest of shareholders.

(B) Shareholders would want to be served only in ways that are in their own best interest.

(C) A corporate manager's obligations to shareholders take precedence over any other obligations the manager may have.

(D) The shareholders have interests that can best be served by corporate managers.

(E) All shareholders want to be served in identical ways.

GO ON TO THE NEXT PAGE.

14. Astronomer: Does a recent meteorite from Mars contain fossilized bacteria? Professor Tagar, a biologist, argues that the bacteria-like structures found in the meteorite cannot be fossilized bacteria, on the grounds that they are one-tenth of 1 percent the volume of the smallest earthly bacteria. However, Tagar's view cannot be right. Tagar does not accept the views of biologists Swiderski and Terrada, who maintain that Martian bacteria would shrink to one-tenth of 1 percent of their normal volume when water or other nutrients were in short supply.

Which one of the following most accurately describes a flaw in the reasoning in the astronomer's argument?

(A) The argument presumes, without providing justification, that the authorities cited have always held the views attributed to them.

(B) The argument provides no justification for giving preference to the views of one rather than the other of two competing sets of authorities.

(C) The argument takes for granted that the number of authorities supporting a particular hypothesis is an indication of how accurate that hypothesis is.

(D) The argument appeals to views that contradict rather than support one another.

(E) The argument presumes, without providing justification, that the opinions of all experts are equally justified.

15. Any good garden compost may appropriately be used for soil drainage and fertility. The best compost is 40 to 60 percent organic matter and is dark brown in color. However, compost that emits a strong ammonia smell should not be used for drainage and fertility, for that smell means that the organic matter has not sufficiently decomposed.

Which one of the following is most strongly supported by the information above?

(A) Compost that is 80 percent organic matter has probably not decomposed sufficiently.

(B) If compost is less than 40 percent organic matter and is not dark brown in color, then it will make soil less fertile and will worsen soil drainage.

(C) If compost is 50 percent organic matter and that organic matter is sufficiently decomposed, then the compost is good.

(D) In the best garden compost, the organic matter is completely decomposed.

(E) Compost that is dark brown in color and emits a strong ammonia smell is not good garden compost.

16. Professor: Unfortunately, pharmaceutical companies and other profit-driven institutions provide nearly all of the funding for the chemistry department's research. Moreover, unless we can secure more funding for basic science research, it is highly unlikely that any significant advances in basic research will come out of the department. Thus, without increased funding from sources other than profit-driven institutions, the chemistry department is unlikely to gain the prestige that only achievements in basic science research confer.

Which one of the following is an assumption on which the professor's argument relies?

(A) If the chemistry department secures more funding for basic science research, its members will make significant advances in basic science.

(B) If the chemistry department's prestige increases substantially, then it is highly likely that the department's funding from sources other than profit-driven institutions will subsequently increase.

(C) Members of the chemistry department are unlikely to make significant advances in basic science research if the department does not forego the funding it currently receives from profit-driven institutions.

(D) The chemistry department's funding for basic science research is not likely to increase if its funding from sources other than profit-driven institutions does not increase.

(E) The profit-driven institutions that currently provide almost all of the chemistry department's funding are not likely to benefit from basic scientific research.

GO ON TO THE NEXT PAGE.

17. In order to save money, many consumers redeem coupons that are distributed by retail stores. However, in general, retail stores that distribute and accept store coupons as a way of discounting the prices on certain products charge more for their products, on average, than other retail stores charge for the same products—even after lower prices available on coupon-discounted products are factored in. This is because producing and distributing coupons usually costs a great deal. To compensate for this expense without reducing profits, retail stores must pass it on to consumers.

Which one of the following can be properly inferred from the information above?

(A) Many consumers who redeem coupons save little if any money, overall, by doing so.
(B) Retail stores that distribute coupons generally compensate for the expense of producing and distributing coupons by charging higher prices for certain products.
(C) The profits of retail stores that use coupons are not significantly lower, on average, than the profits of similar stores that do not use coupons.
(D) At least some retail stores that do not use coupons do not have expenses that they pass on to consumers.
(E) The undiscounted price charged for a good for which a retail store offers a coupon will be higher than the price charged for that same good by a retail store that does not offer a coupon for it.

18. Psychologist: Birth-order effects, the alleged effects of when one was born relative to the births of siblings, have not been detected in studies of adult personality that use standard personality tests. However, they have been detected in birth-order studies that are based on parents' and siblings' reports of the subjects' personalities. All of these birth-order studies, taken together, show that birth order has no lasting effect on personality; instead, birth order affects merely how a sibling's behavior is perceived.

Which one of the following is an assumption required by the psychologist's argument?

(A) Standard personality tests will detect at least some birth-order effects on personality, if those effects exist.
(B) The behavior patterns people display when they are with family are significantly different from those they display otherwise.
(C) Parents' and siblings' perceptions of a person's personality tend not to change between that person's early childhood and adulthood.
(D) Standard personality tests have detected significant birth-order effects in some studies of young children's personalities.
(E) Parents and siblings have accurate perceptions of the behavior patterns of other family members.

19. If the jury did not return a verdict, there would still be media trucks outside the courthouse. There are no media trucks outside the courthouse, so the jury must have returned a verdict.

The pattern of reasoning in the argument above is most similar to that in which one of the following arguments?

(A) If a hurricane arises off the coast this summer, our town will see less tourism than usual. But since there will be no hurricane this summer, there will be no less tourism than usual.
(B) If Peter did not buy a house, he would have rented an apartment. Peter did not rent an apartment, so he must have bought a house.
(C) Renate promised Linus that if his car was not working, she would drive him to work. Linus's car is not working, so Renate must have driven him to work.
(D) If Kay's television was not working last night, she would have gone to a movie. Her television has not been working for the past week, so she must have gone to a movie last night.
(E) If Ralph had told Manuela about the problem, Manuela would have solved it. But Ralph did not tell Manuela about the problem, so someone else must have solved it.

GO ON TO THE NEXT PAGE.

20. A salesperson who makes a sale does not change the desires of the customer. Rather, the salesperson finds out what these desires are and then convinces the customer that a particular product will satisfy them. Persuading people to vote for a politician to whom they are initially indifferent is not significantly different. After discovering what policies the prospective voter would like to see in place, one tries to _____ .

Which one of the following most logically completes the argument?

(A) show that the opponents of the politician in question do not favor all of those policies

(B) disguise any difference between the policies the politician supports and the policies supported by other candidates

(C) convince the voter that the policies favored by the politician in question are preferable to those favored by the voter

(D) demonstrate that the politician is a person of outstanding character and is interested in some of the same issues as the voter

(E) persuade the voter that voting for the politician in question is the best way to get these policies adopted

21. Farmer: My neighbor claims that my pesticides are spreading to her farm in runoff water, but she is wrong. I use only organic pesticides, and there is no evidence that they harm either people or domestic animals. Furthermore, I am careful to avoid spraying on my neighbor's land.

Which one of the following most accurately describes a reasoning flaw in the farmer's argument?

(A) It treats lack of evidence that organic pesticides harm people or domestic animals as proof that they cannot do so.

(B) It presumes, without providing justification, that being careful to avoid something usually results in its avoidance.

(C) It does not address the neighbor's claim that pesticides used by the farmer are spreading onto her land.

(D) It fails to provide an alternative explanation for the presence of pesticides on the neighbor's land.

(E) It ignores the possibility that pesticides might have dangerous effects other than harming people or domestic animals.

22. Linguist: One group of art critics claims that postimpressionist paintings are not really art and so should be neither studied nor displayed. Another group of critics disagrees, insisting that these paintings are works of art. But since the second group grants that there are paintings that are not works of art and should therefore be ignored in the manner suggested by the first group, their disagreement is not over the meaning of the word "art."

The claim that there are paintings that are not works of art plays which one of the following roles in the linguist's argument?

(A) It is a contention that the argument purports to show is the main point of disagreement between the two groups of critics mentioned.

(B) It is cited as a commonly accepted reason for accepting a hypothesis for which the argument offers independent evidence.

(C) It is a claim whose acceptance by critics who differ on other issues is cited by the argument as evidence of its truth.

(D) It is a claim about the nature of art that according to the argument accounts for disputes that only appear to concern the aesthetic merits of certain types of paintings.

(E) It is a claim whose acceptance by both of the two disputing parties is cited as evidence for a conclusion the argument draws about the disagreement.

GO ON TO THE NEXT PAGE.

23. Biologists found that off the northeast coast of a certain country the P-plankton population has recently dropped 10 percent. Additionally, fish species X, Y, and Z are beginning to show extraordinarily high death rates in the region. Since these species of fish are known to sometimes eat P-plankton, biologists believe the two phenomena are connected, but the exact nature of the connection is unknown. No other species in the ecosystem appear to be affected.

Which one of the following, if true, most helps to explain the biologists' findings?

(A) Several major pharmaceutical companies in the region have been secretly dumping large amounts of waste into the ocean for many years.

(B) A new strain of bacteria is attacking P-plankton by destroying their cell walls and is attacking the respiratory systems of fish species X, Y, and Z.

(C) A powerful toxin in the water is killing off P-plankton by inhibiting their production of a chemical they use in reproduction.

(D) Fish species X, Y, and Z are all experiencing widespread starvation within the affected region, and the loss of P-plankton is driving their death rates up even higher.

(E) Global warming has changed the climatic conditions of the ocean all along the northeast coast of the country.

24. *Nightbird* is an unsigned painting that some attribute to the celebrated artist Larocque. Experts agree that it was painted in a style indistinguishable from that of Larocque and that if it was not painted by Larocque, it was undoubtedly painted by one of his students. A recent analysis showed that the painting contains orpiment, a pigment never yet found in a work attributed to Larocque. Therefore, the painting must have been done by one of Larocque's students.

Which one of the following, if true, most weakens the argument?

(A) Few of Larocque's students ever used painting techniques that differed from Larocque's.

(B) Larocque never signed any of his paintings.

(C) No painting currently recognized as the work of one of Larocque's students contains orpiment.

(D) None of Larocque's students is considered to be an important artist.

(E) The use of orpiment became more popular in the years after Larocque's death.

25. Advertisement: The dental profession knows that brushing with Blizzard toothpaste is the best way to fight cavities. We surveyed five dentists, and each agreed that the tartar control formula found in Blizzard is the most effective cavity-fighting formula available in a toothpaste.

The flawed reasoning in which one of the following is most similar to the flawed reasoning in the advertisement?

(A) The nation's voters know that Gomez is the candidate whose policies would be best for the nation. Of ten voters polled, each said that Gomez would be a very popular leader.

(B) Some of the nation's voters believe that Gomez is the candidate who would be best for the nation. Of the ten voters we surveyed, each agreed that the policies Gomez is committed to would be the best policies for the nation to adopt.

(C) The nation's voters generally believe that Gomez is the candidate who would be best for the nation. We polled thousands of voters in the nation, and they agreed that the policies Gomez is committed to would help the nation more than those supported by any of the other candidates.

(D) The nation's voters know that electing Gomez would be the best way to help the nation. The ten voters we polled all agreed that the policies Gomez is committed to would help the nation more than any other policies.

(E) We know that electing Gomez would be the best course for the nation to follow because, of ten voters we surveyed, each agreed that electing Gomez would help the nation.

STOP

IF YOU FINISH BEFORE TIME IS CALLED, YOU MAY CHECK YOUR WORK ON THIS SECTION ONLY.
DO NOT WORK ON ANY OTHER SECTION IN THE TEST.

Computing Your Score

Directions:

1. Use the Answer Key on the next page to check your answers.

2. Use the Scoring Worksheet below to compute your raw score.

3. Use the Score Conversion Chart to convert your raw score into the 120–180 scale.*

Scoring Worksheet

1. Enter the number of questions you answered correctly in each section.

	Number Correct
SECTION I	_____
SECTION II	_____
SECTION III	Unscored
SECTION IV	_____

2. Enter the sum here: _____
   This is your Raw Score.

*Scores are reported on a 120–180 score scale, with 120 being the lowest possible score and 180 being the highest possible score.

Score Conversion Chart

Use the table below to convert your raw score to the corresponding 120–180 scaled score for PrepTest 137.

Raw Score	Scaled Score	Raw Score	Scaled Score
77	180	38	146
76	180	37	146
75	178	36	145
74	176	35	144
73	174	34	143
72	172	33	143
71	171	32	142
70	170	31	141
69	168	30	140
68	167	29	140
67	166	28	139
66	165	27	138
65	164	26	137
64	164	25	136
63	163	24	135
62	162	23	134
61	161	22	133
60	161	21	132
59	160	20	131
58	159	19	129
57	158	18	128
56	158	17	127
55	157	16	125
54	156	15	123
53	156	14	122
52	155	13	120
51	155	12	120
50	154	11	120
49	153	10	120
48	153	9	120
47	152	8	120
46	151	7	120
45	151	6	120
44	150	5	120
43	150	4	120
42	149	3	120
41	148	2	120
40	148	1	120
39	147	0	120

Answer Key

Question	Section I	Section II	Section III*	Section IV
1	B	A	A	B
2	A	A	B	A
3	A	B	A	C
4	C	B	B	C
5	E	E	D	A
6	D	A	D	A
7	D	E	C	E
8	E	E	C	D
9	C	B	C	C
10	C	D	C	B
11	D	C	D	A
12	E	D	E	D
13	A	E	D	B
14	B	A	D	B
15	D	C	D	E
16	E	C	E	D
17	E	B	D	B
18	B	D	C	A
19	D	B	D	B
20	A	C	A	E
21	E	D	E	C
22	B	B	A	E
23	B	B	C	B
24	A	D	B	C
25	D	C	C	D
26	C			
27	E			

*Section III is unscored. The number of items answered correctly in Section III should not be added to the raw score.

PrepTest 138

SECTION I
Time—35 minutes
27 Questions

Directions: Each set of questions in this section is based on a single passage or a pair of passages. The questions are to be answered on the basis of what is **stated** or **implied** in the passage or pair of passages. For some questions, more than one of the choices could conceivably answer the question. However, you are to choose the **best** answer; that is, choose the response that most accurately and completely answers the question and mark that response on your answer sheet.

The *corrido*, a type of narrative folk song, comes from a region half in Mexico and half in the United States known as the Lower Rio Grande Border. Corridos, which flourished from about 1836 to the late 1930s, are part of a long-standing ballad tradition that has roots in eighteenth-century Spain. Sung in Spanish, corridos combine formal features of several different types of folk songs, but their narratives consistently deal with subject matter specific to the Border region. For example, "El Corrido de Kiansis" (c. 1870), the oldest corrido surviving in complete form, records the first cattle drives to Kansas in the late 1860s. A single important event is likely to have inspired several corrido variants, yet the different versions of any given story all partake of standard generic elements. When sung at social gatherings, corridos served to commemorate significant local happenings, but more importantly, their heavy reliance on familiar linguistic and thematic conventions served to affirm the cohesiveness of Border communities.

Corridos take their name from the Spanish verb *correr*, meaning to run or to flow, for corridos tell their stories simply and swiftly, without embellishments. Figures of speech such as metaphors are generally rare in corridos, and when metaphors are used, they usually incorporate everyday images that are familiar to the songs' listeners. In the popular "El Corrido de Gregorio Cortez," for example, the hero Cortez, fighting off pursuers, uses the metaphor of a thunderstorm to boast that he has had harder fights than the one they gave him: "I have weathered thunderstorms; / This little mist doesn't bother me." Similar storm imagery is found in other corridos including "Kiansis," which tells of stampedes caused by thunderstorms during the Kansas cattle drives. Such imagery, highly conventional and readily recognizable to corrido listeners, reflects and strengthens the continuity of the corrido tradition.

The corrido is composed not only of familiar images but also of certain ready-made lines that travel easily from one ballad to another. This is most evident in the corrido's formal closing verse, or *despedida*. The despedida of one variant of "Gregorio Cortez" is translated as follows: "Now with this I say farewell / In the shade of a cypress tree; / This is the end of the ballad / Of Don Gregorio Cortez." The first and third lines are a set convention. The second and fourth lines are variable, the fourth carrying the name of the corrido or expressing its subject, and the second varying according to exigencies of rhyme. In the despedida,

perhaps the clearest marker of both the corrido's uniqueness and its generic continuity, the corrido's maker asserts that the task of relating an authentic Border tale has been accomplished.

1. Which one of the following most accurately expresses the main point of the passage?

    (A) Corrido imagery is one of the clearest indicators of the unique cohesiveness of Border communities.
    (B) The roots of the corrido in the eighteenth-century Spanish ballad tradition are revealed in corridos' conventional themes and language.
    (C) The corrido form, which depends on conventions such as ready-made lines, finds its ideal representation in "Gregorio Cortez."
    (D) Corridos are noted for their vivid use of imagery and their attention to local events.
    (E) The corrido is a type of folk song that promotes cohesiveness in Border communities through the use of familiar conventions.

2. According to the passage, which one of the following is characteristic of corridos?

    (A) use of exaggeration to embellish Border events
    (B) use of numerous figures of speech
    (C) use of a formal closing verse
    (D) use of complex rhyme schemes
    (E) use of verses that combine Spanish and English

GO ON TO THE NEXT PAGE.

3. Given its tone and content, from which one of the following was the passage most likely drawn?

(A) a brochure for contemporary tourists to the Lower Rio Grande Border
(B) a study focusing on the ballad's influence on the music of eighteenth-century Spain
(C) an editorial in a contemporary newspaper from the Lower Rio Grande Border
(D) a treatise on the lives of famous natives of the Lower Rio Grande Border
(E) a book describing various North American folk song forms

4. Which one of the following is mentioned in the passage as an example of the use of metaphor in corridos?

(A) cattle drives
(B) mist
(C) a cypress tree
(D) a fight
(E) stampedes

5. The author discusses metaphor in the second paragraph primarily in order to

(A) elaborate on a claim about the directness of the language used in corridos
(B) counter the commonplace assertion that narrative is the main object of corridos
(C) emphasize the centrality of poetic language to corridos
(D) point out the longevity of the corrido tradition
(E) identify an element common to all variants of a particular corrido

6. The passage provides the most support for inferring which one of the following?

(A) "El Corrido de Gregorio Cortez" was rarely sung at Border social gatherings.
(B) Most surviving corridos do not exist in complete form.
(C) All complete corridos have some lines in common.
(D) Most corrido variants have the same despedida.
(E) "El Corrido de Kiansis" was composed by someone not from the Border region.

7. The passage most strongly suggests that the author would agree with which one of the following statements?

(A) In at least some cases, the dependence of corridos on ready-made lines hindered the efforts of corrido makers to use metaphor effectively.
(B) The corrido is unique among ballad forms because it uses language that is familiar mainly to local audiences.
(C) Much of the imagery used in corridos can also be identified in ballads from Spain.
(D) The reportorial capability of corridos was probably enhanced by their freedom from the constraints of rhymed ballad forms.
(E) A corrido without a surviving despedida would probably still be identifiable as a corrido.

GO ON TO THE NEXT PAGE.

The characteristic smell or taste of a plant, to insects as well as to humans, depends on its chemical composition. Broadly speaking, plants contain two categories of chemical substances: primary and secondary. The primary substances, such as proteins, carbohydrates, vitamins, and hormones, are required for growth and proper functioning and are found in all plants. The secondary substances are a diverse and multitudinous array of chemicals that have no known role in the internal chemical processes of plants' growth or metabolism. Only a few of these substances occur in any one species of plant, but the same or similar ones tend to occur in related plants such as the various species that constitute a single family. It is these secondary substances that give plants their distinctive tastes and smells.

Insects appear to have played a major role in many plants' having the secondary substances they have today. Such substances undoubtedly first appeared, and new ones continue to appear, as the result of genetic mutations in individual plants. But if a mutation is to survive and be passed on to subsequent generations, it must pass the muster of natural selection—that is, it must increase the likelihood of the organism's surviving and reproducing. Some secondary substances are favored by natural selection because they are scents that attract pollinating insects to blossoms. Such scents signal the presence of nectar, which nourishes the insects without damage to the plants. Other secondary substances that arose by mutation were conserved by natural selection because they proved to be biochemical defenses against the enemies of plants, the majority of which are insects. Some of these defensive substances cause insects to suffer unpleasant symptoms or even to die. Still other secondary substances are not in themselves harmful to insects, but are characteristic smells or tastes that dissuade the insect from feeding by warning it of the presence of some other substance that is harmful.

For hundreds of millions of years there has been an evolutionary competition for advantage between plants and plant-eating insects. If insects are to survive as the plants they eat develop defenses against them, they must switch to other foods or evolve ways to circumvent the plants' defenses. They may evolve a way to detoxify a harmful substance, to store it in their bodies out of harm's way, or to avoid its effects in some other manner. Insects quickly come to prefer the plants whose defenses they can circumvent, and they eventually evolve the ability to identify them by their characteristic flavors or odors, or both. As the competition has progressed, fewer and fewer plants have remained as suitable food sources for any one species of insect; species of insects have thus tended to become associated with narrowly defined and often botanically restricted groups of plants.

8. Which one of the following most accurately expresses the main point of the passage?

(A)   Although the secondary substances in plants do not take part in the plants' basic biological processes, these substances operate as natural defenses against damage and destruction by insects.

(B)   Long-term competition between plants and insects has led to a narrowing of the range of secondary substances present in plants and, thus, also to a narrowing of the range of insect species that eat each species of plant.

(C)   The particular secondary substances possessed by different plants, and thus the distinctive tastes and smells that present-day plants have, result in large part from an evolutionary process of interaction between plants and insects.

(D)   Due to long-term evolutionary pressures exerted by insects, the secondary substances in plants have become numerous and diverse but tend to be similar among closely related species.

(E)   Because plant mutations have led to the development of secondary substances, plants have come to participate in a continuing process of competition with plant-eating insects.

9. Which one of the following is mentioned in the passage as a way in which insects can adapt when a plant develops defenses against them?

(A)   to start eating something else instead
(B)   to avoid plants with certain distinctive leaf or flower structures
(C)   to increase their rate of reproduction
(D)   to pollinate other species of plants
(E)   to avoid contact with the dangerous parts of the plant

10. In the passage, the author discusses primary substances mainly in order to

(A)   provide information about how plants grow and metabolize nutrients
(B)   help explain what secondary substances are
(C)   help distinguish between two ways that insects have affected plant evolution
(D)   indicate the great diversity of chemicals that occur in various species of plants
(E)   provide evidence of plants' adaptation to insects

GO ON TO THE NEXT PAGE.

11. The passage provides the most support for inferring which one of the following?

    (A)   Some chemicals that are not known to be directly involved in the growth or metabolism of any species of plant play vital roles in the lives of various kinds of plants.

    (B)   Most plants that have evolved chemical defense systems against certain insect species are nevertheless used as food by a wide variety of insects that have evolved ways of circumventing those defenses.

    (C)   Most insects that feed exclusively on certain botanically restricted groups of plants are able to identify these plants by means other than their characteristic taste or smell.

    (D)   Many secondary substances that are toxic to insects are thought by scientists to have evolved independently in various unrelated species of plants but to have survived in only a few species.

    (E)   Some toxic substances that are produced by plants evolved in correlation with secondary substances but are not themselves secondary substances.

12. Which one of the following describes a set of relationships that is most closely analogous to the relationships between plants and their primary and secondary substances?

    (A)   Electrical power for the operation of devices such as lights and medical instruments is essential to the proper functioning of hospitals; generators are often used in hospitals to provide electricity in case their usual source of power is temporarily unavailable.

    (B)   Mechanical components such as engines and transmissions are necessary for automobiles to run; features such as paint and taillights give a car its distinctive look and serve functions such as preventing rust and improving safety, but automobiles can run without them.

    (C)   Mechanical components such as gears and rotors are required for the operation of clothing factories; electrical components such as wires and transformers supply the power needed to run the mechanical components, but they do not participate directly in the manufacturing process.

    (D)   Some type of braking system is necessary for trains to be able to decelerate and stop; such systems comprise both friction components that directly contact the trains' wheels and pneumatic components that exert pressure on the friction components.

    (E)   Specially designed word processing programs are necessary for computers to be able to function as word processors; such programs can be stored either in the computers' internal memory system or on external disks that are inserted temporarily into the computers.

13. The passage most strongly suggests that which one of the following is true of secondary substances in plants?

    (A)   Some of them are the results of recent natural mutations in plants.

    (B)   They typically contribute to a plant's taste or smell, but not both.

    (C)   Some of them undergo chemical reactions with substances produced by insects, thus altering the plants' chemical composition.

    (D)   Some species of plants produce only one such substance.

    (E)   A few of them act as regulators of plants' production of primary substances.

14. Based on the passage, the author would be most likely to agree with which one of the following statements about the relationship between plants and insects?

    (A)   The diversity of secondary substances that develop in a plant population is proportional to the number of insects with which that plant population has interacted throughout its evolutionary history.

    (B)   Although few species of plants have benefited from evolutionary interaction with insects, many species of insects use plants without either harming the plants or increasing the plants' chances of survival.

    (C)   Throughout the process of evolutionary change, the number of plant species within each family has generally increased while the number of families of plants has decreased.

    (D)   No particular secondary substance has appeared in plants in direct response to insects, though in many instances insects have influenced which particular secondary substances are present in a plant species.

    (E)   While many species of insects have evolved ways of circumventing plants' chemical defenses, none has done this through outright immunity to plants' secondary substances.

GO ON TO THE NEXT PAGE.

David Warsh's book describes a great contradiction inherent in economic theory since 1776, when Adam Smith published *The Wealth of Nations*. Warsh calls it the struggle between the Pin Factory and the Invisible Hand.

Using the example of a pin factory, Smith emphasized the huge increases in efficiency that could be achieved through increased size. The pin factory's employees, by specializing on narrow tasks, produce far more than they could if each worked independently. Also, Smith was the first to recognize how a market economy can harness self-interest to the common good, leading each individual as though "by an invisible hand to promote an end which was no part of his intention." For example, businesses sell products that people want, at reasonable prices, not because the business owners inherently want to please people but because doing so enables them to make money in a competitive marketplace.

These two concepts, however, are opposed to each other. The parable of the pin factory says that there are increasing returns to scale—the bigger the pin factory, the more specialized its workers can be, and therefore the more pins the factory can produce per worker. But increasing returns create a natural tendency toward monopoly, because a large business can achieve larger scale and hence lower costs than a small business. So given increasing returns, bigger firms tend to drive smaller firms out of business, until each industry is dominated by just a few players. But for the invisible hand to work properly, there must be many competitors in each industry, so that nobody can exert monopoly power. Therefore, the idea that free markets always get it right depends on the assumption that returns to scale are diminishing, not increasing.

For almost two centuries, the assumption of diminishing returns dominated economic theory, with the Pin Factory de-emphasized. Why? As Warsh explains, it wasn't about ideology; it was about following the line of least mathematical resistance. Economics has always had scientific aspirations; economists have always sought the rigor and clarity that comes from representing their ideas using numbers and equations. And the economics of diminishing returns lend themselves readily to elegant formalism, while those of increasing returns—the Pin Factory—are notoriously hard to represent mathematically.

Many economists tried repeatedly to bring the Pin Factory into the mainstream of economic thought to reflect the fact that increasing returns obviously characterized many enterprises, such as railroads. Yet they repeatedly failed because they could not state their ideas rigorously enough. Only since the late 1970s has this "underground river"—a term used to describe the role of increasing returns in economic thought—surfaced into the mainstream of economic thought. By then, economists had finally found ways to describe the Pin Factory with the rigor needed to make it respectable.

15. Which one of the following most accurately expresses the main point of the passage?

(A) Mainstream economists have always assumed that returns to scale are generally increasing rather than decreasing.

(B) The functioning of the Invisible Hand is accepted primarily because diminishing returns can be described with mathematical rigor.

(C) Recent developments in mathematics have enabled the Pin Factory to be modeled even more rigorously than the Invisible Hand.

(D) Adam Smith was the first economist to understand how a market economy can enable individual self-interest to serve the common good.

(E) Economists have, until somewhat recently, failed to account for the increasing returns to scale common in many industries.

16. The author's attitude towards the idea that the Pin Factory model should be part of the mainstream of economic thought could most accurately be described as one of

(A) hostility
(B) uncertainty
(C) curiosity
(D) indifference
(E) receptivity

17. The main purpose of the fourth paragraph is to

(A) critique a theory purporting to resolve the tensions between two economic assumptions

(B) explain a difficulty associated with modeling a particular economic assumption

(C) outline the intuitions supporting a particular economic assumption

(D) describe the tensions resulting from attempts to model two competing economic assumptions

(E) refute an argument against a particular economic assumption

GO ON TO THE NEXT PAGE.

18. It can be inferred from the passage that the Pin Factory model would continue to be an "underground river" (middle of the final paragraph) were it not for

(A) the fact that economics has always been a discipline with scientific aspirations
(B) David Warsh's analysis of the work of Adam Smith
(C) economists' success in representing the Pin Factory model with mathematical rigor
(D) a sudden increase in the tendency of some industries toward monopoly
(E) a lowering of the standards used by economists to assess economic models

19. In the first sentence of the final paragraph, the reference to railroads serves to

(A) resolve an ambiguity inherent in the metaphor of the Invisible Hand
(B) illustrate the difficulty of stating the concept of the Pin Factory with mathematical rigor
(C) call attention to the increasing prevalence of industries that have characteristics of the Pin Factory
(D) point to an industry that illustrates the shortcomings of economists' emphasis on the Invisible Hand
(E) present an example of the high levels of competition achieved in transportation industries

20. Which one of the following best illustrates the concept of increasing returns to scale described in the second paragraph of the passage?

(A) A publishing house is able to greatly improve the productivity of its editors by relaxing the standards to which those editors must adhere. This allows the publishing house to employ many fewer editors.
(B) A large bee colony is able to use some bees solely to guard its nectar sources. This enables the colony to collect more nectar, which can feed a larger colony that can better divide up the work of processing the nectar.
(C) A school district increases the total number of students that can be accommodated in a single building by switching to year-round operation, with a different quarter of its student body on vacation at any given time.
(D) The lobster industry as a whole is able to catch substantially more lobsters a day with the same number of traps because advances in technology make the doors to the traps easier for lobsters to get through.
(E) A large ant colony divides and produces two competing colonies that each eventually grow large and prosperous enough to divide into more colonies. These colonies together contain more ants than could have existed in one colony.

21. The passage states which one of the following?

(A) The only way that increasing returns to scale could occur is through increases in the specialization of workers.
(B) Economics fails in its quest to be scientific because its models lack mathematical rigor.
(C) The Pin Factory model's long-standing failure to gain prominence among economists was not a problem of ideology.
(D) Under the Pin Factory model no one is in a position to exert monopoly power.
(E) Adam Smith did not recognize any tension between the Pin Factory model and the Invisible Hand model.

22. Which one of the following, if true, would most undermine the connection that the author draws between increased size and monopoly power?

(A) In some industries, there are businesses that are able to exert monopoly power in one geographical region even though there are larger businesses in the same industry in other regions.
(B) As the tasks workers focus on become narrower, the workers are not able to command as high a salary as when they were performing a greater variety of tasks.
(C) When an industry is dominated by only a few players, these businesses often collude in order to set prices as high as a true monopoly would.
(D) The size that a business must reach in order to begin to achieve increasing returns to scale varies widely from industry to industry.
(E) If a business has very specialized workers, any gains in productivity achieved by making workers even more specialized are offset by other factors such as higher training costs and increased turnover.

GO ON TO THE NEXT PAGE.

Passage A

Law enforcement agencies can effectively nullify particular laws, or particular applications of law, simply by declining to prosecute violators. This power appears to be exercised frequently and I attempt here to explain why.

Rules of law are almost always overinclusive: read literally, they forbid some conduct that the legislature that formulated the rule did not want to forbid. The costs of precisely tailoring a rule to the conduct intended to be forbidden would be prohibitive given the limitations of human foresight and the inherent ambiguities of language. The more particularly the legislature tries to describe the forbidden conduct, the more loopholes it will create. Enforcing an overinclusive rule to the letter could impose very heavy social costs. The effect would be like punishing an innocent person in order to reduce the probability of acquitting a guilty one. Of course, the danger of punishing the innocent is not a decisive blow against the use of a particular method of law enforcement; the danger must be traded off against the costs of alternative methods that would reduce it. But there is a technique—discretionary nonenforcement—by which the costs of overinclusion can be reduced without a corresponding increase in underinclusion (loopholes).

Of course, allowing discretionary nonenforcement does not determine the principle by which the law enforcement agency will select its cases. Conceivably the agency could concentrate its resources on those areas of conduct that had been brought inadvertently within the scope of the rule. But this seems unlikely. Capricious enforcement is not unknown (or even rare) but it does not appear to be the central tendency since legislative oversight assures that the agency does not stray too far from the intended, as distinct from the enacted, regulation being enforced.

Passage B

The newspaper reported that 231,000 water customers in the city are late paying their bills—some by months, others by decades. In all, these water delinquents owe the city more than $625 million in overdue bills and penalties. So officials are planning to selectively cut the water to a few residences with outstanding bills to show that they are serious about collecting those debts. Officials plan to target only high-income neighborhoods, to make examples of a few privileged residents who will be in no position to complain since they were caught stiffing the system.

But property owners are responsible for water bills. So why not just do what every other property-related creditor or tax authority does—attach a lien to the property? The money owed would automatically be available whenever a property was sold, and the threat of negative credit implications would be a powerful incentive to keep current with one's water obligations.

Well, here's an answer: a loophole prohibits debts other than taxes from being subject to liens by the city, and, technically, water charges are not taxes. But if the problem is with the law, then why not change the law? Wouldn't that be easier, and politically smarter, than shutting off people's water?

23. Both passages explicitly mention which one of the following?

(A) legal technicalities
(B) incentives
(C) loopholes
(D) language
(E) overinclusive laws

24. Which one of the following statements can be inferred from the material in passage B?

(A) Most water customers in the city are late paying their water bills.
(B) Most of the residences with outstanding water bills are in the city's high-income neighborhoods.
(C) It is appropriate to turn off the water of high-income residents in the city who pay their water bills a few days late.
(D) In recent years, the city has rarely, if ever, turned off the water of customers who were late paying their water bills.
(E) The only reasonable solution to the problem of overdue water bills in the city is to enact a law that classifies water bills as taxes.

25. The role of the word "selectively" in passage B (second to last sentence of the first paragraph) is most closely related to the role of which one of the following words in passage A?

(A) Word from third sentence of the second paragraph: "particularly"
(B) Word from fifth sentence of the second paragraph: "probability"
(C) Word from sixth sentence of the second paragraph: "alternative"
(D) Word from final sentence of the second paragraph: "discretionary"
(E) Word from final sentence of the third paragraph: "capricious"

GO ON TO THE NEXT PAGE.

26. The author of passage A would be most likely to agree with which one of the following statements concerning the plan described in the final two sentences of the first paragraph of passage B?

(A) Officials should not implement the plan until just after the legislature's annual appropriations hearing.

(B) At least the plan would have a lower social cost than would turning off the water of all 231,000 households that have not paid on time.

(C) The plan is a reasonable response to the water department's history of enforcing overinclusive rules to the letter.

(D) A better plan would have been to place liens on the properties owned by those who are late paying their bills.

(E) Instead of implementing the plan, specific laws regarding the payment of water bills should be introduced to provide a more effective set of incentives.

27. Passage A suggests that an instance of "capricious enforcement" (final sentence of the third paragraph) most likely involves

(A) enforcing the law only to the degree that municipal resources make possible

(B) enforcing the law according to the legislature's intent in passing the laws

(C) prioritizing enforcement of the law according to the amount of damage caused by the crimes

(D) not understanding the difference between the letter of the law and the intent of the law

(E) not following the intent of the legislature in enforcing the law

S T O P

IF YOU FINISH BEFORE TIME IS CALLED, YOU MAY CHECK YOUR WORK ON THIS SECTION ONLY.
DO NOT WORK ON ANY OTHER SECTION IN THE TEST.

SECTION II
Time—35 minutes
26 Questions

Directions: Each question in this section is based on the reasoning presented in a brief passage. In answering the questions, you should not make assumptions that are by commonsense standards implausible, superfluous, or incompatible with the passage. For some questions, more than one of the choices could conceivably answer the question. However, you are to choose the **best** answer; that is, choose the response that most accurately and completely answers the question and mark that response on your answer sheet.

1. Technician: Laboratory mice that are used for research aimed at improving human health are usually kept in small cages. Such an environment is neither normal nor healthy for mice. Moreover, the reliability of research using animals is diminished if those animals are not in an environment that is normal for them.

   Which one of the following can be properly inferred from the technician's statements?

   (A) The conditions under which laboratory mice are kept are not likely to change in the near future.
   (B) If laboratory mice were kept under better conditions, it would be appropriate to use them for research aimed at improving human health.
   (C) Research using laboratory mice that is aimed at improving human health is compromised by the conditions under which the mice are kept.
   (D) Those who conduct research aimed at improving human health will develop new research techniques.
   (E) Laboratory mice that are used for research that is not directly related to human health are not usually kept in small cages.

2. "Dumping" is defined as selling a product in another country for less than production cost. Shrimp producers from Country F are selling shrimp in Country G below the cost of producing shrimp in Country G. So Country F's producers are dumping shrimp.

   In order to evaluate the argument above, it is necessary to determine whether

   (A) "production cost" in the definition of dumping refers to the cost of producing the product in the country where it originates or in the country where it is sold
   (B) there is agreement among experts about whether dumping is harmful to the economy of the country in which products are sold for less than production cost
   (C) shrimp producers from Country F charge more for shrimp that they sell within their own country than for shrimp that they sell in Country G
   (D) shrimp producers from Country F will eventually go out of business if they continue to sell shrimp in Country G for less than production cost
   (E) shrimp producers from Country F are selling shrimp in Country G for considerably less than production cost or just slightly less

GO ON TO THE NEXT PAGE.

3. Scientist: Venus contains a hot molten core, like that of Earth. Also like Earth, Venus must expel the excess heat the core generates. On Earth, this occurs entirely through active volcanos and fissures created when tectonic plates separate. Yet Venus has neither active volcanos nor fissures caused by the movement of tectonic plates.

Which one of the following, if true, does the most to resolve the apparent discrepancy described by the scientist?

(A) Rock on the surface of Venus remains solid at much higher temperatures than does rock on Earth.

(B) The surface of Venus is relatively thin, allowing internally produced heat to radiate into space.

(C) The interior of Venus undergoes greater fluctuations in temperature than does that of Earth.

(D) Though Venus lacks active volcanoes and heat-diffusing fissures, it has surface movement somewhat like that of Earth.

(E) The atmosphere of Venus is significantly hotter than that of Earth.

4. Columnist: The managers of some companies routinely donate a certain percentage of their companies' profits each year to charity. Although this practice may seem totally justified and even admirable, it is not. After all, corporate profits are not the property of the managers, but of the companies' owners. The legendary Robin Hood may have stolen from the rich to give to the poor, but he was nevertheless stealing.

Which one of the following, if true, most weakens the analogy used in the argument?

(A) The profits that a company makes in a given year are, in part, returned to the owners of the company.

(B) Managers who routinely donate a certain percentage of corporate profits to charity do so with the owners' tacit consent.

(C) Company managers often donate part of their own income to charities or other philanthropic organizations.

(D) Any charity that accepts corporate donations needs to be able to account for how that money is spent.

(E) Charities often solicit contributions from companies as well as private individuals.

5. Principle: A law whose purpose is to protect wild animal populations should not be enforced against those whose actions do not threaten wild animal populations.

Application: Even though there is a law against capturing wild snakes, which was enacted to protect wild snake populations, snake charmers who violate this law should not be prosecuted.

Which one of the following, if true, most justifies the above application of the principle?

(A) Since there are relatively few snake charmers and they each capture relatively few snakes per year, snake charmers have a minimal effect on wild populations.

(B) Many attempts to prosecute snake charmers under this law have failed because prosecutors lacked adequate knowledge of the procedures used to capture snakes.

(C) Very few, if any, snake charmers are aware that there is a law that prohibits the capture of wild snakes.

(D) Snake populations are much less threatened than the populations of several other species for which capture is legal.

(E) Snake charmers capture wild snakes only because they believe they would be unable to earn a living otherwise.

GO ON TO THE NEXT PAGE.

6. A film makes a profit if the number of people who see it is sufficient to generate revenues from ticket sales greater than the amount spent to make it. Hence, the primary goal of movie executives is to maximize the number of people who see a film. However, it is not the primary goal of television executives to maximize the number of viewers for their shows.

Which one of the following, if true, most helps to explain the difference between the goals of movie executives and those of television executives?

(A) More people are willing to see a film more than once than are willing to watch a television show more than once.

(B) There is no analog in television to the large profits that owners of movie theaters make by selling refreshments to their customers.

(C) The average cost of producing an hour of film is much greater than the average cost of producing an hour of television.

(D) Television shows make their profits from sponsors, who are chiefly concerned with the purchasing power of the people who watch a television show.

(E) Over half of the most popular television shows are shows that viewers do not have to pay to watch.

7. Several companies that make herbal teas containing ginseng assert in their marketing that ginseng counteracts the effects of stress. As a result, many people buy these products hoping to improve their health. Yet no definitive scientific study links ginseng with the relief of stress. Thus, these marketing campaigns make false claims.

The reasoning in the argument is flawed in that the argument

(A) rejects an argument because of its source without evaluating the argument's logical strength

(B) concludes that a claim is false merely on the grounds that it has not been shown to be true

(C) draws an inference on the basis of a sample that is likely to be unrepresentative

(D) fails to address the possibility that many people buy herbal teas containing ginseng because they enjoy drinking the tea

(E) fails to address the possibility that some ingredients other than ginseng in the herbal teas containing ginseng counteract the effects of stress

8. Scientists conjecture that certain microbes consume organic molecules in exposed shale and similar sediments. In so doing, the microbes remove oxygen from the atmosphere and generate carbon dioxide, a gas that, evidence indicates, promotes global warming. They also conjecture that these microbes reproduce more quickly at higher temperatures.

The scientists' conjectures, if true, provide the most support for which one of the following statements?

(A) The microbes' activity will soon diminish as the organic molecules in exposed sediments are depleted.

(B) Every organism that generates carbon dioxide reproduces more quickly at high temperatures.

(C) If global warming occurs, it will be exacerbated by the activity of the microbes.

(D) The microbes do not remove any element other than oxygen from the atmosphere.

(E) A significant portion of the carbon dioxide in Earth's atmosphere was produced by the microbes.

GO ON TO THE NEXT PAGE.

9. A diet whose protein comes from fish is much healthier than one whose protein comes from red meat. Yet if everyone were to adopt this healthier diet, most of the marine species on which it is based would become extinct, making it impossible. Hence, we should not recommend the universal adoption of such a diet.

The reasoning in which one of the following arguments most closely resembles that in the argument above?

(A) Some studies have provided evidence that taking a vitamin E supplement every day reduces one's risk of heart attack. However, it has not been conclusively established that vitamin E supplements are safe for all people. So we should not recommend that everyone take vitamin E supplements every day.

(B) Governments are within their rights to tax tobacco heavily and spend this tax revenue on education. If these taxes become too high, however, people might smoke less, thereby reducing the funding thus generated for education. So such taxes might eventually have to be supplemented by other sources of revenue.

(C) A consumer is better off when limiting purchases to what he or she truly needs and saving or investing any remaining income. If everyone did this, however, the economy would be thrown into a severe recession, thereby making saving and investing impossible for most people. So we should not recommend this spending pattern to everyone.

(D) If legislators spent less time campaigning, they would have more time to do the jobs for which they were elected. But if they did not spend so much time campaigning, they probably would not get reelected. So it is not surprising that legislators spend so much time campaigning.

(E) If we restrict land development in wilderness areas, we help preserve many of the species that now inhabit these areas. But we also thereby reduce the proliferation of the admittedly smaller number of species, such as deer, that flourish in developed areas. So it is not always clear which areas should be designated as wilderness areas.

10. People who are allergic to cats are actually allergic to certain proteins found in the animals' skin secretions and saliva; which particular proteins are responsible, however, varies from allergy sufferer to allergy sufferer. Since all cats shed skin and spread saliva around their environment, there is no such thing as a cat incapable of provoking allergic reactions, although it is common for a given cat to cause an allergic reaction in some—but not all—people who are allergic to cats.

Which one of the following statements is most strongly supported by the information above?

(A) Any particular individual will be allergic to some breeds of cat but not to others.

(B) No cat is capable of causing an allergic reaction in all types of allergy sufferers.

(C) Not all cats are identical with respect to the proteins contained in their skin secretions and saliva.

(D) The allergic reactions of some people who are allergic to cats are more intense than the allergic reactions of other allergy sufferers.

(E) There is no way to predict whether a given cat will produce an allergic reaction in a particular allergy sufferer.

11. Cartographer: Maps are like language: they can be manipulated in order to mislead. That most people are not generally misled by words, however, should not lead us to think that most people are not susceptible to being misled by maps. Most people are taught to be cautious interpreters of language, but education in the sophisticated use of maps is almost nonexistent.

Which one of the following most accurately describes how the statement that most people are taught to be cautious interpreters of language functions in the cartographer's argument?

(A) It is offered as an analogical case that helps to clarify the meaning of the argument's conclusion.

(B) It is a conclusion drawn from the claim that education in the sophisticated use of maps is almost nonexistent.

(C) It is part of a distinction drawn in order to support the argument's conclusion.

(D) It is offered as support for the contention that maps have certain relevant similarities to language.

(E) It is the conclusion drawn in the argument.

GO ON TO THE NEXT PAGE.

12. Journalist: A book claiming that a new drug has dangerous side effects has recently been criticized by a prominent physician. However, the physician is employed by the company that manufactures that drug, and hence probably has personal reasons to deny that the drug is dangerous. Therefore, the critique does not provide legitimate grounds to reject the book's claims about the drug's side effects.

The reasoning in the journalist's argument is most vulnerable to criticism on which one of the following grounds?

(A) It fails to address adequately the possibility that the critique of the book called into question other claims made in the book in addition to the claim that the drug has dangerous side effects.

(B) It takes for granted that anyone even remotely associated with a company that manufactures a drug is unable to fairly weigh evidence concerning possible dangerous side effects of that drug.

(C) It overlooks the possibility that the author of the book was biased for personal reasons in favor of the claim that the drug has dangerous side effects.

(D) It fails to address adequately the possibility that someone who has personal reasons to deny a claim may nonetheless provide legitimate grounds for denying that claim.

(E) It overlooks the possibility that even if a critique does not provide legitimate grounds to reject a claim, this failure need not be the result of any personal biases of the author.

13. A computer game publisher has recently released its latest adventure game. The game's inventive puzzles and compelling plot induce even casual players to become preoccupied with completing it. The game can be purchased from retail outlets or rented for two-day intervals. The publisher offers a rebate equal to the cost of one rental for renters who go on to purchase the game, saving them a significant portion of the purchase price. Since the rate of sales now meets expectations and rentals are exceeding expectations, the publisher predicts that soon sales of the game will also exceed expectations.

Which one of the following, if true, most helps to justify the publisher's prediction?

(A) The game can be purchased directly from the publisher as well as from retailers.

(B) It takes several weeks for most players to complete the game.

(C) The publisher's games are among the most popular computer games on the market.

(D) Most people who complete the game do not play it extensively afterward.

(E) Some people buy and complete the game and then give it away to a friend.

14. City dog licensing records show that more cocker spaniels are registered to addresses in the Flynn Heights neighborhood than to addresses in all other neighborhoods combined. So if an animal control officer finds a stray cocker spaniel anywhere near Flynn Heights, it is likely that the dog belongs to someone in Flynn Heights.

Which one of the following would be most useful to know in order to evaluate the argument?

(A) whether cocker spaniels are more likely than dogs of other breeds to stray from their owners

(B) whether there are more cocker spaniels registered to addresses in Flynn Heights than any other breed of dog

(C) whether the city's animal control officers find more stray dogs in and around Flynn Heights than in any other part of the city

(D) whether the number of pets owned, per capita, is greater for residents of Flynn Heights than for residents of any other neighborhood

(E) whether residents of Flynn Heights are more likely to license their dogs than residents of other neighborhoods are

GO ON TO THE NEXT PAGE.

15. Psychologists recently conducted a study in which people from widely disparate cultures were asked to examine five photographs. Each photograph depicted the face of a person expressing one of five basic human emotions—fear, happiness, disgust, anger, and sadness. The people in the study were asked to identify the emotion being expressed in each photograph. For each photograph, everyone identified the same emotion. This shows that people are genetically predisposed to associate certain facial expressions with certain basic emotions.

Which one of the following is an assumption on which the argument depends?

(A) For each photograph, the emotion that the subjects agreed was being expressed was the emotion that the person photographed was, in fact, feeling.

(B) One's emotional disposition is not influenced by one's culture.

(C) Some behaviors that are present in people from widely disparate cultures are nonetheless culturally influenced.

(D) If there is a behavior common to people of widely disparate cultures, then there is probably a genetic predisposition to that behavior.

(E) The people whose faces were depicted in the photographs were not all from the same culture.

16. Judge: The defendant admits noncompliance with national building codes but asks that penalties not be imposed because he was confused as to whether national or local building codes applied to the area in which he was building. This excuse might be acceptable had he been charged with noncompliance with local codes, but since he is charged with noncompliance with national codes, his excuse is unacceptable.

Which one of the following principles, if valid, most helps to justify the judge's reasoning?

(A) Local codes and national codes must not overlap with each other.

(B) Local codes may be less strict, but not more strict, than national codes.

(C) Any behavior required by national codes is also required by local codes.

(D) Ignorance of the difference between two codes is not an adequate excuse for noncompliance.

(E) A behavior that is in compliance with one law is not necessarily in compliance with another.

17. Brianna: It would have been better to buy a tree last summer rather than this summer. The one we bought this summer is struggling to survive this summer's drought. If we had bought one last summer, it would have been able to survive this summer's drought, because last summer's normal rainfall would have enabled it to develop established roots. Trees with established roots can better withstand droughts.

Which one of the following most accurately expresses the overall conclusion drawn in Brianna's argument?

(A) It would have been better to buy a tree last summer rather than this summer.

(B) The tree purchased this summer is struggling to survive this summer's drought.

(C) If a tree had been purchased last summer, it would be better able to survive this summer's drought.

(D) A tree purchased last summer would have established roots.

(E) Trees with established roots can better withstand droughts.

18. Every delegate to the convention is a party member. Some delegates to the convention are government officials, and each government official who is at the convention is a speaker at the convention, as well.

If the statements above are true, then which one of the following statements must be true?

(A) Every party member at the convention is a delegate to the convention.

(B) At least some speakers at the convention are neither delegates nor party members.

(C) At least some speakers at the convention are delegates to the convention.

(D) All speakers at the convention are government officials.

(E) Every government official at the convention is a party member.

GO ON TO THE NEXT PAGE.

19. Research into artificial intelligence will fail to produce truly intelligent machines unless the focus of the discipline is radically changed. Progress has been made in creating devices of tremendous computational sophistication, but the present focus on computational ability to the exclusion of other abilities will produce devices only as capable of displaying true intelligence as a human being would be who was completely devoid of emotional and other noncognitive responses.

Which one of the following most accurately expresses the main conclusion argued for above?

(A) The current focus of research into artificial intelligence will produce devices no more capable of displaying true intelligence than a person would be who lacked emotions and other noncognitive responses.

(B) If the current focus of research into artificial intelligence is not radically changed, this research will not be able to produce machines capable of true intelligence.

(C) Despite progress in creating machines of great computational sophistication, current research into artificial intelligence has failed to fulfill its objectives.

(D) The capacity to express noncognitive responses such as emotion is at least as important for true intelligence as is computational sophistication.

(E) If a machine is not capable of producing humanlike noncognitive responses, then it cannot be regarded as truly intelligent.

20. A study found that when rating the educational value of specific children's television shows parents tend to base their judgments primarily on how much they themselves enjoyed the shows, and rarely took into account the views of educational psychologists as to the shows' educational value. Accordingly, if the psychologists' views are sound, parents have little reason to trust their own ratings of the educational value of children's television shows.

The argument is most vulnerable to criticism on the grounds that it

(A) relies on a sample that is likely to be unrepresentative of the population with which the conclusion is concerned

(B) takes for granted that parents do not enjoy the same sort of children's television shows that children themselves enjoy

(C) takes for granted that the educational value of a television show should be the only consideration for a parent trying to decide whether a child should watch the show

(D) fails to rule out the possibility that parents' ratings of the shows based on their own enjoyment coincide closely with the educational psychologists' views of the shows' educational values

(E) takes for granted that educational psychologists are the only people who can judge the educational value of children's television shows with a high degree of accuracy

GO ON TO THE NEXT PAGE.

21. Justine: Pellman, Inc. settled the lawsuit out of court by paying $1 million. That Pellman settled instead of going to trial indicates their corporate leaders expected to lose in court.

 Simon: It's unclear whether Pellman's leaders expected to lose in court. But I think they expected that, whether they won or lost the case, the legal fees involved in going to trial would have been more costly than the settlement. So settling the lawsuit seemed the most cost-effective solution.

The dialogue provides the most support for the claim that Justine and Simon disagree with each other about which one of the following?

(A) If the lawsuit against Pellman had gone to trial, it is likely that Pellman would have lost in court.

(B) Pellman's corporate leaders were able to accurately estimate their chances of winning in court.

(C) If Pellman's legal fees for going to trial would have been more costly than the settlement, then settling the lawsuit was the most cost-effective solution for the corporation.

(D) If Pellman's corporate leaders had expected that the legal fees for going to trial would have been less costly than the settlement, they would have taken the lawsuit to trial.

(E) If Pellman's corporate leaders had expected to win in court, then they would not have settled the lawsuit out of court for $1 million.

22. Astrologer: Although some scientists have claimed that there is no correlation between people's astrological signs and their personality types, this claim is scientifically unjustified. Since science does not have precise criteria for distinguishing one personality type from another, scientific studies cannot be used to disprove a correlation between personality type and any other phenomenon.

Which one of the following most accurately describes the role played in the astrologer's argument by the statement that scientific studies cannot be used to disprove a correlation between personality type and any other phenomenon?

(A) It is a claim offered as support for a conclusion that is in turn offered as support for the overall conclusion drawn in the argument.

(B) It is a conclusion for which support is offered and that in turn is offered as support for the overall conclusion drawn in the argument.

(C) It is the overall conclusion drawn in the argument.

(D) It summarizes a position that the argument as a whole is directed toward discrediting.

(E) It provides a specific instance of the general principle that the argument as a whole is directed toward establishing.

23. Ethicist: Only when we know a lot about the events that led to an action are we justified in praising or blaming a person for that action—as we sometimes are. We must therefore reject Tolstoy's rash claim that if we knew a lot about the events leading up to any action, we would cease to regard that action as freely performed.

Which one of the following, if assumed, enables the conclusion of the ethicist's argument to be properly drawn?

(A) People should not be regarded as subject to praise or blame for actions that were caused by conditions beyond their control.

(B) Whether an act is one for which the person doing it is genuinely responsible is not determined by how much information others possess about that act.

(C) We can be justified in praising or blaming a person for an action only when we regard that action as freely performed.

(D) The responsibility a person bears for an action is not a matter of degree; however, our inclination to blame or praise whoever performed the action varies with the amount of information available.

(E) If we do not know much about the events leading up to any given action, we will regard that action as freely performed.

24. Studies have found that human tears contain many of the same hormones that the human body produces in times of emotional stress. Hence, shedding tears removes significant quantities of these hormones from the body. Therefore, crying must have the effect of reducing emotional stress.

The reasoning in the argument is most vulnerable to criticism on the grounds that the argument

(A) overlooks the possibility that if crying has a tendency to reduce emotional stress, this tendency might arise because of something other than the shedding of tears

(B) confuses a condition that is required for the production of a given phenomenon with a condition that in itself would be sufficient to cause the production of that phenomenon

(C) fails to adequately address the possibility that, even if one phenomenon causally contributes to a second phenomenon, the second phenomenon may causally influence the first as well

(D) fails to adequately distinguish between two distinct factors that are jointly responsible for causing a given phenomenon

(E) takes for granted that because certain substances are present whenever a condition occurs, those substances are a cause of that condition

GO ON TO THE NEXT PAGE.

25. If squirrels eat from a bird feeder, it will not attract many birds. However, squirrels eat from a bird feeder only if it lacks a protective cover. So a bird feeder will not attract many birds if it does not have a protective cover.

The flawed pattern of reasoning in the argument above is most similar to that in which one of the following arguments?

(A) If a tire's pressure is too low, the tire will wear out prematurely, and if a tire wears out prematurely, a likely cause is that the pressure was too low. So if a car owner checks the tire pressure regularly, the tires will not wear out prematurely.

(B) If a tire's pressure is too low, the tire will wear out prematurely. But tire pressure will become too low only if the car owner neglects to check the pressure regularly. So a tire will wear out prematurely if the car owner neglects to check the pressure regularly.

(C) Tires wear out prematurely if car owners neglect to check the tire pressure regularly. Unless car owners are unaware of this fact, they check the tire pressure regularly. So car owners need to be made aware of the consequences of neglecting to check the tire pressure.

(D) If a tire's pressure is too low, the tire will wear out prematurely. But tire pressure will become too low if the car owner neglects to check the pressure regularly. Therefore, if the car owner neglects to check the pressure regularly, a tire will wear out prematurely.

(E) If a tire's pressure is too low, the tire will wear out prematurely. But it will also wear out prematurely if it is often driven on gravel roads. Therefore, if a tire is often driven on gravel roads, keeping its pressure from becoming too low will not help it to last longer.

26. Sarah: When commercial fishing boats with permits to fish for certain species accidentally catch a type of fish for which they have no permit, the latter must be thrown back. This is a very wasteful practice because many, if not most, of the rejected fish do not survive. Fishing permits should therefore be altered so that fishers can keep fish caught accidentally.

Amar: Making it legal to keep those fish would probably lead to a lot more "accidents."

The technique Amar uses in responding to Sarah's argument is to

(A) question whether Sarah's recommendation can be put into practice

(B) point out that Sarah used a crucial term in two distinct senses

(C) allude to a factor that supposedly strengthens the case for Sarah's recommendation

(D) contend that Sarah's recommendation has an important negative consequence

(E) maintain that Sarah overlooks important lessons from past policies

STOP

IF YOU FINISH BEFORE TIME IS CALLED, YOU MAY CHECK YOUR WORK ON THIS SECTION ONLY.
DO NOT WORK ON ANY OTHER SECTION IN THE TEST.

NO TEST MATERIAL ON THIS PAGE.
GO ON TO THE NEXT PAGE

SECTION III
Time—35 minutes
25 Questions

Directions: Each question in this section is based on the reasoning presented in a brief passage. In answering the questions, you should not make assumptions that are by commonsense standards implausible, superfluous, or incompatible with the passage. For some questions, more than one of the choices could conceivably answer the question. However, you are to choose the **best** answer; that is, choose the response that most accurately and completely answers the question and mark that response on your answer sheet.

1. Curator: Critics have rightly claimed that removing the centuries-old grime from the frescoes of Michelangelo will expose them to acids formed by the combination of water vapor in human breath with pollutants in the air. Notwithstanding this fact, the restoration should continue, for the frescoes in their present condition cannot be seen as they appeared when painted by Michelangelo.

    Which one of the following principles, if valid, most helps to justify the curator's reasoning?

    (A) The decision as to whether an artwork merits restoration or not should depend on its greatness as judged by aesthetic standards alone.

    (B) An artwork possesses aesthetic value only if there are people who observe and appreciate it.

    (C) It is acceptable to risk future damage to an artwork if the purpose is to enable it to be appreciated in its original form.

    (D) It is right to spend large amounts of money on the restoration of an old artwork if this restoration makes the artwork accessible to large numbers of people.

    (E) A picture that has become encrusted with grime over a long period can no longer be regarded as the same work of art as that painted by the artist.

2. Forest fragmentation occurs when development severs a continuous area of forest, breaking it down into small patches. Some animals, such as white-footed mice, thrive in conditions of forest fragmentation, reaching their highest population densities in small forest patches. These mice are the main carrier of the bacteria that cause Lyme disease, a debilitating illness that is often transmitted from white-footed mice to humans by deer ticks.

    Which one of the following is most strongly supported by the information above?

    (A) White-footed mice are very rarely found in unfragmented forests.

    (B) The population density for most species of small animals increases when a continuous area of forest becomes fragmented.

    (C) Forest fragmentation reduces the number and variety of animal species that an area can support.

    (D) Efforts to stop the fragmentation of forests can have a beneficial effect on human health.

    (E) Deer ticks reach their highest population densities in small forest patches.

GO ON TO THE NEXT PAGE.

3. Statistics reveal that more collisions between bicycles and motor vehicles occur on roads having specifically designated bicycle lanes than on roads having no such lanes. Hence, adding such lanes to existing roads is unlikely to enhance the safety of bicyclists.

The argument is most vulnerable to criticism on the grounds that it

(A) overlooks the possibility that injuries sustained by bicyclists in accidents on roads with bicycle lanes are as serious, on average, as those sustained by bicyclists in accidents on roads without such lanes

(B) fails to address the possibility that there are more bicyclists riding on roads with bicycle lanes than there are riding on roads without such lanes

(C) takes for granted that any road alteration that enhances the safety of bicyclists also enhances the safety of motorists

(D) concludes that adding bicycle lanes to roads will fail to enhance the safety of bicyclists on the grounds that only some roads that currently have such lanes are safe

(E) takes statistical evidence that fails to support a conclusion concerning the safety of bicyclists as evidence that proves the opposite conclusion

4. Over the last few decades, public outcries against pollution have brought about stricter regulations of emissions. The cities that had the most polluted air 30 years ago now have greatly improved air quality. This would not have happened without these stricter regulations.

Which one of the following can be properly inferred from the statements above?

(A) In the city with the worst air pollution today, the air quality is better than it was 30 years ago.

(B) No city has worse air pollution today than it did 30 years ago.

(C) Most of the public outcries against pollution came from people in the cities that had the most polluted air.

(D) The most polluted cities today are not the cities that were the most polluted 30 years ago.

(E) Public criticism led to an improvement in the air quality of the cities that had the most polluted air 30 years ago.

5. Editorialist: Many professional musicians claim that unauthorized music-sharing services, which allow listeners to obtain music for free, rob musicians of royalties. While it is true that musicians are deprived of royalties they deserve, music-sharing services are not to blame since record companies, publishers, managers, and other intermediaries take an inequitably large cut of the revenues from music sales.

The reasoning in the editorialist's argument is most vulnerable to criticism on the grounds that the argument

(A) concludes that one party is not blameworthy merely because another party is blameworthy

(B) attempts to promote a particular behavior simply by showing that many people engage in that behavior

(C) attacks a position based solely on the character of the people who hold that position

(D) tries to show that a position is false simply by pointing out an undesirable consequence of holding that position

(E) treats a necessary condition for blameworthiness as though it were a sufficient condition for blameworthiness

GO ON TO THE NEXT PAGE.

6. Medical columnist: Some doctors recommend taking vitamin C to help maintain overall health because vitamin C is an antioxidant, a substance that protects the body from certain types of oxygen particles that can trigger disease. People suffering from various ailments are encouraged to take vitamin C to guard against developing other health problems. However, doctors are now discouraging some cancer patients from taking vitamin C, even when they are undergoing therapies with side effects that are detrimental to their overall health.

Which one of the following, if true, most helps to explain why the doctors' recommendation to some cancer patients differs from the general recommendation regarding vitamin C?

(A) Some kinds of cancer cells absorb large amounts of vitamin C, which interferes with the oxidation mechanism by which many cancer therapies kill cancer cells.

(B) Vitamin C has not been shown to reduce people's risk of developing cancer, even at the very high dosage levels recommended by some doctors.

(C) Cancer cells that are susceptible to certain types of cancer therapies are not likely to be affected by the presence of vitamin C.

(D) The better the overall health of cancer patients while undergoing therapy, the more likely they are to experience a full recovery.

(E) Certain side effects of cancer therapies that are detrimental to patients' overall health are not affected by vitamin C.

7. Researcher: Accurate readings of air pollution are expensive to obtain. Lichens are complex plantlike organisms that absorb airborne pollutants and so may offer a cheaper way to monitor air quality. To investigate this, I harvested lichens at sites plagued by airborne copper pollution, determined the lichens' copper concentration, and compared the results with those acquired using mechanical monitoring devices. The lichens were as accurate as the best equipment available. Thus, lichens can effectively replace expensive pollution-monitoring devices without loss of information.

Which one of the following, if true, most strengthens the researcher's argument?

(A) Mechanical monitoring devices have not already been installed in areas where air pollution is a serious problem.

(B) Copper particles are a component of air pollution in several locales.

(C) Experiments have shown that lichens thrive in areas where air pollution is minimal.

(D) Lichens can easily be grown in laboratories.

(E) Lichens absorb all other significant air pollutants in a manner similar to their absorption of copper.

8. Some claim that migratory birds have an innate homing sense that allows them to return to the same areas year after year. However, there is little evidence to support this belief, since the studies testing whether the accuracy of birds' migratory patterns is due to such an innate ability are inconclusive. After all, birds may simply navigate using landmarks, just as humans do, and we do not say that humans have an innate sense of direction simply because they find their way home time after time.

Which one of the following statements most accurately expresses the main conclusion drawn in the argument?

(A) Neither migratory birds nor humans have an innate homing sense.

(B) There is as yet little reason to accept that birds have an innate homing sense.

(C) Studies testing whether the accuracy of birds' migratory patterns is due to an innate homing sense are inconclusive.

(D) The ability to use landmarks to find one's way home is probably not an innate ability in birds.

(E) It is as false to claim that humans have an innate sense of direction as it is to claim that birds have an innate homing sense.

GO ON TO THE NEXT PAGE.

9. All laundry detergents contain surfactants, which can harm aquatic life. However, the environmental effects of most ingredients in laundry detergents, including most of those in so-called "ecologically friendly" detergents, are unknown. Therefore, there is no reason to suppose that laundry detergents advertised as ecologically friendly are less damaging to the environment than other laundry detergents are.

Which one of the following, if true, most weakens the argument?

(A) Laundry detergents that are advertised as ecologically friendly contain much lower amounts of surfactants, on average, than do other laundry detergents.

(B) There is no reason to suppose that most of the ingredients in laundry detergents not advertised as ecologically friendly harm the environment significantly.

(C) Different kinds of laundry detergents contain different kinds of surfactants, which differ in the degree to which they could potentially harm aquatic life.

(D) There is reason to suppose that ingredients in laundry detergents other than surfactants harm the environment more than surfactants do.

(E) Laundry detergents advertised as environmentally friendly are typically less effective than other detergents, so that larger amounts must be used.

10. Fishery officials are still considering options for eliminating Lake Davis's population of razor-toothed northern pike, a fierce game fish that could threaten salmon and trout populations if it slips into the adjoining river system. Introducing pike-specific diseases and draining the lake have been ruled out. Four years ago, poison was added to the lake in order to eliminate the pike. This outraged local residents, because the water remained tainted for months and the region's tourism economy suffered.

Which one of the following is most strongly supported by the information above?

(A) Draining the lake would not cause the region's tourism economy to suffer.

(B) Four years ago was the only time that poison was used against the pike in the lake.

(C) The poison added to the lake four years ago was not successful in ridding the lake of the pike.

(D) Four years ago, fishery officials did not consider any options other than using poison.

(E) Salmon and trout populations in the Lake Davis area are essential to the region's economy.

11. Counselor: Many people assume that personal conflicts are inevitable, but that assumption is just not so. Personal conflicts arise primarily because people are being irrational. For instance, people often find it easier to ascribe bad qualities to a person than good ones—even when there is more evidence of the latter. If someone suspects that a friend is unreliable, for example, a single instance may turn this suspicion into a feeling of certainty, whereas a belief that someone is reliable is normally built up only after many years of personal interaction.

Which one of the following most accurately expresses the main conclusion drawn in the argument?

(A) Many people assume that personal conflicts are inevitable.

(B) Even when there is more evidence of good qualities than of bad ones, people find it easier to ascribe bad qualities than good ones.

(C) It is irrational to allow a single instance to turn one's suspicion that a friend is unreliable into a feeling of certainty.

(D) Personal conflicts are not inevitable.

(E) Unlike a suspicion that a friend is unreliable, a belief that someone is reliable is normally built up only after many years of personal interaction.

12. Dried parsley should never be used in cooking, for it is far less tasty and healthful than fresh parsley is.

Which one of the following principles, if valid, most clearly helps to justify the argument above?

(A) Fresh ingredients should be used in cooking whenever possible.

(B) Only the tastiest ingredients should ever be used in cooking.

(C) Ingredients that should never be used in cooking are generally neither tasty nor healthful.

(D) Parsley that is not both tasty and healthful should never be used in cooking.

(E) In cooking, dried ingredients are inferior to fresh ingredients.

GO ON TO THE NEXT PAGE.

13. The size of northern fur seals provides a reliable indication of their population levels—the smaller the average body size of seals in a population, the larger the population. Archaeologists studied seal fossils covering an 800-year period when the seals were hunted for food by Native peoples in North America and found that the average body size of the seals did not vary significantly.

The statements above, if true, provide the most support for which one of the following?

(A) During the 800-year period studied, seal hunting practices did not vary substantially between different groups of Native peoples in North America.

(B) The body size of northern fur seals is not strongly correlated with the overall health of the seals.

(C) Before the 800-year period studied, the average body size of northern fur seals fluctuated dramatically.

(D) Native peoples in North America made an effort to limit their hunting of northern fur seals in order to prevent depletion of seal populations.

(E) Hunting by Native peoples in North America did not significantly reduce the northern fur seal population over the 800-year period studied.

14. Mayor: Our city faces a difficult environmental problem caused by the enormous amount of garbage that we must dispose of. Although new recycling projects could greatly reduce this amount, these projects would actually be counterproductive to the goal of minimizing the overall amount of environmental damage.

Which one of the following, if true, would most help to resolve the apparent inconsistency in the mayor's claims about new recycling projects?

(A) The vehicles that pick up materials for recycling create less pollution than would be caused by incinerating those materials.

(B) The great costs of new recycling projects would prevent other pollution-reducing projects from being undertaken.

(C) The mayor's city has nearly exhausted its landfill space and therefore must incinerate much of its garbage.

(D) More recycling would give industries in the mayor's city a greater incentive to use recycled materials in their manufacturing processes.

(E) People who recycle feel less justified in consuming more than they need than do people who do not recycle.

15. Anyone who knows Ellsworth knows that he is bursting with self-righteousness, touting the idealism of his generation over the greed of the previous generation. So no one who knows him will be surprised that Ellsworth is offended by the suggestions in the media that he has engaged in unethical business practices.

The conclusion drawn above follows logically if which one of the following is assumed?

(A) Everyone suspects self-righteous people of being, in actuality, unethical.

(B) Ellsworth has been accused of unethical business practices before.

(C) Hypocrites often hide behind righteous indignation.

(D) Ellsworth is in fact innocent of all wrongdoing.

(E) Everyone expects self-righteous people to be easily offended.

16. Political scientist: People become unenthusiastic about voting if they believe that important problems can be addressed only by large numbers of people drastically changing their attitudes and that such attitudinal changes generally do not result from government action. The decreasing voter turnout is thus entirely due to a growing conviction that politicians cannot solve the most important problems.

The reasoning in the political scientist's argument is most vulnerable to criticism on the grounds that the argument

(A) presumes, without providing justification, that there is no cause of decreasing voter turnout other than the belief that few important problems can be solved by government action

(B) presumes, without providing justification, that there are no political solutions to the most important problems

(C) infers that important problems can be seriously addressed if people's attitudes do change from the premise that these problems cannot be addressed if people's attitudes do not change

(D) undermines its claim that people no longer believe there are political solutions to important problems by suggesting that people are dissatisfied with politicians

(E) presumes, without providing justification, that voter apathy prevents the attitudinal changes that result in finding solutions to important problems

GO ON TO THE NEXT PAGE.

17. The conventional view is that asteroids strike the earth at random locations, thereby randomly affecting various aspects of the earth's evolution. One iconoclastic geophysicist claims instead that asteroids have struck the earth through a highly organized natural process. Cited as evidence is the unusual pattern of impact craters that form a halo-like swath across the Northern Hemisphere. There is a consensus that these craters appeared at the end of the Cretaceous period, followed by a mass extinction of much land and ocean life.

Which one of the following, if true, would most help to support the iconoclastic geophysicist's claim?

(A) Several asteroid strikes within a short period could produce both volcanic activity that warms the oceans and atmospheric debris that blocks sunlight, and such changes could cause mass extinctions.

(B) If asteroids repeatedly pummel the same spots, the beating may affect the flow of molten rock inside the earth, which would affect the degree to which continents drift around the earth's surface.

(C) The impact craters that form a halo-like swath across the Northern Hemisphere were the result of a single cluster of meteors striking the earth.

(D) Lumpy masses within the earth cause gravitational interactions with approaching asteroids that force them into specific orbits before impact.

(E) No similar pattern of impact craters was created during any other period of the earth's history.

18. The chairperson of Acme Corporation has decided to move the company from its current location in Milltown to Ocean View. Most Acme employees cannot afford housing within a 30-minute commute of Ocean View. So once the company has moved, most Acme employees will have a commute of more than 30 minutes.

The argument requires assuming which one of the following?

(A) All Acme employees can afford housing within a 30-minute commute of Milltown.

(B) The chairperson of Acme has good financial reasons for wanting to move the company to Ocean View.

(C) None of Acme's employees except the chairperson are in favor of moving the company to Ocean View.

(D) Currently, most Acme employees have a commute of less than 30 minutes.

(E) Acme's move to Ocean View will not be accompanied by a significant pay raise for Acme employees.

19. Editorial: Painting involves a sequential application of layers, each of which adheres satisfactorily only if the underlying layer has been properly applied. Education is, in this respect, like the craft of painting. Since the most important steps in painting are preparation of the surface to be painted and application of the primer coat, it makes sense to suppose that _____.

Which one of the following most logically completes the editorial's argument?

(A) in the educator's initial contact with a student, the educator should be as undemanding as possible

(B) students who have a secure grasp of the fundamentals of a subject are likely to make progress in that subject

(C) educators who are not achieving the goals they intended should revise their teaching methods

(D) teaching new students is rewarding but much more difficult than teaching more advanced students

(E) the success of a student's overall educational experience depends above all upon that student's initial educational experience

20. Scientist: Given the human tendency to explore and colonize new areas, some people believe that the galaxy will eventually be colonized by trillions of humans. If so, the vast majority of humans ever to live would be alive during this period of colonization. Since all of us are humans and we have no reason to think we are unrepresentative, the odds are overwhelming that we would be alive during this period, too. But, because we are not alive during this period, the odds are slim that such colonization will ever happen.

The scientist's argument proceeds by

(A) reasoning that because an event has not occurred, that event has a low probability of occurring

(B) drawing a conclusion that implicitly contradicts one of the premises that the argument accepts

(C) taking for granted that dependable predictions about the future cannot ever be made simply on the basis of the present facts

(D) inferring that since an event that is taken to be likely on a given hypothesis has not occurred, the hypothesis is probably false

(E) making a prediction far into the future based on established human tendencies

GO ON TO THE NEXT PAGE.

21. Professor Riley characterized the university president's speech as inflammatory and argued that it was therefore inappropriate. However, Riley has had a long-standing feud with the president, and so we should not conclude that her speech was inflammatory solely on the basis of Riley's testimony. Therefore, unless there are independent reasons to deem the president's speech inflammatory, it is not true that her speech was inappropriate.

The argument is flawed in that it

(A) takes for granted that the speech could not be inappropriate if it was not inflammatory

(B) fails to adequately address the possibility that inflammatory speeches may be appropriate for some audiences

(C) favors the university president's side in a dispute simply because of the president's privileged standing

(D) concludes that Riley's claim is false merely on the grounds that Riley has something to gain if the claim is accepted as true

(E) fails to adequately address the possibility that Riley's animosity toward the university president is well founded

22. Radio producer: Our failure to attract new listeners over the past several years has forced us to choose between devoting some airtime to other, more popular genres of music, and sticking with classical music that appeals only to our small but loyal audience. This audience, however loyal, did not generate enough advertising revenue for us to pay our bills, so if we appeal to them alone, our station risks going out of business. We should not take that risk. We should, therefore, devote some airtime to other, more popular genres of music.

Which one of the following arguments is most similar in its pattern of reasoning to that used by the radio producer?

(A) We should either buy blinds for the windows or make full-length curtains. Blinds would be very expensive to purchase. Thus, if cost is our greatest concern, we should make curtains.

(B) We should either make curtains for the windows or buy blinds. Since the windows are not standard sizes, if we buy blinds we will have to special order them. Since we do not have time to wait for special orders, we should make the curtains.

(C) For the living room windows, we can make curtains or valances or both. We want to have privacy; and while curtains provide privacy, valances do not. So we should make curtains but not valances.

(D) Since we have very little fabric, we will have to either buy more, or make valances instead of curtains. However, if we use this fabric to make valances, then we will have to buy blinds. Since it would be hard to buy fabric that matches what we already have, we should buy blinds.

(E) We should either buy blinds or make curtains for the windows. If we buy blinds but do not make valances, the windows will look bare. We should not have bare windows. So if we do not make the curtains, we should make the valances.

GO ON TO THE NEXT PAGE.

23. Art historian: This painting, purportedly by Mary Cassatt, is a forgery. Although the canvas and other materials are consistent with most of Cassatt's work, and the subject matter is similar to that of Cassatt's finest paintings, the brush style of this painting is not found in any work known to be Cassatt's. Hence this painting is definitely not a genuine Cassatt.

The art historian's argument depends on assuming which one of the following?

(A) The type of canvas and other materials that Cassatt used in most of her work were readily available to others.

(B) None of Cassatt's works is painted using a brush style that is not exhibited in any of her known works.

(C) Cassatt's work generally had a characteristic subject matter that distinguished it from the work of other painters of her era.

(D) The most characteristic feature of Cassatt's work is her brush style.

(E) No painter other than Cassatt would be able to match Cassatt's brush style perfectly.

24. In the Riverview Building, every apartment that has a balcony also has a fireplace. None of the apartments with balconies is a one-bedroom apartment. So none of the one-bedroom apartments has a fireplace.

The flawed nature of the argument above can most effectively be demonstrated by noting that, by parallel reasoning, we could conclude that

(A) every fish has fur since no cat lacks fur and no cat is a fish

(B) some cats lack fur since every dog has fur and no cat is a dog

(C) no dog has fur since every cat has fur and no cat is a dog

(D) every cat is a fish since no cat is a dog and no dog is a fish

(E) no fish is a dog since every dog is a mammal and no fish is a mammal

25. Alissa: If, as the mayor says, the city can no longer continue to fund both the children's museum and local children's television programming, then it should cease funding the television programming. The interactive character of the exhibits at the museum makes for a richer educational experience than watching television, which is largely passive.

Greta: We should stop funding the museum, not the television programming, because, as the mayor has also pointed out, the museum reaches a much smaller audience.

On the basis of their statements, it can be inferred that Alissa and Greta disagree on which one of the following?

(A) whether the city will need to cease funding local children's television programming if it continues funding the children's museum

(B) whether the mayor has spoken truthfully about what will need to happen if the city does not cease funding local children's television programming

(C) whether the city should cease funding local children's television programming if continuing to fund it would mean that the city would have to cease funding the children's museum

(D) whether local children's television programming provides a beneficial educational experience to a greater number of children in the city than does the children's museum

(E) whether the children's museum provides a rich educational experience for those children who visit it

S T O P

IF YOU FINISH BEFORE TIME IS CALLED, YOU MAY CHECK YOUR WORK ON THIS SECTION ONLY.
DO NOT WORK ON ANY OTHER SECTION IN THE TEST.

SECTION IV
Time—35 minutes
25 Questions

Directions: Each question in this section is based on the reasoning presented in a brief passage. In answering the questions, you should not make assumptions that are by commonsense standards implausible, superfluous, or incompatible with the passage. For some questions, more than one of the choices could conceivably answer the question. However, you are to choose the **best** answer; that is, choose the response that most accurately and completely answers the question and mark that response on your answer sheet.

1. Jim's teacher asked him to determine whether a sample of a substance contained iron. Jim knew that magnets attract iron, so he placed a magnet near the substance. Jim concluded that the substance did contain iron, because the substance became attached to the magnet.

   Jim's reasoning is questionable in that it fails to consider the possibility that

   (A) iron sometimes fails to be attracted to magnets
   (B) iron is attracted to other objects besides magnets
   (C) the magnet needed to be oriented in a certain way
   (D) magnets attract substances other than iron
   (E) some magnets attract iron more strongly than others

2. All the books in the library have their proper shelf locations recorded in the catalog. The book Horatio wants is missing from its place on the library shelves, and no one in the library is using it. Since it is not checked out to a borrower nor awaiting shelving nor part of a special display, it must have been either misplaced or stolen.

   Which one of the following most accurately describes the method of reasoning used in the argument?

   (A) An observation about one object is used as a basis for a general conclusion regarding the status of similar objects.
   (B) A deficiency in a system is isolated by arguing that the system failed to control one of the objects that it was intended to control.
   (C) A conclusion about a particular object is rebutted by observing that a generalization that applies to most such objects does not apply to the object in question.
   (D) A generalization is rejected by showing that it fails to hold in one particular instance.
   (E) The conclusion is supported by ruling out other possible explanations of an observed fact.

3. The level of sulfur dioxide in the atmosphere is slightly higher than it was ten years ago. This increase is troubling because ten years ago the Interior Ministry imposed new, stricter regulations on emissions from coal-burning power plants. If these regulations had been followed, then the level of sulfur dioxide in the atmosphere would have decreased.

   Which one of the following can be properly inferred from the statements above?

   (A) If current regulations on emissions from coal-burning power plants are not followed from now on, then the level of sulfur dioxide in the atmosphere will continue to increase.
   (B) There have been violations of the regulations on emissions from coal-burning power plants that were imposed ten years ago.
   (C) If the regulations on emissions from coal-burning power plants are made even stronger, the level of sulfur dioxide in the atmosphere still will not decrease.
   (D) Emissions from coal-burning power plants are one of the main sources of air pollution.
   (E) Government regulations will never reduce the level of sulfur dioxide in the atmosphere.

GO ON TO THE NEXT PAGE.

4. Ecologist: Landfills are generally designed to hold ten years' worth of waste. Some people maintain that as the number of active landfills consequently dwindles over the coming decade, there will inevitably be a crisis in landfill availability. However, their prediction obviously relies on the unlikely assumption that no new landfills will open as currently active ones close and is therefore unsound.

The claim that there will be a crisis in landfill availability plays which one of the following roles in the ecologist's argument?

(A) It follows from the claim stated in the argument's first sentence.
(B) It is the main conclusion of the argument.
(C) It establishes the truth of the argument's conclusion.
(D) It is a claim on which the argument as a whole is designed to cast doubt.
(E) It is an intermediate conclusion of the argument.

5. Recent epidemiological studies report that Country X has the lowest incidence of disease P of any country. Nevertheless, residents of Country X who are reported to have contracted disease P are much more likely to die from it than are residents of any other country.

Which one of the following, if true, most helps to resolve the apparent discrepancy described above?

(A) There are several forms of disease P, some of which are more contagious than others.
(B) Most of the fatal cases of disease P found in Country X involve people who do not reside in Country X.
(C) In Country X, diagnosis of disease P seldom occurs except in the most severe cases of the disease.
(D) The number of cases of disease P that occur in any country fluctuates widely from year to year.
(E) Because of its climate, more potentially fatal illnesses occur in Country X than in many other countries.

6. After an oil spill, rehabilitation centers were set up to save sea otters by removing oil from them. The effort was not worthwhile, however, since 357 affected live otters and 900 that had died were counted, but only 222 affected otters, or 18 percent of those counted, were successfully rehabilitated and survived. Further, the percentage of all those affected that were successfully rehabilitated was much lower still, because only a fifth of the otters that died immediately were ever found.

Which one of the following, as potential challenges, most seriously calls into question evidence offered in support of the conclusion above?

(A) Do sea otters of species other than those represented among the otters counted exist in areas that were not affected by the oil spill?
(B) How is it possible to estimate, of the sea otters that died, how many were not found?
(C) Did the process of capturing sea otters unavoidably involve trapping and releasing some otters that were not affected by the spill?
(D) Were other species of wildlife besides sea otters negatively affected by the oil spill?
(E) What was the eventual cost, per otter rehabilitated, of the rehabilitation operation?

7. Psychologist: Research has shown that a weakened immune system increases vulnerability to cancer. So, cancer-patient support groups, though derided by those who believe that disease is a purely biochemical phenomenon, may indeed have genuine therapeutic value, as it is clear that participation in such groups reduces participants' stress levels.

Which one of the following is an assumption required by the psychologist's argument?

(A) Cancer patients can learn to function well under extreme stress.
(B) Disease is not a biochemical phenomenon at all.
(C) Stress can weaken the immune system.
(D) Discussing one's condition eliminates the stress of being in that condition.
(E) Stress is a symptom of a weakened immune system.

GO ON TO THE NEXT PAGE.

8. Adobe is an ideal material for building in desert environments. It conducts heat very slowly. As a result, a house built of adobe retains the warmth of the desert sun during the cool evenings and then remains cool during the heat of the day, thereby helping to maintain a pleasant temperature. In contrast, houses built of other commonly used building materials, which conduct heat more rapidly, grow hot during the day and cold at night.

Which one of the following most accurately expresses the main conclusion drawn in the argument above?

(A) Adobe is a suitable substitute for other building materials where the heat-conduction properties of the structure are especially important.

(B) In the desert, adobe buildings remain cool during the heat of the day but retain the warmth of the sun during the cool evenings.

(C) Because adobe conducts heat very slowly, adobe houses maintain a pleasant, constant temperature.

(D) Ideally, a material used for building houses in desert environments should enable those houses to maintain a pleasant, constant temperature.

(E) Adobe is an especially suitable material to use for building houses in desert environments.

9. In one study of a particular plant species, 70 percent of the plants studied were reported as having patterned stems. In a second study, which covered approximately the same geographical area, only 40 percent of the plants of that species were reported as having patterned stems.

Which one of the following, if true, most helps to resolve the apparent discrepancy described above?

(A) The first study was carried out at the time of year when plants of the species are at their most populous.

(B) The first study, but not the second study, also collected information about patterned stems in other plant species.

(C) The second study included approximately 15 percent more individual plants than the first study did.

(D) The first study used a broader definition of "patterned."

(E) The focus of the second study was patterned stems, while the first study collected information about patterned stems only as a secondary goal.

10. Letter to the editor: Sites are needed for disposal of contaminated dredge spoils from the local harbor. However, the approach you propose would damage commercial fishing operations. One indication of this is that over 20,000 people have signed petitions opposing your approach and favoring instead the use of sand-capped pits in another area.

Which one of the following most accurately describes a reasoning flaw in the letter's argument?

(A) The argument distorts the editor's view in a manner that makes that view seem more vulnerable to criticism.

(B) The argument fails to establish that the alternative approach referred to is a viable one.

(C) The argument attempts to establish a particular conclusion because doing so is in the letter writer's self-interest rather than because of any genuine concern for the truth of the matter.

(D) The argument's conclusion is based on the testimony of people who have not been shown to have appropriate expertise.

(E) The argument takes for granted that no third option is available that will satisfy all the interested parties.

GO ON TO THE NEXT PAGE.

11. Most universities today offer students a more in-depth and cosmopolitan education than ever before. Until recently, for example, most university history courses required only the reading of textbooks that hardly mentioned the history of Africa or Asia after the ancient periods, or the history of the Americas' indigenous cultures. The history courses at most universities no longer display such limitations.

Which one of the following, if true, most strengthens the argument above?

(A) The history courses that university students find most interesting are comprehensive in their coverage of various periods and cultures.

(B) Many students at universities whose history courses require the reading of books covering all periods and world cultures participate in innovative study-abroad programs.

(C) The extent to which the textbooks of university history courses are culturally inclusive is a strong indication of the extent to which students at those universities get an in-depth and cosmopolitan education.

(D) Universities at which the history courses are quite culturally inclusive do not always have courses in other subject areas that show the same inclusiveness.

(E) University students who in their history courses are required only to read textbooks covering the history of a single culture will not get an in-depth and cosmopolitan education from these courses alone.

12. The government has recently adopted a policy of publishing airline statistics, including statistics about each airline's number of near collisions and its fines for safety violations. However, such disclosure actually undermines the government's goal of making the public more informed about airline safety, because airlines will be much less likely to give complete reports if such information will be made available to the public.

The reasoning in the argument is most vulnerable to criticism on the grounds that it

(A) fails to consider that, even if the reports are incomplete, they may nevertheless provide the public with important information about airline safety

(B) presumes, without providing justification, that the public has a right to all information about matters of public safety

(C) presumes, without providing justification, that information about airline safety is impossible to find in the absence of government disclosures

(D) presumes, without providing justification, that airlines, rather than the government, should be held responsible for accurate reporting of safety information

(E) fails to consider whether the publication of airline safety statistics will have an effect on the revenues of airlines

13. Many economists claim that financial rewards provide the strongest incentive for people to choose one job over another. But in many surveys, most people do not name high salary as the most desirable feature of a job. This shows that these economists overestimate the degree to which people are motivated by money in their job choices.

Which one of the following, if true, most weakens the argument?

(A) Even high wages do not enable people to obtain all the goods they desire.

(B) In many surveys, people say that they would prefer a high-wage job to an otherwise identical job with lower wages.

(C) Jobs that pay the same salary often vary considerably in their other financial benefits.

(D) Many people enjoy the challenge of a difficult job, as long as they feel that their efforts are appreciated.

(E) Some people are not aware that jobs with high salaries typically leave very little time for recreation.

GO ON TO THE NEXT PAGE.

14. Editorial: A proposed new law would limit elementary school class sizes to a maximum of 20 students. Most parents support this measure and argue that making classes smaller allows teachers to devote more time to each student, with the result that students become more engaged in the learning process. However, researchers who conducted a recent study conclude from their results that this reasoning is questionable. The researchers studied schools that had undergone recent reductions in class size, and found that despite an increase in the amount of time teachers spent individually with students, the students' average grades were unchanged.

Which one of the following is an assumption required by the researchers' argument?

(A) The only schools appropriate for study are large elementary schools.
(B) Teachers generally devote the same amount of individualized attention to each student in a class.
(C) Reductions in class size would also involve a decrease in the number of teachers.
(D) Degree of student engagement in the learning process correlates well with students' average grades.
(E) Parental support for the proposed law rests solely on expectations of increased student engagement in the learning process.

15. Camille: Manufacturers of water-saving faucets exaggerate the amount of money such faucets can save. Because the faucets handle such a low volume of water, people using them often let the water run longer than they would otherwise.

Rebecca: It is true that showering now takes longer. Nevertheless, I have had lower water bills since I installed a water-saving faucet. Thus, it is not true that the manufacturers' claims are exaggerated.

The reasoning in Rebecca's argument is questionable in that she takes for granted that

(A) the cost of installing her water-saving faucet was less than her overall savings on her water bill
(B) she saved as much on her water bills as the manufacturers' claims suggested she would
(C) the manufacturers' claims about the savings expected from the installation of water-saving faucets are consistent with one another
(D) people who use water-saving faucets are satisfied with the low volume of water handled by such faucets
(E) installing more water-saving faucets in her house would increase her savings

16. Company spokesperson: In lieu of redesigning our plants, our company recently launched an environmental protection campaign to buy and dispose of old cars, which are generally highly pollutive. Our plants account for just 4 percent of the local air pollution, while automobiles that predate 1980 account for 30 percent. Clearly, we will reduce air pollution more by buying old cars than we would by redesigning our plants.

Which one of the following, if true, most seriously weakens the company spokesperson's argument?

(A) Only 1 percent of the automobiles driven in the local area predate 1980.
(B) It would cost the company over $3 million to reduce its plants' toxic emissions, while its car-buying campaign will save the company money by providing it with reusable scrap metal.
(C) Because the company pays only scrap metal prices for used cars, almost none of the cars sold to the company still run.
(D) Automobiles made after 1980 account for over 30 percent of local air pollution.
(E) Since the company launched its car-buying campaign, the number of citizen groups filing complaints about pollution from the company's plants has decreased.

GO ON TO THE NEXT PAGE.

17. Humankind would not have survived, as it clearly has, if our ancestors had not been motivated by the desire to sacrifice themselves when doing so would ensure the survival of their children or other close relatives. But since even this kind of sacrifice is a form of altruism, it follows that our ancestors were at least partially altruistic.

Which one of the following arguments is most similar in its reasoning to the argument above?

(A) Students do not raise their grades if they do not increase the amount of time they spend studying. Increased study time requires good time management. However, some students do raise their grades. So some students manage their time well.

(B) Organisms are capable of manufacturing their own carbohydrate supply if they do not consume other organisms to obtain it. So plants that consume insects must be incapable of photosynthesis, the means by which most plants produce their carbohydrate supplies.

(C) If fragile ecosystems are not protected by government action their endemic species will perish, for endemic species are by definition those that exist nowhere else but in those ecosystems.

(D) The natural resources used by human beings will be depleted if they are not replaced by alternative materials. But since such replacement generally requires more power, the resources used to create that power will become depleted.

(E) Public buildings do not harmonize with their surroundings if they are not well designed. But any well-designed building is expensive to construct. Thus, either public buildings are expensive to construct or else they do not harmonize with their surroundings.

18. Bus driver: Had the garbage truck not been exceeding the speed limit, it would not have collided with the bus I was driving. I, on the other hand, was abiding by all traffic regulations—as the police report confirms. Therefore, although I might have been able to avoid the collision had I reacted more quickly, the bus company should not reprimand me for the accident.

Which one of the following principles, if valid, most helps to justify the reasoning in the bus driver's argument?

(A) If a vehicle whose driver is violating a traffic regulation collides with a vehicle whose driver is not, the driver of the first vehicle is solely responsible for the accident.

(B) A bus company should not reprimand one of its drivers whose bus is involved in a collision if a police report confirms that the collision was completely the fault of the driver of another vehicle.

(C) Whenever a bus driver causes a collision to occur by violating a traffic regulation, the bus company should reprimand that driver.

(D) A company that employs bus drivers should reprimand those drivers only when they become involved in collisions that they reasonably could have been expected to avoid.

(E) When a bus is involved in a collision, the bus driver should not be reprimanded by the bus company if the collision did not result from the bus driver's violating a traffic regulation.

GO ON TO THE NEXT PAGE.

19. Item Removed From Scoring.

20. Historian: Radio drama requires its listeners to think about what they hear, picturing for themselves such dramatic elements as characters' physical appearances and spatial relationships. Hence, while earlier generations, for whom radio drama was the dominant form of popular entertainment, regularly exercised their imaginations, today's generation of television viewers do so less frequently.

Which one of the following is an assumption required by the historian's argument?

(A) People spend as much time watching television today as people spent listening to radio in radio's heyday.

(B) The more familiar a form of popular entertainment becomes, the less likely its consumers are to exercise their imaginations.

(C) Because it inhibits the development of creativity, television is a particularly undesirable form of popular entertainment.

(D) For today's generation of television viewers, nothing fills the gap left by radio as a medium for exercising the imagination.

(E) Television drama does not require its viewers to think about what they see.

21. Each of the candidates in this year's mayoral election is a small-business owner. Most small-business owners are competent managers. Moreover, no competent manager lacks the skills necessary to be a good mayor. So, most of the candidates in this year's mayoral election have the skills necessary to be a good mayor.

The pattern of flawed reasoning in which one of the following is most similar to that in the argument above?

(A) Anyone who has worked in sales at this company has done so for at least a year. Most of this company's management has worked in its sales department. So, since no one who has worked in the sales department for more than a year fails to understand marketing, most of this company's upper management understands marketing.

(B) Everything on the menu at Maddy's Shake Shop is fat-free. Most fat-free foods and drinks are sugar-free. And all sugar-free foods and drinks are low in calories. Hence, most items on the menu at Maddy's are low in calories.

(C) All the books in Ed's apartment are hardcover books. Most hardcover books are more than 100 pages long. Ed has never read a book longer than 100 pages in its entirety in less than 3 hours. So, Ed has never read any of his books in its entirety in less than 3 hours.

(D) Each of the avant-garde films at this year's film festival is less than an hour long. Most films less than an hour long do not become commercially successful. So, since no movie less than an hour long has an intermission, it follows that most of the movies at this year's film festival do not have an intermission.

(E) All of the bicycle helmets sold in this store have some plastic in them. Most of the bicycle helmets sold in this store have some rubber in them. So, since no helmets that have rubber in them do not also have plastic in them, it follows that most of the helmets in this store that have plastic in them have rubber in them.

GO ON TO THE NEXT PAGE.

4 4 4 4 4 -75- 4

22. One of the most useful social conventions is money, whose universality across societies is matched only by language. Unlike language, which is rooted in an innate ability, money is an artificial, human invention. Hence, it seems probable that the invention of money occurred independently in more than one society.

The argument's conclusion is properly drawn if which one of the following is assumed?

(A) Some societies have been geographically isolated enough not to have been influenced by any other society.

(B) Language emerged independently in different societies at different times in human history.

(C) Universal features of human society that are not inventions are rooted in innate abilities.

(D) If money were not useful, it would not be so widespread.

(E) No human society that adopted the convention of money has since abandoned it.

23. Libel is defined as damaging the reputation of someone by making false statements. Ironically, strong laws against libel can make it impossible for anyone in the public eye to have a good reputation. For the result of strong libel laws is that, for fear of lawsuits, no one will say anything bad about public figures.

Which one of the following principles, if valid, most helps to justify the reasoning in the argument?

(A) The absence of laws against libel makes it possible for everyone in the public eye to have a good reputation.

(B) Even if laws against libel are extremely strong and rigorously enforced, some public figures will acquire bad reputations.

(C) If one makes statements that one sincerely believes, then those statements should not be considered libelous even if they are in fact false and damaging to the reputation of a public figure.

(D) In countries with strong libel laws, people make negative statements about public figures only when such statements can be proved.

(E) Public figures can have good reputations only if there are other public figures who have bad reputations.

24. Mammals cannot digest cellulose and therefore cannot directly obtain glucose from wood. Mushrooms can, however; and some mushrooms use cellulose to make highly branched polymers, the branches of which are a form of glucose called beta-glucans. Beta-glucan extracts from various types of mushrooms slow, reverse, or prevent the growth of cancerous tumors in mammals, and the antitumor activity of beta-glucans increases as the degree of branching increases. These extracts prevent tumor growth not by killing cancer cells directly but by increasing immune-cell activity.

Which one of the following is most strongly supported by the information above?

(A) Mammals obtain no beneficial health effects from eating cellulose.

(B) If extracts from a type of mushroom slow, reverse, or prevent the growth of cancerous tumors in mammals, then the mushroom is capable of using cellulose to make beta-glucans.

(C) The greater the degree of branching of beta-glucans, the greater the degree of immune-cell activity it triggers in mammals.

(D) Immune-cell activity in mammals does not prevent tumor growth by killing cancer cells.

(E) Any organism capable of obtaining glucose from wood can use cellulose to make beta-glucans.

25. A law is successful primarily because the behavior it prescribes has attained the status of custom. Just as manners are observed not because of sanctions attached to them but because, through repetition, contrary behavior becomes unthinkable, so societal laws are obeyed not because the behavior is ethically required or because penalties await those who act otherwise, but because to act otherwise would be uncustomary.

Which one of the following comparisons is utilized by the argument?

(A) As with manners and other customs, laws vary from society to society.

(B) As with manners, the primary basis for a society to consider when adopting a law is custom.

(C) As with manners, the main factor accounting for compliance with laws is custom.

(D) As with manners, most laws do not prescribe behavior that is ethically required.

(E) As with manners, most laws do not have strict penalties awaiting those who transgress them.

S T O P

IF YOU FINISH BEFORE TIME IS CALLED, YOU MAY CHECK YOUR WORK ON THIS SECTION ONLY.
DO NOT WORK ON ANY OTHER SECTION IN THE TEST.

Computing Your Score

Directions:

1. Use the Answer Key on the next page to check your answers.

2. Use the Scoring Worksheet below to compute your raw score.

3. Use the Score Conversion Chart to convert your raw score into the 120–180 scale.*

Scoring Worksheet

1. Enter the number of questions you answered correctly in each section.

	Number Correct
SECTION I	_____
SECTION II	_____
SECTION III	_____
SECTION IV	Unscored

2. Enter the sum here: _____
   This is your Raw Score.

Score Conversion Chart

Use the table below to convert your raw score to the corresponding 120–180 scaled score for PrepTest 138.

Raw Score	Scaled Score	Raw Score	Scaled Score
78	180	38	146
77	180	37	145
76	179	36	144
75	177	35	144
74	176	34	143
73	174	33	142
72	173	32	141
71	172	31	140
70	170	30	140
69	169	29	139
68	168	28	138
67	167	27	137
66	167	26	136
65	166	25	135
64	165	24	134
63	164	23	134
62	163	22	133
61	162	21	131
60	162	20	130
59	161	19	129
58	160	18	128
57	159	17	127
56	159	16	125
55	158	15	123
54	157	14	122
53	157	13	120
52	156	12	120
51	155	11	120
50	154	10	120
49	154	9	120
48	153	8	120
47	152	7	120
46	152	6	120
45	151	5	120
44	150	4	120
43	149	3	120
42	149	2	120
41	148	1	120
40	147	0	120
39	147		

*Scores are reported on a 120–180 score scale, with 120 being the lowest possible score and 180 being the highest possible score.

Answer Key

Question	Section I	Section II	Section III	Section IV*
1	E	C	C	D
2	C	A	D	E
3	E	B	B	B
4	B	B	E	D
5	A	A	A	C
6	C	D	A	B
7	E	B	E	C
8	C	C	B	E
9	A	C	A	D
10	B	C	C	D
11	A	C	D	C
12	B	D	B	A
13	A	B	E	C
14	D	E	B	D
15	E	D	E	B
16	E	C	A	C
17	B	A	D	A
18	C	C	E	E
19	D	B	E	**
20	B	D	D	D
21	C	E	A	B
22	E	B	B	A
23	C	C	B	E
24	D	E	C	C
25	D	B	C	C
26	B	D		
27	E			

*Section IV is unscored. The number of items answered correctly in Section IV should not be added to the raw score.
** Item removed from scoring

PrepTest 139

SECTION I

Time—35 minutes

25 Questions

Directions: Each question in this section is based on the reasoning presented in a brief passage. In answering the questions, you should not make assumptions that are by commonsense standards implausible, superfluous, or incompatible with the passage. For some questions, more than one of the choices could conceivably answer the question. However, you are to choose the **best** answer; that is, choose the response that most accurately and completely answers the question and mark that response on your answer sheet.

1. Police chief: This department's officers are, of course, prohibited from drinking on the job. However, there is one exception: it is extremely valuable for officers to work undercover to investigate nightclubs that have chronic crime problems, and officers may drink in moderation during such work.

   Which one of the following, if true, most helps to justify the exception to the police department's rule stated above?

   (A) Only very experienced police officers are allowed to work undercover investigating nightclubs.

   (B) Many nightclub patrons would suspect that people in a nightclub who refrained from drinking were police officers.

   (C) Over the last several years, the police department has significantly increased its undercover operations in nightclubs.

   (D) Most police officers believe that allowing officers to drink during undercover work in nightclubs does not cause significant problems.

   (E) For the most part, the public is aware that police officers are allowed to drink during undercover operations in nightclubs.

2. Jake: Companies have recently introduced antibacterial household cleaning products that kill common bacteria on surfaces like countertops and floors. It's clear that people who want to minimize the amount of bacteria in their homes should use cleaning products that contain antibacterial agents.

   Karolinka: But studies also suggest that the use of these antibacterial cleaning products can be harmful, since common bacteria that survive the use of these products will eventually produce strains of bacteria that are resistant to antibiotics. That's why antibacterial agents should not be used in household cleaning products.

   The discussion above indicates that Jake and Karolinka agree with each other that which one of the following is true?

   (A) Household cleaning products with antibacterial agents kill some common bacteria.

   (B) Household cleaning products with antibacterial agents remove dirt better than do products lacking those agents.

   (C) The use of antibacterial agents in household cleaning products can produce antibiotic-resistant strains of bacteria.

   (D) Common household bacteria are a serious health concern.

   (E) People should use household cleaning products with antibacterial agents to clean their homes.

GO ON TO THE NEXT PAGE.

3. A study of the dietary habits of a group of people who had recently developed cancer and a group without cancer found that during the previous five years the diets of the two groups' members closely matched each other in the amount of yogurt they contained. Yogurt contains galactose, which is processed in the body by an enzyme. In the people with cancer the levels of this enzyme were too low to process the galactose in the yogurt they were consuming. It can be concluded that galactose in amounts exceeding the body's ability to process it is carcinogenic.

Of the following, which one constitutes the strongest objection to the reasoning in the argument?

(A) The argument fails to consider whether the dietary habits of everyone in the two groups were the same in all other respects.

(B) The argument neglects to recommend that people with low levels of the enzyme avoid eating yogurt.

(C) The argument focuses on only one substance that can increase the risk of cancer, when it is well known that there are many such substances.

(D) The argument overlooks the possibility that cancer causes low levels of the enzyme.

(E) The argument does not specify whether any member of either group lacked the enzyme entirely.

4. Chemical-company employee: A conservation group's study of the pollutants released into the environment by 30 small chemical companies reveals that our company and four other companies together account for 60 percent of the total. Clearly, our company releases more pollutants than most chemical companies similar to us in size.

Which one of the following is an assumption required by the employee's argument?

(A) The conservation group that produced the study is not hostile to the chemical industry.

(B) The employee's company does not produce chemicals whose processing naturally produces more pollutants than the chemicals produced by other small chemical companies.

(C) The total pollution produced by all small chemical companies combined is not greatly outweighed by that produced by large chemical companies.

(D) The four other companies mentioned by the employee do not together account for very close to 60 percent of the total pollution by the 30 companies.

(E) There is no significant variation in the quantities of pollutants released by the other 25 small chemical companies.

5. Journalist: A recent study showed that people who drink three cups of decaffeinated coffee per day are twice as likely to develop arthritis—inflammation of joints resulting from damage to connective tissue—as those who drink three cups of regular coffee per day. Clearly, decaffeinated coffee must contain something that damages connective tissue and that is not present in regular coffee.

Which one of the following would be most useful to know in order to evaluate the journalist's argument?

(A) whether people who exercise regularly are more likely to drink decaffeinated beverages than those who do not

(B) whether people who drink decaffeinated coffee tend to drink coffee less often than those who drink regular coffee

(C) whether the degeneration of connective tissue is slowed by consumption of caffeine and other stimulants

(D) whether most coffee drinkers drink more than three cups of coffee per day

(E) whether people who have arthritis are less likely than the general population to drink coffee of any kind

6. A company that imports and sells collectibles sought to have some of its collectible figurines classified as toys, which are subject to lower import tariffs than collectibles. The company argued that the figurines amuse customers, just as toys do. However, the government agency responsible for tariffs rejected the company's request on the grounds that the figurines are marketed as collector's items rather than toys.

Which one of the following principles, if valid, most helps to justify the government agency's decision?

(A) The tariff classification of an item should depend primarily on how the item is marketed.

(B) When importing products, a company should seek the tariff classification that results in the lowest tariffs.

(C) An object should not be classified as a collectible if it is typically used as a toy.

(D) Objects that are developed primarily to provide amusement should be subject to lower tariffs than other objects.

(E) A company should market its products as collectibles rather than toys if doing so enables it to sell them for higher prices.

GO ON TO THE NEXT PAGE.

7. The photographs that the store developed were quite unsatisfactory. The customer claims to have handled the film correctly. Neither the film nor the camera was defective. If a store does not process pictures properly, the customer is owed a refund, so if the customer's claim is correct, the store owes her a refund.

The argument relies on assuming which one of the following?

(A) If the store owes the customer a refund, then neither the camera nor the film was defective.

(B) If neither the film nor the camera was defective, and the customer handled the film correctly, then the store processed it improperly.

(C) If pictures are taken with a defective camera, then it is not possible for the store to develop those pictures improperly.

(D) If the customer handled the film incorrectly, that is what caused the photographs that the store developed to be unsatisfactory.

(E) If the customer's claim was not correct, then the store does not owe her a refund.

8. When weeding a vegetable garden, one should not try to remove all the weeds. It is true that the more weeds, the less productive the garden. Nevertheless, avoiding the painstaking effort of finding and pulling every single weed more than compensates for the slight productivity loss resulting from leaving a few.

The principle underlying which one of the following arguments is most similar to the principle underlying the argument above?

(A) It is a mistake to try to remove every imperfection from one's personality. Personality imperfections make life difficult sometimes, but people cannot be truly happy if their personalities lack defects.

(B) One should not try to change every aspect of one's personality. Such a radical change is more likely to make one worse off than better off.

(C) If one is trying to improve one's personality by removing imperfections, one should not try to remove them all. For while each imperfection makes one's personality worse, it is no longer worth one's time to remove imperfections if there are only a few left.

(D) One who is trying to improve one's personality by removing imperfections should not try to remove them all. Granted, the fewer imperfections one's personality has, the happier one will be. However, it is never possible to remove all of the imperfections from one's personality.

(E) When one is trying to improve one's personality, one should not try to remove imperfections that do not cause one serious difficulties. Often, removing such an imperfection will only lead to greater imperfections.

9. Doctor: It would benefit public health if junk food were taxed. Not only in this country but in many other countries as well, the excessive proportion of junk food in people's diets contributes to many common and serious health problems. If junk food were much more expensive than healthful food, people would be encouraged to make dietary changes that would reduce these problems.

Which one of the following most accurately expresses the conclusion drawn in the doctor's argument?

(A) Taxing junk food would benefit public health.

(B) In many countries, the excessive proportion of junk food in people's diets contributes to many common and serious health problems.

(C) If junk food were much more expensive than healthful food, people would be encouraged to make dietary changes that would reduce many common and serious health problems.

(D) Taxing junk food would encourage people to reduce the proportion of junk food in their diets.

(E) Junk food should be taxed if doing so would benefit public health.

10. Large deposits of the rare mineral nahcolite formed in salty lakes 50 million to 52 million years ago during the Eocene epoch. Laboratory tests found that, in salty water, nahcolite can form only when the atmosphere contains at least 1,125 parts per million of carbon dioxide.

The statements above, if true, most strongly support which one of the following?

(A) For most of the time since the Eocene epoch, the level of carbon dioxide in the atmosphere has been lower than it was during most of the Eocene epoch.

(B) Levels of carbon dioxide in the atmosphere fluctuated greatly during the Eocene epoch.

(C) Lakes were more likely to be salty during periods when the level of carbon dioxide in the atmosphere was at least 1,125 parts per million.

(D) The atmosphere contained at least 1,125 parts per million of carbon dioxide during at least some part of the Eocene epoch.

(E) No significant deposits of nahcolite have formed at any time since the Eocene epoch.

GO ON TO THE NEXT PAGE.

11. Editor: When asked to name a poet contemporaneous with Shakespeare, 60 percent of high school students picked a twentieth-century poet. Admittedly, it is hard to interpret this result accurately. Does it show that most high school students do not know any poets of Shakespeare's era, or do they just not know what "contemporaneous" means? However, either way, there is clearly something deeply wrong with the educational system.

The statement that the majority of students picked a twentieth-century poet functions primarily in the argument

(A) as evidence that the educational system is producing students who are ignorant of the history of poetry
(B) as evidence of the ambiguity of some questions
(C) to illustrate that research results are difficult to interpret
(D) as evidence that the ambiguity of data should not prevent us from drawing conclusions from them
(E) as evidence that something is deeply wrong with the educational system

12. One should apologize only to a person one has wronged, and only for having wronged that person. To apologize sincerely is to acknowledge that one has acted wrongfully. One cannot apologize sincerely unless one intends not to repeat that wrongful act. To accept an apology sincerely is to acknowledge a wrong, but also to vow not to hold a grudge against the wrongdoer.

The statements above, if true, most strongly support which one of the following?

(A) If one apologizes and subsequently repeats the wrongful act for which one has apologized, then one has not apologized sincerely.
(B) One cannot sincerely accept an apology that was not sincerely offered.
(C) If one commits a wrongful act, then one should sincerely apologize for that act.
(D) An apology that cannot be sincerely accepted cannot be sincerely offered.
(E) An apology cannot be both sincerely offered and sincerely accepted unless each person acknowledges that a wrongful act has occurred.

13. A small collection of copper-alloy kitchen implements was found in an abandoned Roman-era well. Beneath them was a cache of coins, some of which dated to 375 A.D. The implements, therefore, were dropped into the well no earlier than 375 A.D.

Which one of the following, if true, most strengthens the argument?

(A) The coins used in the Roman Empire often remained in circulation for many decades.
(B) The coins were found in a dense cluster that could not have been formed by coins slipping through an accumulation of larger objects.
(C) The coins had far more value than the kitchen implements did.
(D) The items in the well were probably thrown there when people evacuated the area and would have been retrieved if the people had returned.
(E) Items of jewelry found beneath the coins were probably made around 300 A.D.

14. Investigators have not proved that the forest fire was started by campers. Nor have they proved that lightning triggered the fire. So the investigators have not proved that the blaze was caused by campers or lightning.

The flawed pattern of reasoning in which one of the following arguments most closely resembles the flawed pattern of reasoning in the argument above?

(A) Kim has no reason to believe that Sada will win the election. Kim also has no reason to believe that Brown will win the election. So Kim has no reason to believe that either Sada or Brown will win the election.
(B) We have no proof either for the theory that the thief escaped through the vent in the ceiling or for the theory that the thief escaped through the window. Therefore, one theory is as plausible as the other.
(C) Most of the students in my dormitory are engineering majors, and most of the students in my dormitory are from out of town. So most of the engineering majors in my dormitory are from out of town.
(D) In some parts of the forest camping is permitted. Also, hunting is permitted in some parts of the forest. So there are some parts of the forest in which both hunting and camping are permitted.
(E) The evidence shows that the car could have been driven by Jones at the time of the accident; however, it also shows that it could have been driven by Katsarakis at the time of the accident. Therefore, the evidence shows that the car could have been driven by both Jones and Katsarakis at the time of the accident.

GO ON TO THE NEXT PAGE.

15. To reduce the mosquito population in a resort area, hundreds of trees were planted that bear fruit attractive to birds. Over the years, as the trees matured, they attracted a variety of bird species and greatly increased the summer bird population in the area. As expected, the birds ate many mosquitoes. However, the planting of the fruit trees had the very opposite of its intended effect.

Which one of the following, if true, most helps to explain the apparently paradoxical result?

(A) Most of the species of birds that were attracted by the trees that were planted did not eat mosquitoes.

(B) The species of birds that were attracted in the greatest number by the fruit of the trees that were planted did not eat mosquitoes.

(C) The birds attracted to the area by the trees ate many more insects that prey on mosquitoes than they did mosquitoes.

(D) Since the trees were planted, the annual precipitation has been below average, and drier weather tends to keep mosquito populations down.

(E) Increases and decreases in mosquito populations tend to follow a cyclical pattern.

16. Roxanne promised Luke that she would finish their report while he was on vacation; however, the deadline for that report was postponed. Clearly, if you promised a friend that you would meet them for lunch but just before lunch you felt ill, it would not be wrong for you to miss the lunch; your friend would not expect you to be there if you felt ill. Similarly, _____.

Which one of the following most logically completes the argument?

(A) if Roxanne believes that Luke would not expect her to finish the report under the circumstances, then it would be wrong for Roxanne to finish it

(B) it would not be wrong for Roxanne to finish the report if Luke did not expect the deadline to be postponed

(C) if Luke would expect Roxanne to finish the report even after the deadline has been postponed, then it would be wrong for Roxanne not to finish it

(D) if Luke would not expect Roxanne to finish the report under the circumstances, then it would not be wrong for Roxanne to fail to finish it

(E) Luke would not expect Roxanne to finish the report and it would be wrong if she did finish it

17. Politician: A major social problem is children hurting other children. The results of a recent experiment by psychologists establish that watching violent films is at least partly responsible for this aggressive behavior. The psychologists conducted an experiment in which one group of children watched a film of people punching Bobo the Clown dolls. A second group of children was not shown the film. Afterward, both groups of children played together in a room containing a Bobo doll. Most of the children who had seen the film punched the Bobo doll, while most of the other children did not.

Which one of the following, if true, most weakens the politician's argument?

(A) Some of the children who did not punch the Bobo doll, including some who had been shown the film, chastised those who did punch the doll.

(B) The child who punched the Bobo doll the hardest and the most frequently had not been shown the film.

(C) The children who had been shown the film were found to be no more likely than the children who had not been shown the film to punch other children.

(D) Some children who had not been shown the film imitated the behavior of those who had been shown the film and who punched the doll.

(E) Many of the children who participated in the experiment had never seen a Bobo doll before the experiment.

GO ON TO THE NEXT PAGE.

18. Editorial: In order to encourage personal responsibility in adults, society should not restrict the performance of any of the actions of adults or interfere with the likely results except to prevent negative effects on others.

Which one of the following expresses a view that is inconsistent with the principle stated in the editorial?

(A) We should not prevent the students from wasting the classroom time set aside for homework. But this does not mean that they may spend the time any way they wish. Activities disruptive to others should not be tolerated.

(B) The scientist who invented this technology is not the only one who should be allowed to profit from it. After all, there is no evidence that allowing others to profit from this technology will reduce the scientist's own profits.

(C) Even though public smoking may lead to indirect harm to others, it should not be banned. There are several other ways to eliminate this harm that do not restrict the conduct of smokers and hence are preferable to a complete ban on public smoking.

(D) Highway speed limits are a justified restriction of freedom. For drivers who speed do not risk only their own lives; such drivers often injure or kill other people. Moreover, speed limits have been shown to significantly reduce highway accident and fatality rates.

(E) It is not enough that consumable products containing harmful substances have warning labels. Many adults simply ignore such warnings and continue to consume these substances in spite of the harm it may cause them. This is why consuming such substances should be illegal.

19. The goblin fern, which requires a thick layer of leaf litter on the forest floor, is disappearing from North American forests. In spots where it has recently vanished, the leaf litter is unusually thin and, unlike those places where this fern still thrives, is teeming with the European earthworm *Lumbricus rubellus*, which eats leaf litter. *L. rubellus* is thus probably responsible for the fern's disappearance.

Which one of the following is an assumption on which the argument depends?

(A) Wherever there is a thick layer of leaf litter in North American forests, goblin ferns can be found.

(B) None of the earthworms that are native to North America eat leaf litter.

(C) Dead leaves from goblin ferns make up the greater part of the layer of leaf litter on the forest floors where the goblin fern has recently vanished.

(D) There are no spots in the forests of North America where both goblin ferns and earthworms of the species *L. rubellus* can be found.

(E) *L. rubellus* does not favor habitats where the leaf litter layer is considerably thinner than what is required by goblin ferns.

20. Medical reporter: Studies have consistently found that taking an aspirin a day thins the blood slightly, thereby helping to prevent or reduce the severity of heart disease. Since heart disease is one of the most common types of ill health in industrialized nations, most people in such nations would therefore be in better health if they took an aspirin a day.

The reasoning in the doctor's argument is most vulnerable to criticism on which one of the following grounds?

(A) It takes for granted that if medication can reduce the severity of heart disease, it can also prevent some cases of heart disease.

(B) It overlooks the possibility that even if a disease is one of the most common in a nation, most people in that nation are not in significant danger of developing that disease.

(C) It overlooks the possibility that preventing or reducing the severity of heart disease has little or no effect on any of the other most common diseases in industrialized nations.

(D) It fails to address the possibility that taking an aspirin a day is not the single most effective measure for preventing heart disease.

(E) It fails to address the possibility that the studies on the beneficial effects of aspirin were conducted only in industrialized nations.

GO ON TO THE NEXT PAGE.

21. Essayist: Winners of a Nobel prize for science, who are typically professional scientists, have all made significant contributions to science. But amateur scientists have also provided many significant contributions. And unlike professional scientists, who are often motivated by economic necessity or a desire for fame, amateur scientists are motivated by the love of discovery alone.

If the essayist's statements are true, then which one of the following must also be true?

(A) Some amateur scientists who did not win a Nobel prize for science nevertheless made significant contributions to science.

(B) Typically, winners of a Nobel prize for science are not motivated at all by the love of discovery.

(C) The love of discovery is the motive behind many significant contributions to science.

(D) Professional scientists have made a greater overall contribution to science than have amateur scientists.

(E) A professional scientist is more likely to make a significant contribution to science if he or she is motivated by the love of discovery.

22. Company president: Most of our best sales representatives came to the job with a degree in engineering but little or no sales experience. Thus, when we hire sales representatives, we should favor applicants who have engineering degrees but little or no sales experience over applicants with extensive sales experience but no engineering degrees.

Which one of the following, if true, most seriously weakens the company president's argument?

(A) Some of the company's sales representatives completed a degree in engineering while working for the company.

(B) Most of the people hired by the company as sales representatives have had a degree in engineering but no sales experience.

(C) Most of the customers that the company's sales representatives work with have a degree in engineering.

(D) Most of the people who apply for a sales representative position with the company do not have a degree in engineering.

(E) Some of the people who the company has hired as sales representatives and who were subsequently not very good at the job did not have extensive previous sales experience.

23. Anthropologist: Every human culture has taboos against eating certain animals. Some researchers have argued that such taboos originated solely for practical reasons, pointing out, for example, that in many cultures it is taboo to eat domestic animals that provide labor and that are therefore worth more alive than dead. But that conclusion is unwarranted; taboos against eating certain animals might instead have arisen for symbolic, ritualistic reasons, and the presence of the taboos might then have led people to find other uses for those animals.

In the argument, the anthropologist

(A) calls an explanation of a phenomenon into question by pointing out that observations cited as evidence supporting it are also compatible with an alternative explanation of the phenomenon

(B) establishes that an explanation of a phenomenon is false by demonstrating that the evidence that had been cited in support of that explanation was inadequate

(C) rejects the reasoning used to justify a hypothesis about the origins of a phenomenon, on the grounds that there exists another, more plausible hypothesis about the origins of that phenomenon

(D) argues in support of one explanation of a phenomenon by citing evidence incompatible with a rival explanation

(E) describes a hypothesis about the sequence of events involved in the origins of a phenomenon, and then argues that those events occurred in a different sequence

GO ON TO THE NEXT PAGE.

24. In an effort to reduce underage drinking, the Department of Health has been encouraging adolescents to take a pledge not to drink alcohol until they reach the legal age. This seems to be successful. A survey of seventeen-year-olds has found that many who do not drink report having taken a pledge to refrain from drinking, whereas almost all who drink report having never taken such a pledge.

The reasoning in the argument is most vulnerable to criticism because the argument

(A) bases a conclusion about the efficacy of a method to reduce underage drinking merely on a normative judgment about the morality of underage drinking
(B) fails to consider that an alternative method of reducing underage drinking might be more effective
(C) infers from an association between pledging not to drink and refraining from drinking that the pledging was the cause of refraining from drinking
(D) treats a condition that is sufficient to produce an outcome as though it were necessary for the outcome to occur
(E) confuses the claim that many adolescents who do not drink report having taken the pledge with the claim that many who report having taken the pledge do not drink

25. Literary critic: A folktale is a traditional story told in an entertaining way, which may lead some to think that folktales lack deeper meaning. But this is not the case. A folktale is passed along by a culture for generations, and each storyteller adds something of his or her own to the story, and in this way folktales provide great insight into the wisdom of the culture.

The main conclusion of the literary critic's argument can be properly inferred if which one of the following is assumed?

(A) Any tale that is passed along by a culture for generations can provide great insight into the wisdom of that culture.
(B) Any tale that provides insight into the wisdom of a culture is deeply meaningful in some respect.
(C) Not every tale that lacks deep meaning or beauty is told solely for entertainment.
(D) Any tale with deep meaning provides great insight into the wisdom of the culture by which it has been passed on.
(E) A story that is told primarily for entertainment does not necessarily lack deeper meaning.

STOP

IF YOU FINISH BEFORE TIME IS CALLED, YOU MAY CHECK YOUR WORK ON THIS SECTION ONLY.
DO NOT WORK ON ANY OTHER SECTION IN THE TEST.

SECTION II
Time—35 minutes
27 Questions

Directions: Each set of questions in this section is based on a single passage or a pair of passages. The questions are to be answered on the basis of what is **stated** or **implied** in the passage or pair of passages. For some questions, more than one of the choices could conceivably answer the question. However, you are to choose the **best** answer; that is, choose the response that most accurately and completely answers the question and mark that response on your answer sheet.

Over the past 50 years, expansive, low-density communities have proliferated at the edges of many cities in the United States and Canada, creating a phenomenon known as suburban sprawl. Andres Duany, Elizabeth Plater-Zyberk, and Jeff Speck, a group of prominent town planners belonging to a movement called New Urbanism, contend that suburban sprawl contributes to the decline of civic life and civility. For reasons involving the flow of automobile traffic, they note, zoning laws usually dictate that suburban homes, stores, businesses, and schools be built in separate areas, and this separation robs people of communal space where they can interact and get to know one another. It is as difficult to imagine the concept of community without a town square or local pub, these town planners contend, as it is to imagine the concept of family independent of the home.

Suburban housing subdivisions, Duany and his colleagues add, usually contain homes identical not only in appearance but also in price, resulting in a de facto economic segregation of residential neighborhoods. Children growing up in these neighborhoods, whatever their economic circumstances, are certain to be ill prepared for life in a diverse society. Moreover, because the widely separated suburban homes and businesses are connected only by "collector roads," residents are forced to drive, often in heavy traffic, in order to perform many daily tasks. Time that would in a town center involve social interaction within a physical public realm is now spent inside the automobile, where people cease to be community members and instead become motorists, competing for road space, often acting antisocially. Pedestrians rarely act in this manner toward each other. Duany and his colleagues advocate development based on early-twentieth-century urban neighborhoods that mix housing of different prices and offer residents a "gratifying public realm" that includes narrow, tree-lined streets, parks, corner grocery stores, cafes, small neighborhood schools, all within walking distance. This, they believe, would give people of diverse backgrounds and lifestyles an opportunity to interact and thus develop mutual respect.

Opponents of New Urbanism claim that migration to sprawling suburbs is an expression of people's legitimate desire to secure the enjoyment and personal mobility provided by the automobile and the lifestyle that it makes possible. However, the New Urbanists do not question people's right to their own values; instead, they suggest that we should take a more critical view of these values and of the sprawl-conducive zoning and subdivision policies that reflect them. New Urbanists are fundamentally concerned with the long-term social costs of the now-prevailing attitude that individual mobility, consumption, and wealth should be valued absolutely, regardless of their impact on community life.

1. Which one of the following most accurately expresses the main point of the passage?

   (A) In their critique of policies that promote suburban sprawl, the New Urbanists neglect to consider the interests and values of those who prefer suburban lifestyles.

   (B) The New Urbanists hold that suburban sprawl inhibits social interaction among people of diverse economic circumstances, and they advocate specific reforms of zoning laws as a solution to this problem.

   (C) The New Urbanists argue that most people find that life in small urban neighborhoods is generally more gratifying than life in a suburban environment.

   (D) The New Urbanists hold that suburban sprawl has a corrosive effect on community life, and as an alternative they advocate development modeled on small urban neighborhoods.

   (E) The New Urbanists analyze suburban sprawl as a phenomenon that results from short-sighted traffic policies and advocate changes to these traffic policies as a means of reducing the negative effects of sprawl.

2. According to the passage, the New Urbanists cite which one of the following as a detrimental result of the need for people to travel extensively every day by automobile?

   (A) It imposes an extra financial burden on the residents of sprawling suburbs, thus detracting from the advantages of suburban life.

   (B) It detracts from the amount of time that people could otherwise devote to productive employment.

   (C) It increases the amount of time people spend in situations in which antisocial behavior occurs.

   (D) It produces significant amounts of air pollution and thus tends to harm the quality of people's lives.

   (E) It decreases the amount of time that parents spend in enjoyable interactions with their children.

GO ON TO THE NEXT PAGE.

3. The passage most strongly suggests that the New Urbanists would agree with which one of the following statements?

(A) The primary factor affecting a neighborhood's conduciveness to the maintenance of civility is the amount of time required to get from one place to another.

(B) Private citizens in suburbs have little opportunity to influence the long-term effects of zoning policies enacted by public officials.

(C) People who live in suburban neighborhoods usually have little difficulty finding easily accessible jobs that do not require commuting to urban centers.

(D) The spatial configuration of suburban neighborhoods both influences and is influenced by the attitudes of those who live in them.

(E) Although people have a right to their own values, personal values should not affect the ways in which neighborhoods are designed.

4. Which one of the following most accurately describes the author's use of the word "communities" in the first sentence of the first paragraph and "community" in the last sentence of the first paragraph?

(A) They are intended to be understood in almost identical ways, the only significant difference being that one is plural and the other is singular.

(B) The former is intended to refer to dwellings—and their inhabitants—that happen to be clustered together in particular areas; in the latter, the author means that a group of people have a sense of belonging together.

(C) In the former, the author means that the groups referred to are to be defined in terms of the interests of their members; the latter is intended to refer generically to a group of people who have something else in common.

(D) The former is intended to refer to groups of people whose members have professional or political ties to one another; the latter is intended to refer to a geographical area in which people live in close proximity to one another.

(E) In the former, the author means that there are informal personal ties among members of a group of people; the latter is intended to indicate that a group of people have similar backgrounds and lifestyles.

5. Which one of the following, if true, would most weaken the position that the passage attributes to critics of the New Urbanists?

(A) Most people who spend more time than they would like getting from one daily task to another live in central areas of large cities.

(B) Most people who often drive long distances for shopping and entertainment live in small towns rather than in suburban areas surrounding large cities.

(C) Most people who have easy access to shopping and entertainment do not live in suburban areas.

(D) Most people who choose to live in sprawling suburbs do so because comparable housing in neighborhoods that do not require extensive automobile travel is more expensive.

(E) Most people who vote in municipal elections do not cast their votes on the basis of candidates' positions on zoning policies.

6. The passage most strongly suggests that which one of the following would occur if new housing subdivisions in suburban communities were built in accordance with the recommendations of Duany and his colleagues?

(A) The need for zoning laws to help regulate traffic flow would eventually be eliminated.

(B) There would be a decrease in the percentage of suburban buildings that contain two or more apartments.

(C) The amount of time that residents of suburbs spend traveling to the central business districts of cities for work and shopping would increase.

(D) The need for coordination of zoning policies between large-city governments and governments of nearby suburban communities would be eliminated.

(E) There would be an increase in the per capita number of grocery stores and schools in those suburban communities.

7. The second paragraph most strongly supports the inference that the New Urbanists make which one of the following assumptions?

(A) Most of those who buy houses in sprawling suburbs do not pay drastically less than they can afford.

(B) Zoning regulations often cause economically uniform suburbs to become economically diverse.

(C) City dwellers who do not frequently travel in automobiles often have feelings of hostility toward motorists.

(D) Few residents of suburbs are aware of the potential health benefits of walking, instead of driving, to carry out daily tasks.

(E) People generally prefer to live in houses that look very similar to most of the other houses around them.

GO ON TO THE NEXT PAGE.

Passage A

In ancient Greece, Aristotle documented the ability of foraging honeybees to recruit nestmates to a good food source. He did not speculate on how the communication occurred, but he and naturalists since then have observed that a bee that finds a new food source returns to the nest and "dances" for its nestmates. In the 1940s, von Frisch and colleagues discovered a pattern in the dance. They observed a foraging honeybee's dance, deciphered it, and thereby deduced the location of the food source the bee had discovered. Yet questions still remained regarding the precise mechanism used to transmit that information.

In the 1960s, Wenner and Esch each discovered independently that dancing honeybees emit low-frequency sounds, which we now know to come from wing vibrations. Both researchers reasoned that this might explain the bees' ability to communicate effectively even in completely dark nests. But at that time many scientists mistakenly believed that honeybees lack hearing, so the issue remained unresolved. Wenner subsequently proposed that smell rather than hearing was the key to honeybee communication. He hypothesized that honeybees derive information not from sound, but from odors the forager conveys from the food source.

Yet Gould has shown that foragers can dispatch bees to sites they had not actually visited, something that would not be possible if odor were in fact necessary to bees' communication. Finally, using a honeybee robot to simulate the forager's dance, Kirchner and Michelsen showed that sounds emitted during the forager's dance do indeed play an essential role in conveying information about the food's location.

Passage B

All animals communicate in some sense. Bees dance, ants leave trails, some fish emit high-voltage signals. But some species—bees, birds, and primates, for example—communicate symbolically. In an experiment with vervet monkeys in the wild, Seyfarth, Cheney, and Marler found that prerecorded vervet alarm calls from a loudspeaker elicited the same response as did naturally produced vervet calls alerting the group to the presence of a predator of a particular type. Vervets looked upward upon hearing an eagle alarm call, and they scanned the ground below in response to a snake alarm call. These responses suggest that each alarm call represents, for vervets, a specific type of predator.

Karl von Frisch was first to crack the code of the honeybee's dance, which he described as "language." The dance symbolically represents the distance, direction, and quality of newly discovered food. Adrian Wenner and others believed that bees rely on olfactory cues, as well as the dance, to find a food source, but this has turned out not to be so.

While it is true that bees have a simple nervous system, they do not automatically follow just any information. Biologist James Gould trained foraging bees to find food in a boat placed in the middle of a lake and then allowed them to return to the hive to indicate this new location. He found that hive members ignored the foragers' instructions, presumably because no pollinating flowers grow in such a place.

8. The passages have which one of the following aims in common?

(A) arguing that certain nonhuman animals possess human-like intelligence
(B) illustrating the sophistication with which certain primates communicate
(C) describing certain scientific studies concerned with animal communication
(D) airing a scientific controversy over the function of the honeybee's dance
(E) analyzing the conditions a symbolic system must meet in order to be considered a language

9. Which one of the following statements most accurately characterizes a difference between the two passages?

(A) Passage A is concerned solely with honeybee communication, whereas passage B is concerned with other forms of animal communication as well.
(B) Passage A discusses evidence adduced by scientists in support of certain claims, whereas passage B merely presents some of those claims without discussing the support that has been adduced for them.
(C) Passage B is entirely about recent theories of honeybee communication, whereas passage A outlines the historic development of theories of honeybee communication.
(D) Passage B is concerned with explaining the distinction between symbolic and nonsymbolic communication, whereas passage A, though making use of the distinction, does not explain it.
(E) Passage B is concerned with gaining insight into human communication by considering certain types of nonhuman communication, whereas passage A is concerned with these types of nonhuman communication in their own right.

GO ON TO THE NEXT PAGE.

10. Which one of the following statements is most strongly supported by Gould's research, as reported in the two passages?

(A) When a forager honeybee does not communicate olfactory information to its nestmates, they will often disregard the forager's directions and go to sites of their own choosing.

(B) Forager honeybees instinctively know where pollinating flowers usually grow and will not dispatch their nestmates to any other places.

(C) Only experienced forager honeybees are able to locate the best food sources.

(D) A forager's dances can draw other honeybees to sites that the forager has not visited and can fail to draw other honeybees to sites that the forager has visited.

(E) Forager honeybees can communicate with their nestmates about a newly discovered food source by leaving a trail from the food source to the honeybee nest.

11. It can be inferred from the passages that the author of passage A and the author of passage B would accept which one of the following statements?

(A) Honeybees will ignore the instructions conveyed in the forager's dance if they are unable to detect odors from the food source.

(B) Wenner and Esch established that both sound and odor play a vital role in most honeybee communication.

(C) Most animal species can communicate symbolically in some form or other.

(D) The work of von Frisch was instrumental in answering fundamental questions about how honeybees communicate.

(E) Inexperienced forager honeybees that dance to communicate with other bees in their nest learn the intricacies of the dance from more experienced foragers.

12. Which one of the following most accurately describes a relationship between the two passages?

(A) Passage A discusses and rejects a position that is put forth in passage B.

(B) Passage A gives several examples of a phenomenon for which passage B gives only one example.

(C) Passage A is concerned in its entirety with a phenomenon that passage B discusses in support of a more general thesis.

(D) Passage A proposes a scientific explanation for a phenomenon that passage B argues cannot be plausibly explained.

(E) Passage A provides a historical account of the origins of a phenomenon that is the primary concern of passage B.

GO ON TO THE NEXT PAGE.

Most scholars of Mexican American history mark César Chávez's unionizing efforts among Mexican and Mexican American farm laborers in California as the beginning of Chicano political activism in the 1960s. By 1965, Chávez's United Farm Workers Union gained international recognition by initiating a worldwide boycott of grapes in an effort to get growers in California to sign union contracts. The year 1965 also marks the birth of contemporary Chicano theater, for that is the year Luis Valdez approached Chávez about using theater to organize farm workers. Valdez and the members of the resulting Teatro Campesino are generally credited by scholars as having initiated the Chicano theater movement, a movement that would reach its apex in the 1970s.

In the fall of 1965, Valdez gathered a group of striking farm workers and asked them to talk about their working conditions. A former farm worker himself, Valdez was no stranger to the players in the daily drama that was fieldwork. He asked people to illustrate what happened on the picket lines, and the less timid in the audience delighted in acting out their ridicule of the strikebreakers. Using the farm workers' basic improvisations, Valdez guided the group toward the creation of what he termed "actos," skits or sketches whose roots scholars have traced to various sources that had influenced Valdez as a student and as a member of the San Francisco Mime Troupe. Expanding beyond the initial setting of flatbed-truck stages at the fields' edges, the acto became the quintessential form of Chicano theater in the 1960s. According to Valdez, the acto should suggest a solution to the problems exposed in the brief comic statement, and, as with any good political theater, it should satirize the opposition and inspire the audience to social action. Because actos were based on participants' personal experiences, they had palpable immediacy.

In her book El Teatro Campesino, Yolanda Broyles-González rightly criticizes theater historians for having tended to credit Valdez individually with inventing actos as a genre, as if the striking farm workers' improvisational talent had depended entirely on his vision and expertise for the form it took. She traces especially the actos' connections to a similar genre of informal, often satirical shows known as carpas that were performed in tents to mainly working-class audiences. Carpas had flourished earlier in the twentieth century in the border area of Mexico and the United States. Many participants in the formation of the Teatro no doubt had substantial cultural links to this tradition and likely adapted it to their improvisations. The early development of the Teatro Campesino was, in fact, a collective accomplishment; still, Valdez's artistic contribution was a crucial one, for the resulting actos were neither carpas nor theater in the European tradition of Valdez's academic training, but a distinctive genre with connections to both.

13. Which one of the following most accurately expresses the main point of the passage?

(A) Some theater historians have begun to challenge the once widely accepted view that in creating the Teatro Campesino, Luis Valdez was largely uninfluenced by earlier historical forms.

(B) In crediting Luis Valdez with founding the Chicano theater movement, theater historians have neglected the role of César Chávez in its early development.

(C) Although the creation of the early material of the Teatro Campesino was a collective accomplishment, Luis Valdez's efforts and expertise were essential factors in determining the form it took.

(D) The success of the early Teatro Campesino depended on the special insights and talents of the amateur performers who were recruited by Luis Valdez to participate in creating actos.

(E) Although, as Yolanda Broyles-González has pointed out, the Teatro Campesino was a collective endeavor, Luis Valdez's political and academic connections helped bring it recognition.

14. The author uses the word "immediacy" (last sentence of the second paragraph) most likely in order to express

(A) how little physical distance there was between the performers in the late 1960s actos and their audiences

(B) the sense of intimacy created by the performers' technique of addressing many of their lines directly to the audience

(C) the ease with which the Teatro Campesino members were able to develop actos based on their own experiences

(D) how closely the director and performers of the Teatro Campesino worked together to build a repertoire of actos

(E) how vividly the actos conveyed the performers' experiences to their audiences

GO ON TO THE NEXT PAGE.

15. The second sentence of the passage functions primarily in which one of the following ways?

(A) It helps explain both a motivation of those who developed the first *actos* and an important aspect of their subject matter.

(B) It introduces a major obstacle that Valdez had to overcome in gaining public acceptance of the work of the Teatro Campesino.

(C) It anticipates and counters a possible objection to the author's view that the *actos* developed by Teatro Campesino were effective as political theater.

(D) It provides an example of the type of topic on which scholars of Mexican American history have typically focused to the exclusion of theater history.

(E) It helps explain why theater historians, in their discussions of Valdez, have often treated him as though he were individually responsible for inventing *actos* as a genre.

16. The passage indicates that the early *actos* of the Teatro Campesino and the *carpas* were similar in that

(A) both had roots in theater in the European tradition

(B) both were studied by the San Francisco Mime Troupe

(C) both were initially performed on farms

(D) both often involved satire

(E) both were part of union organizing drives

17. It can be inferred from the passage that Valdez most likely held which one of the following views?

(A) As a theatrical model, the *carpas* of the early twentieth century were ill-suited to the type of theater that he and the Teatro Campesino were trying to create.

(B) César Chávez should have done more to support the efforts of the Teatro Campesino to use theater to organize striking farm workers.

(C) Avant-garde theater in the European tradition is largely irrelevant to the theatrical expression of the concerns of a mainly working-class audience.

(D) Actors do not require formal training in order to achieve effective and artistically successful theatrical performances.

(E) The aesthetic aspects of a theatrical work should be evaluated independently of its political ramifications.

18. Based on the passage, it can be concluded that the author and Broyles-González hold essentially the same attitude toward

(A) the influences that shaped *carpas* as a dramatic genre

(B) the motives of theater historians in exaggerating the originality of Valdez

(C) the significance of *carpas* for the development of the genre of the *acto*

(D) the extent of Valdez's acquaintance with *carpas* as a dramatic form

(E) the role of the European tradition in shaping Valdez's contribution to the development of *actos*

19. The information in the passage most strongly supports which one of the following statements regarding the Teatro Campesino?

(A) Its efforts to organize farm workers eventually won the acceptance of a few farm owners in California.

(B) It included among its members a number of individuals who, like Valdez, had previously belonged to the San Francisco Mime Troupe.

(C) It did not play a major role in the earliest efforts of the United Farm Workers Union to achieve international recognition.

(D) Although its first performances were entirely in Spanish, it eventually gave some performances partially in English, for the benefit of non-Spanish-speaking audiences.

(E) Its work drew praise not only from critics in the United States but from critics in Mexico as well.

20. The passage most strongly supports which one of the following?

(A) The *carpas* tradition has been widely discussed and analyzed by both U.S. and Mexican theater historians concerned with theatrical performance styles and methods.

(B) Comedy was a prominent feature of Chicano theater in the 1960s.

(C) In directing the *actos* of the Teatro Campesino, Valdez went to great lengths to simulate or recreate certain aspects of what audiences had experienced in the *carpas*.

(D) Many of the earliest *actos* were based on scripts composed by Valdez, which the farm-worker actors modified to suit their own diverse aesthetic and pragmatic interests.

(E) By the early 1970s, Valdez was using *actos* as the basis for other theatrical endeavors and was no longer directly associated with the Teatro Campesino.

GO ON TO THE NEXT PAGE.

In October 1999, the Law Reform Commission of Western Australia (LRCWA) issued its report, "Review of the Civil and Criminal Justice System." Buried within its 400 pages are several important recommendations for introducing contingency fees for lawyers' services into the state of Western Australia. Contingency-fee agreements call for payment only if the lawyer is successful in the case. Because of the lawyer's risk of financial loss, such charges generally exceed regular fees.

Although there are various types of contingency-fee arrangements, the LRCWA has recommended that only one type be introduced: "uplift" fee arrangements, which in the case of a successful outcome require the client to pay the lawyer's normal fee plus an agreed-upon additional percentage of that fee. This restriction is intended to prevent lawyers from gaining disproportionately from awards of damages and thus to ensure that just compensation to plaintiffs is not eroded. A further measure toward this end is found in the recommendation that contingency-fee agreements should be permitted only in cases where two conditions are satisfied: first, the contingency-fee arrangement must be used only as a last resort when all means of avoiding such an arrangement have been exhausted; and second, the lawyer must be satisfied that the client is financially unable to pay the fee in the event that sufficient damages are not awarded.

Unfortunately, under this recommendation, lawyers wishing to enter into an uplift fee arrangement would be forced to investigate not only the legal issues affecting any proposed litigation, but also the financial circumstances of the potential client and the probable cost of the litigation. This process would likely be onerous for a number of reasons, not least of which is the fact that the final cost of litigation depends in large part on factors that may change as the case unfolds, such as strategies adopted by the opposing side.

In addition to being burdensome for lawyers, the proposal to make contingency-fee agreements available only to the least well-off clients would be unfair to other clients. This restriction would unjustly limit freedom of contract and would, in effect, make certain types of litigation inaccessible to middle-income people or even wealthy people who might not be able to liquidate assets to pay the costs of a trial. More importantly, the primary reasons for entering into contingency-fee agreements hold for all clients. First, they provide financing for the costs of pursuing a legal action. Second, they shift the risk of not recovering those costs, and of not obtaining a damages award that will pay their lawyer's fees, from the client to the lawyer. Finally, given the convergence of the lawyer's interest and the client's interest under a contingency-fee arrangement, it is reasonable to assume that such arrangements increase lawyers' diligence and commitment to their cases.

21. As described in the passage, the uplift fee agreements that the LRCWA's report recommends are most closely analogous to which one of the following arrangements?

(A) People who join together to share the costs of purchasing lottery tickets on a regular basis agree to share any eventual proceeds from a lottery drawing in proportion to the amounts they contributed to tickets purchased for that drawing.

(B) A consulting firm reviews a company's operations. The consulting firm will receive payment only if it can substantially reduce the company's operating expenses, in which case it will be paid double its usual fee.

(C) The returns that accrue from the assumption of a large financial risk by members of a business partnership formed to develop and market a new invention are divided among them in proportion to the amount of financial risk each assumed.

(D) The cost of an insurance policy is determined by reference to the likelihood and magnitude of an eventual loss covered by the insurance policy and the administrative and marketing costs involved in marketing and servicing the insurance policy.

(E) A person purchasing a property receives a loan for the purchase from the seller. In order to reduce risk, the seller requires the buyer to pay for an insurance policy that will pay off the loan if the buyer is unable to do so.

22. The passage states which one of the following?

(A) Contingency-fee agreements serve the purpose of transferring the risk of pursuing a legal action from the client to the lawyer.

(B) Contingency-fee agreements of the kind the LRCWA's report recommends would normally not result in lawyers being paid larger fees than they deserve.

(C) At least some of the recommendations in the LRCWA's report are likely to be incorporated into the legal system in the state of Western Australia.

(D) Allowing contingency-fee agreements of the sort recommended in the LRCWA's report would not affect lawyers' diligence and commitment to their cases.

(E) Usually contingency-fee agreements involve an agreement that the fee the lawyer receives will be an agreed-upon percentage of the client's damages.

GO ON TO THE NEXT PAGE.

23. The author's main purpose in the passage is to

(A) defend a proposed reform against criticism

(B) identify the current shortcomings of a legal system and suggest how these should be remedied

(C) support the view that a recommended change would actually worsen the situation it was intended to improve

(D) show that a legal system would not be significantly changed if certain proposed reforms were enacted

(E) explain a suggested reform and critically evaluate it

24. Which one of the following is given by the passage as a reason for the difficulty a lawyer would have in determining whether—according to the LRCWA's recommendations—a prospective client was qualified to enter into an uplift agreement?

(A) The length of time that a trial may last is difficult to predict in advance.

(B) Not all prospective clients would wish to reveal detailed information about their financial circumstances.

(C) Some factors that may affect the cost of litigation can change after the litigation begins.

(D) Uplift agreements should only be used as a last resort.

(E) Investigating whether a client is qualified to enter into an uplift agreement would take time away from investigating the legal issues of the case.

25. The phrase "gaining disproportionately from awards of damages" (near the middle of the second paragraph) is most likely intended by the author to mean

(A) receiving a payment that is of greater monetary value than the legal services rendered by the lawyer

(B) receiving a higher portion of the total amount awarded in damages than is reasonable compensation for the professional services rendered and the amount of risk assumed

(C) receiving a higher proportion of the damages awarded to the client than the client considers fair

(D) receiving a payment that is higher than the lawyer would have received had the client's case been unsuccessful

(E) receiving a higher proportion of the damages awarded to the client than the judge or the jury that awarded the damages intended the lawyer to receive

26. According to the passage, the LRCWA's report recommended that contingency-fee agreements

(A) be used only when it is reasonable to think that such arrangements will increase lawyers' diligence and commitment to their cases

(B) be used only in cases in which clients are unlikely to be awarded enormous damages

(C) be used if the lawyer is not certain that the client seeking to file a lawsuit could pay the lawyer's regular fee if the suit were to be unsuccessful

(D) not be used in cases in which another type of arrangement is practicable

(E) not be used except in cases where the lawyer is reasonably sure that the client will win damages sufficiently large to cover the lawyer's fees

27. Which one of the following, if true, most seriously undermines the author's criticism of the LRCWA's recommendations concerning contingency-fee agreements?

(A) The proportion of lawsuits filed by the least well-off litigants tends to be higher in areas where uplift fee arrangements have been widely used than in areas in which uplift agreements have not been used.

(B) Before the LRCWA's recommendations, lawyers in Western Australia generally made a careful evaluation of prospective clients' financial circumstances before accepting cases that might involve complex or protracted litigation.

(C) There is strong opposition in Western Australia to any legal reform perceived as favoring lawyers, so it is highly unlikely that the LRCWA's recommendations concerning contingency-fee agreements will be implemented.

(D) The total fees charged by lawyers who successfully litigate cases under uplift fee arrangements are, on average, only marginally higher than the total fees charged by lawyers who litigate cases without contingency agreements.

(E) In most jurisdictions in which contingency-fee agreements are allowed, those of the uplift variety are used much less often than are other types of contingency-fee agreements.

S T O P

IF YOU FINISH BEFORE TIME IS CALLED, YOU MAY CHECK YOUR WORK ON THIS SECTION ONLY.
DO NOT WORK ON ANY OTHER SECTION IN THE TEST.

SECTION III
Time—35 minutes
27 Questions

Directions: Each set of questions in this section is based on a single passage or a pair of passages. The questions are to be answered on the basis of what is **stated** or **implied** in the passage or pair of passages. For some questions, more than one of the choices could conceivably answer the question. However, you are to choose the **best** answer; that is, choose the response that most accurately and completely answers the question and mark that response on your answer sheet.

The prevailing trend in agriculture toward massive and highly mechanized production, with its heavy dependence on debt and credit as a means of raising capital, has been linked to the growing problem of bankruptcy among small farms. African American horticulturalist Booker T. Whatley has proposed a comprehensive approach to small farming that runs counter to this trend. Whatley maintains that small farms can operate profitably despite these economic obstacles, and he provides guidelines that he believes will bring about such profitability when combined with smart management and hard work.

Whatley emphasizes that small farms must generate year-round cash flow. To this end, he recommends growing at least ten different crops, which would alleviate financial problems should one crop fail completely. To minimize the need to seek hard-to-obtain loans, the market for the farm products should be developed via a "clientele membership club" (CMC), whereby clients pay in advance for the right to go to the farm and harvest what they require. To help guarantee small farmers a market for all of their crops, Whatley encourages them to grow only crops that clients ask for, and to comply with client requests regarding the use of chemicals.

Whatley stresses that this "pick-your-own" farming is crucial for profitability because 50 percent of a farmer's production cost is tied up with harvesting, and using clients as harvesters allows the farmer to charge 60 percent of what supermarkets charge and still operate the farm at a profit. Whatley's plan also affords farmers the advantage of selling directly to consumers, thus eliminating distribution costs. To realize profits on a 25-acre farm, for example, Whatley suggests that a CMC of about 1,000 people is needed. The CMC would consist primarily of people from metropolitan areas who value fresh produce.

The success of this plan, Whatley cautions, depends in large part on a farm's location: the farm should be situated on a hard-surfaced road within 40 miles of a population center of at least 50,000 people, as studies suggest that people are less inclined to travel any greater distances for food. In this way, Whatley reverses the traditional view of hard-surfaced roads as farm-to-market roads, calling them instead "city-to-farm" roads. The farm should also have well-drained soil and a ready water source for irrigation, since inevitably certain preferred crops will not be drought resistant. Lastly, Whatley recommends carrying liability insurance upwards of $1 million to cover

anyone injured on the farm. Adhering to this plan, Whatley contends, will allow small farms to exist as a viable alternative to sprawling corporate farms while providing top-quality agricultural goods to consumers in most urban areas.

1. Which one of the following most accurately states the main point of the passage?

(A) In reaction to dominant trends in agriculture, Booker T. Whatley has advanced a set of recommendations he claims will enable small farms to thrive.

(B) Booker T. Whatley's approach to farming is sensitive to the demands of the consumer, unlike the dominant approach to farming that focuses on massive and efficient production and depends on debt and credit.

(C) As part of a general critique of the trend in agriculture toward massive production, Booker T. Whatley assesses the ability of small farms to compete against large corporate farms.

(D) While CMCs are not the only key to successful small farming, Booker T. Whatley shows that without them small farms risk failure even with a diversity of crops and a good location.

(E) The adoption of Booker T. Whatley's methods of small farming will eventually threaten the dominance of large-scale production and reliance on debt and credit that mark corporate farming.

GO ON TO THE NEXT PAGE.

2. Based on the information in the passage, which one of the following would Whatley be most likely to view as facilitating adherence to an aspect of his plan for operating a small farm?

    (A) a farmer's planting a relatively unknown crop to test the market for that crop
    (B) a farmer's leaving large lanes between plots of each crop to allow people easy access at harvest time
    (C) a farmer's traveling into the city two afternoons a week to sell fresh produce at a farmer's market
    (D) a farmer's using an honor system whereby produce is displayed on tables in view of the road and passersby can buy produce and leave their money in a box
    (E) a farmer's deciding that for environmental reasons chemicals will no longer be used on the farm to increase yields

3. According to the passage, "pick-your-own" farming is seen by Whatley as necessary to the operation of small farms for which one of the following reasons?

    (A) Customers are given the chance to experience firsthand where their produce comes from.
    (B) It guarantees a substantial year-round cash flow for the farm.
    (C) It allows farmers to maintain profits while charging less for produce than what supermarkets charge.
    (D) Only those varieties of crops that have been specifically selected by clients within the CMC will be grown by the farmer.
    (E) Consumers who are willing to drive to farms to harvest their own food comprise a strong potential market for farmers.

4. The author of the passage is primarily concerned with

    (A) summarizing the main points of an innovative solution to a serious problem
    (B) examining contemporary trends and isolating their strengths and weaknesses
    (C) criticizing widely accepted practices within a key sector of the economy
    (D) demonstrating the advantages and disadvantages of a new strategy within an industry
    (E) analyzing the impact of a new idea on a tradition-driven industry

5. The passage provides the most support for inferring which one of the following statements?

    (A) A corporate farm is more likely to need a loan than a small farm is.
    (B) If small farms charged what supermarkets charge for produce that is fresher than that sold by supermarkets, then small farms would see higher profits in the long term.
    (C) Consumers who live in rural areas are generally less inclined than those who live in metropolitan areas to join a CMC.
    (D) If a CMC requests fewer than ten different crops to be grown, then at least one of Whatley's recommendations will not be followed.
    (E) Distribution costs are accounted for in the budget of a small farm with a CMC and are paid directly by customers.

6. According to the passage, Whatley advocates which one of the following actions because it would help to guarantee that small farms have buyers for all of their produce?

    (A) growing at least ten different crops
    (B) charging 60 percent of what supermarkets charge for the same produce
    (C) recruiting only clients who value fresh produce
    (D) honoring the crop requests and chemical-use preferences of clients
    (E) irrigating crops that are susceptible to drought

7. Which one of the following inferences is most supported by the information in the passage?

    (A) The advance payment to the farmer by CMC members guarantees that members will get the produce they want.
    (B) Hard-surfaced roads are traditionally the means by which some farmers transport their produce to their customers in cities.
    (C) A typical population center of 50,000 should be able to support CMCs on at least fifty 25-acre farms.
    (D) Consumers prefer hard-surfaced roads to other roads because the former cause less wear and tear on their vehicles.
    (E) Most roads with hard surfaces were originally given these surfaces primarily for the sake of farmers.

GO ON TO THE NEXT PAGE.

When Jayne Hinds Bidaut saw her first tintype, she was so struck by its rich creamy tones that she could hardly believe this photographic process had been abandoned. She set out to revive it. Bidaut had been searching for a way to photograph insects from her entomological collection, but paper prints simply seemed too flat to her. The tintype, an image captured on a thin, coated piece of iron (there is no tin in it), provided the detail and dimensionality she wanted. The image-containing emulsion can often create a raised surface on the plate.

For the photographer Dan Estabrook, old albumen prints and tintypes inspired a fantasy. He imagines planting the ones he makes in flea markets and antique shops, to be discovered as "originals" from a bygone time that never existed.

On the verge of a filmless, digital revolution, photography is moving forward into its past. In addition to reviving the tintype process, photographers are polishing daguerreotype plates, coating paper with egg whites, making pinhole cameras, and mixing emulsions from nineteenth-century recipes in order to coax new expressive effects from old photographic techniques. So diverse are the artists returning to photography's roots that the movement is more like a groundswell.

The old techniques are heavily hands-on and idiosyncratic. That is the source of their appeal. It is also the prime reason for their eclipse. Most became obsolete in a few decades, replaced by others that were simpler, cheaper, faster, and more consistent in their results. Only the tintype lasted as a curiosity into the twentieth century. Today's artists quickly discover that to exploit the past is to court the very uncertainty that early innovators sought to banish. Such unpredictability attracted Estabrook to old processes. His work embraces accident and idiosyncrasy in order to foster the illusion of antiquity. In his view, time leaches meaning from every photograph and renders it a lost object, enabling us to project onto it our sentiments and associations. So while the stains and imperfections of prints made from gum bichromate or albumen coatings would probably have been cropped out by a nineteenth-century photographer, Estabrook retains them to heighten the sense of nostalgia.

This preoccupation with contingency offers a clue to the deeper motivations of many of the antiquarian avant-gardists. The widely variable outcome of old techniques virtually guarantees that each production is one of a kind and bears, on some level, the indelible mark of the artist's encounter with a particular set of circumstances. At the same time, old methods offer the possibility of recovering an intimacy with photographic communication that mass media have all but overwhelmed.

8. In the context of the third paragraph, the function of the phrase "on the verge of a filmless, digital revolution" (beginning of the third paragraph) is to

(A) highlight the circumstances that make the renewed interest in early photographic processes ironic

(B) indicate that most photographers are wary of advanced photographic techniques

(C) reveal the author's skeptical views regarding the trend toward the use of old photographic techniques

(D) suggest that most photographers who are artists see little merit in the newest digital technology

(E) imply that the groundswell of interest by photographers in old processes will probably turn out to be a passing fad

9. Based on the passage, which one of the following most accurately describes an attitude displayed by the author toward artists' uses of old photographic techniques?

(A) doubtful hesitation about the artistic value of using old techniques

(B) appreciative understanding of the artists' aesthetic goals

(C) ironic amusement at the continued use of techniques that are obsolete

(D) enthusiastic endorsement of their implicit critique of modern photographic technology

(E) whimsical curiosity about the ways in which the processes work

GO ON TO THE NEXT PAGE.

10. Information in the passage most helps to answer which one of the following questions?

   (A) What are some nineteenth-century photographic techniques that have not been revived?

   (B) What is the chemical makeup of the emulsion applied to the iron plate in the tintype process?

   (C) What are the names of some contemporary photographers who are using pinhole cameras?

   (D) What effect is produced when photographic paper is coated with egg whites?

   (E) What were the perceived advantages of the innovations that led to the obsolescence of many early photographic techniques and processes?

11. Which one of the following most accurately describes the primary purpose of the passage?

   (A) to make a case for the aesthetic value of certain old photographic processes

   (B) to provide details of how certain old methods of photographic processing are used in producing artistic photographs

   (C) to give an account of a surprising recent development in the photographic arts

   (D) to explain the acclaim that photographers using old photographic techniques have received

   (E) to contrast the approaches used by two contemporary photographers

12. Which one of the following is most analogous to the use of old photographic techniques for artistic purposes by late-twentieth-century artists, as described in the passage?

   (A) A biomedical researcher in a pharmaceutical firm researches the potential of certain traditional herbal remedies for curing various skin conditions.

   (B) An architect investigates ancient accounts of classical building styles in order to get inspiration for designing a high-rise office building.

   (C) An engineer uses an early-twentieth-century design for a highly efficient turbocharger in preference to a new computer-aided design.

   (D) A clothing designer uses fabrics woven on old-fashioned looms in order to produce the irregular texture of handwoven garments.

   (E) An artist uses a computer graphics program to reproduce stylized figures from ancient paintings and insert them into a depiction of a modern city landscape.

13. Based on the information in the passage, it can be inferred that Estabrook believes that

   (A) photography in the nineteenth century tended to focus on subjects that are especially striking and aesthetically interesting

   (B) artists can relinquish control over significant aspects of the process of creating their work and still produce the aesthetic effects they desire

   (C) photographs produced in the nineteenth and early twentieth centuries were generally intended to exploit artistically the unpredictability of photographic processing

   (D) it is ethically questionable to produce works of art intended to deceive the viewer into believing that the works are older than they really are

   (E) the aesthetic significance of a photograph depends primarily on factors that can be manipulated after the photograph has been taken

14. The reasoning by which, according to the passage, Estabrook justifies his choice of certain strategies in photographic processing would be most strengthened if which one of the following were true?

   (A) When advanced modern photographic techniques are used to intentionally produce prints with imperfections resembling those in nineteenth-century prints, the resulting prints invariably betray the artifice involved.

   (B) The various feelings evoked by a work of art are independent of the techniques used to produce the work and irrelevant to its artistic value.

   (C) Most people who use photographs as a way of remembering or learning about the past value them almost exclusively for their ability to record their subjects accurately.

   (D) People who are interested in artistic photography seldom see much artistic value in photographs that appear antique but are not really so.

   (E) The latest photographic techniques can produce photographs that are almost completely free of blemishes and highly resistant to deterioration over time.

GO ON TO THE NEXT PAGE.

Passage A is from a 2007 article on the United States patent system; passage B is from a corporate statement.

Passage A

Theoretically, the patent office is only supposed to award patents for "nonobvious" inventions, and the concept of translating between an Internet address and a telephone number certainly seems obvious. Still, a court recently held that a technology company had infringed on patents covering computer servers that perform these translations.

In an ideal world, patents would be narrow enough that companies could "invent around" others' patents if licensing agreements cannot be reached. Unfortunately, the patent system has departed from this ideal. In recent decades, the courts have dramatically lowered the bar for obviousness. As a result, some patents being granted are so broad that inventing around them is practically impossible.

Large technology companies have responded to this proliferation of bad patents with the patent equivalent of nuclear stockpiling. By obtaining hundreds or even thousands of patents, a company can develop a credible deterrent against patent lawsuits: if someone sues it for patent infringement, it can find a patent the other company has infringed and countersue. Often, however, a fundamental mistake is made: not joining this arms race. As a result, a company can find itself defenseless against lawsuits.

Software patents are particularly ripe for abuse because software is assembled from modular components. If the patent system allows those components to be patented, it becomes almost impossible to develop a software product without infringing numerous patents. Moreover, because of the complexity of software, it is often prohibitively expensive to even find all the patents a given software product might in principle be infringing. So even a software maker that wanted to find and license all of the patents relevant to its products is unlikely to be able to do so.

Passage B

Software makers like ours have consistently taken the position that patents generally impede innovation in software development and are inconsistent with open-source/free software. We will continue to work to promote this position and are pleased to join our colleagues in the open-source/free software community, as well as those proprietary vendors who have publicly stated their opposition to software patents.

At the same time, we are forced to live in the world as it is, and that world currently permits software patents. A small number of very large companies have amassed large numbers of software patents. We believe such massive software patent portfolios are ripe for misuse because of the questionable nature of many software patents generally and because of the high cost of patent litigation.

One defense against such misuse is to develop a corresponding portfolio of software patents for defensive purposes. Many software makers, both open-source and proprietary, pursue this strategy. In the interests of our company and in an attempt to protect and promote the open-source community, we have elected to adopt this same stance. We do so reluctantly because of the perceived inconsistency with our stance against software patents; however, prudence dictates this position.

15. Which one of the following pairs would be most appropriate as titles for passage A and passage B, respectively?

(A) "The Use and Abuse of Patents"; "The Necessary Elimination of Software Patents"
(B) "Reforming Patent Laws"; "In Defense of Software Patents"
(C) "Patenting the Obvious"; "Patents: A Defensive Policy"
(D) "A Misunderstanding of Patent Policies"; "Keeping Software Free but Safe"
(E) "Developing a Credible Deterrent Against Patent Lawsuits"; "An Apology to Our Customers"

16. Which one of the following is mentioned in passage A but not in passage B?

(A) the amassing of patents by software companies
(B) the cost of finding all the patents a product may infringe
(C) the negative effect of patents on software development
(D) the high cost of patent litigation in general
(E) the dubious nature of many software patents

17. Which one of the following comes closest to capturing the meaning of the phrase "invent around" (first sentence of the second paragraph of passage A)?

(A) invent a product whose use is so obvious that no one can have a patent on it
(B) conceal the fact that a product infringes a patent
(C) implement a previously patented idea in a way other than that intended by the patent holder
(D) develop new products based on principles that are entirely different from those for products affected by competitors' patents
(E) devise something that serves the same function as the patented invention without violating the patent

GO ON TO THE NEXT PAGE.

18. Which one of the following most accurately describes the relationship between the two passages?

(A) Passage A objectively reports a set of events; passage B subjectively takes issue with aspects of the reported events.

(B) Passage A discusses a problem in an industry; passage B states the position of a party dealing with that problem.

(C) Passage A is highly critical of a defensive strategy used by an industry; passage B is a clarification of that strategy.

(D) Passage A describes an impasse within an industry; passage B suggests a way out of this impasse.

(E) Passage A lays out both sides of a dispute; passage B focuses on one of those sides.

19. The authors of the passages would be most likely to agree that software companies would be well advised to

(A) amass their own portfolios of software patents

(B) attempt to license software patented by other companies

(C) exploit patents already owned by competitors

(D) refrain from infringing on any patents held by other companies

(E) research the patents relevant to their products more thoroughly

20. In terms of what it alludes to, "this same stance" (near the end of the final paragraph of passage B) is most closely related to which one of the following phrases in passage A?

(A) Phrase from first sentence of the passage: nonobvious

(B) Phrase from first sentence of the second paragraph: invent around

(C) Phrase from third sentence of the second paragraph: lowered the bar

(D) Phrase from second sentence of the third paragraph: credible deterrent

(E) Phrase from first sentence of the fourth paragraph: modular components

21. Which one of the following, if true, would cast doubt on the position concerning innovation in software development taken in the first paragraph of passage B?

(A) Most patents for software innovations have a duration of only 20 years or less.

(B) Software companies that do not patent software generally offer products that are more reliable than those that do.

(C) Some proprietary vendors oppose software patents for self-interested reasons.

(D) Software innovation would be less profitable if software could not be patented.

(E) The main beneficiaries of software innovations are large corporations rather than individual innovators.

GO ON TO THE NEXT PAGE.

Calvaria major is a rare but once-abundant tree found on the island of Mauritius, which was also home to the dodo, a large flightless bird that became extinct about three centuries ago. In 1977 Stanley Temple, an ecologist whose investigation of *Calvaria major* was a sidelight to his research on endangered birds of Mauritius, proposed that the population decline of *Calvaria major* was linked to the demise of the dodo, a hypothesis that subsequently gained considerable currency. Temple had found only thirteen *Calvaria major* trees on Mauritius, all overmature and dying, and all estimated by foresters at over 300 years old. These trees produced fruits that appeared fertile but that Temple assumed could no longer germinate, given his failure to find younger trees.

The temporal coincidence between the extinction of the dodo and what Temple considered the last evidence of natural germination of *Calvaria major* seeds led him to posit a causal connection. Specifically, he hypothesized that the fruit of *Calvaria major* had developed its extremely thick-walled pit as an evolutionary response to the dodo's habitual consumption of those fruits, a trait enabling the pits to withstand the abrasive forces exerted on them in the birds' digestive tracts. This defensive thickness, though, ultimately prevented the seeds within the pits from germinating without the thinning caused by abrasion in the dodo's gizzard. What had once been adaptive, Temple maintained, became a lethal imprisonment for the seeds after the dodo vanished.

Although direct proof was unattainable, Temple did offer some additional findings in support of his hypothesis, which lent his argument a semblance of rigor. From studies of other birds, he estimated the abrasive force generated within a dodo's gizzard. Based on this estimate and on test results determining the crush-resistant strength of *Calvaria major* pits, he concluded that the pits could probably have withstood a cycle through a dodo's gizzard. He also fed *Calvaria major* pits to turkeys, and though many of the pits were destroyed, ten emerged, abraded yet intact. Three of these sprouted when planted, which he saw as vindicating his hypothesis.

Though many scientists found this dramatic and intriguing hypothesis plausible, Temple's proposals have been strongly challenged by leading specialists in the field. Where Temple had found only thirteen specimens of *Calvaria major*, Wendy Strahm, the foremost expert on the plant ecology of Mauritius, has identified hundreds, many far younger than three centuries. So *Calvaria major* seeds have in fact germinated, and the tree's reproductive cycle has thus continued, since the dodo's disappearance. Additional counterevidence comes from horticultural research by Anthony Speke, which shows that while only a minority of unabraded *Calvaria major* seeds germinate, the number is still probably sufficient to keep this species from becoming extinct. The population decline, while clearly acute, could easily be due to other factors, including disease and damage done by certain nonindigenous animals introduced onto Mauritius in the past few centuries.

22. Which one of the following most accurately expresses the main point of the passage?

(A) *Calvaria major* germination, though rare, is probably adequate to avoid extinction of the species.

(B) The appeal of Temple's hypothesis notwithstanding, the scarcity of *Calvaria major* is probably not due to the extinction of the dodo.

(C) Temple's experimentation with *Calvaria major* pits, though methodologically unsound, nevertheless led to a probable solution to the mystery of the tree's decline.

(D) Temple's dramatic but speculative hypothesis, though presented without sufficient supporting research, may nevertheless be correct.

(E) *Calvaria major* would probably still be scarce today even if the dodo had not become extinct.

23. The author indicates that Temple's research on birds of the island of Mauritius

(A) was largely concerned with species facing the threat of extinction

(B) furnished him with the basis for his highly accurate estimates of the crush-resistant strength of *Calvaria major* pits

(C) provided experimental evidence that some modern birds' gizzards exert roughly the same amount of abrasive force on their contents as did dodo gizzards

(D) was comprehensive in scope and conducted with methodological precision

(E) was originally inspired by his observation that apparently fertile *Calvaria major* pits were nevertheless no longer able to germinate

GO ON TO THE NEXT PAGE.

24. In saying that Temple's supporting evidence lent his argument a "semblance of rigor" (first sentence of the third paragraph), the author most likely intends to indicate that

(A)   despite his attempts to use strict scientific methodology, Temple's experimental findings regarding *Calvaria major* pits were not carefully derived and thus merely appeared to support his hypothesis

(B)   direct proof of a hypothesis of the sort Temple was investigating is virtually impossible to obtain, even with the most exact measurements and observations

(C)   in contrast to Temple's secondhand information concerning the age of the thirteen overmature *Calvaria major* trees he found, his experiments with turkeys and other birds represented careful and accurate firsthand research

(D)   in his experimentation on *Calvaria major* pits, Temple produced quantitative experimental results that superficially appeared to bolster the scientific credibility of his hypothesis

(E)   although the consensus among experts is that Temple's overall conclusion is mistaken, the scientific precision and the creativity of Temple's experimentation remain admirable

25. The passage indicates which one of the following about the abrasion of *Calvaria major* pit walls?

(A)   Thinning through abrasion is not necessary for germination of *Calvaria major* seeds.

(B)   In Temple's experiment, the abrasion caused by the digestive tracts of turkeys always released *Calvaria major* seeds, undamaged, from their hard coverings.

(C)   Temple was mistaken in believing that the abrasion caused by dodos would have been sufficient to thin the pit walls to any significant degree.

(D)   Abrasion of *Calvaria major* pit walls by the digestive tracts of animals occurred commonly in past centuries but rarely occurs in nature today.

(E)   Temple overlooked the fact that other natural environmental forces have been abrading *Calvaria major* pit walls since the dodo ceased to fulfill this role.

26. It can be most logically inferred from the passage that the author regards Temple's hypothesis that the extinction of the dodo was the cause of *Calvaria major*'s seeming loss of the ability to reproduce as which one of the following?

(A)   essentially correct, but containing some inaccurate details

(B)   initially implausible, but vindicated by his empirical findings

(C)   an example of a valuable scientific achievement outside a researcher's primary area of expertise

(D)   laudable for its precise formulation and its attention to historical detail

(E)   an attempt to explain a state of affairs that did not in fact exist

27. Based on the passage, it can be inferred that the author would be likely to agree with each of the following statements about *Calvaria major* **except**:

(A)   The causes of the evolution of the tree's particularly durable pit wall have not been definitively identified by Temple's critics.

(B)   The notion that the thickness of the pit wall in the tree's fruit has been a factor contributing to the decline of the tree has not been definitively discredited.

(C)   In light of the current rate of germination of seeds of the species, it is surprising that the tree has not been abundant since the dodo's disappearance.

(D)   There is good reason to believe that the tree is not threatened with imminent extinction.

(E)   *Calvaria major* seeds can germinate even if they do not first pass through a bird's digestive system.

S T O P

IF YOU FINISH BEFORE TIME IS CALLED, YOU MAY CHECK YOUR WORK ON THIS SECTION ONLY.
DO NOT WORK ON ANY OTHER SECTION IN THE TEST.

SECTION IV
Time—35 minutes
25 Questions

Directions: Each question in this section is based on the reasoning presented in a brief passage. In answering the questions, you should not make assumptions that are by commonsense standards implausible, superfluous, or incompatible with the passage. For some questions, more than one of the choices could conceivably answer the question. However, you are to choose the **best** answer; that is, choose the response that most accurately and completely answers the question and mark that response on your answer sheet.

1. Scientists generally believe that no deep-sea creature can detect red light, but they need to reassess that view. Researchers recently discovered a foot-long deep-sea creature of the genus *Erenna* with bioluminescent red lights on some of its tentacles. These red lights, which are shaped like a common food source for small, deep-sea fish, probably function as lures to attract prey.

   Which one of the following most accurately expresses the overall conclusion drawn in the argument?

   (A) Red lights on the tentacles of a newly discovered deep-sea creature probably function as lures.
   (B) Red lights on the tentacles of a newly discovered deep-sea creature are shaped like a common food source for small, deep-sea fish.
   (C) A foot-long deep-sea creature of the genus *Erenna* has been discovered recently.
   (D) Scientists generally believe that deep-sea creatures cannot detect red light.
   (E) Scientists need to reconsider the belief that deep-sea creatures cannot detect red light.

2. For house painting, acrylic paints are an excellent choice. They provide everything that a good paint should provide: smooth and even coverage, quick drying time, durability, and easy cleanup. Even acrylics, however, cannot correct such surface defects as badly cracked paint. Such conditions indicate some underlying problem, such as water damage, that needs repair.

   Which one of the following is most strongly supported by the statements above?

   (A) Badly cracked paint is not a result of harsh weather conditions.
   (B) Acrylics are the only paints that provide everything that most homeowners need from a paint.
   (C) Acrylics should not be used to paint over other types of house paint.
   (D) It is not a requirement of house paints that they correct surface defects such as badly cracked paint.
   (E) Acrylic paints come in as wide a range of colors as do any other paints.

3. Letter to the editor: You have asserted that philanthropists want to make the nonprofit sector as efficient as private business in this country. Philanthropists want no such thing, of course. Why would anyone want to make nonprofits as inefficient as Byworks Corporation, which has posted huge losses for years?

   The reasoning of the argument in the letter is most vulnerable to criticism on the grounds that the argument

   (A) draws a conclusion about what ought to be the case from premises that are entirely about what is the case
   (B) takes the condition of one member of a category to be representative of the category in general
   (C) rejects a claim by attacking the proponent of the claim rather than addressing the claim itself
   (D) concludes that a claim must be false because of the mere absence of evidence in its favor
   (E) concludes that a phenomenon will have a certain property merely because the phenomenon's cause has that property

4. Statistical records of crime rates probably often reflect as much about the motives and methods of those who compile or cite them as they do about the actual incidence of crime. The police may underreport crime in order to convey the impression of their own success or overreport crime to make the case for a budget increase. Politicians may magnify crime rates to get elected or minimize them to remain in office. Newspapers, of course, often sensationalize crime statistics to increase readership.

   The argument proceeds by doing which one of the following?

   (A) evaluating evidence for and against its conclusion
   (B) citing examples in support of its conclusion
   (C) deriving implications of a generalization that it assumes to be true
   (D) enumerating problems for which it proposes a general solution
   (E) showing how evidence that apparently contradicts its conclusion actually supports that conclusion

GO ON TO THE NEXT PAGE.

5. Physiologist: The likelihood of developing osteoporosis is greatly increased by a deficiency of calcium in the diet. Dairy products usually contain more calcium per serving than do fruits and vegetables. Yet in countries where dairy products are rare, and fruits and vegetables are the main source of calcium, the incidence of osteoporosis is much lower than in countries where people consume a great deal of calcium from dairy products.

Which one of the following, if true, would most help to resolve the apparent discrepancy described by the physiologist?

(A) A healthy human body eventually loses the excess calcium that it takes in.

(B) Many people who eat large quantities of fruits and vegetables also consume dairy products.

(C) There are more people who have a calcium deficiency than there are who have developed osteoporosis.

(D) People who have calcium deficiencies are also likely to have deficiencies in other minerals.

(E) The fats in dairy products tend to inhibit the body's calcium absorption.

6. A first-term board member should not be on the finance committee unless he or she is an accountant or his or her membership on the committee is supported by all the members of the board.

Which one of the following arguments most closely conforms to the principle stated above?

(A) Simkins is a first-term board member and not an accountant; thus, Simkins should not be on the finance committee.

(B) Timmons is a third-term board member but not an accountant; thus, if all other board members think that Timmons should be on the finance committee, then Timmons should be on that committee.

(C) Ruiz is on the finance committee but is not an accountant; thus, Ruiz's membership must have been supported by all the members of the board.

(D) Klein is a first-term board member who is not an accountant; thus, Klein should not be allowed on the finance committee if any board member opposes Klein's appointment to that committee.

(E) Mabry is a board member who is not an accountant; thus, because Mabry's membership on the finance committee is opposed by most board members, Mabry should not be allowed on that committee.

7. Most respondents to a magazine survey who had recently listened to a taped reading of a certain best-selling novel said that they had enjoyed the novel, while most respondents who had recently read the novel themselves said they had not enjoyed it. These survey results support the contention that a person who listens to a taped reading of a novel is more likely to enjoy the novel than a person who reads it is.

Which one of the following, if true, would most weaken the argument?

(A) Most of the respondents who had listened to a taped reading of the novel had never read it, and most of the respondents who had read the novel had never listened to a taped reading of it.

(B) Most people can read a novel in considerably less time than it would take them to listen to a taped reading of it.

(C) When people are asked their opinion of a best-selling novel that they have read or listened to on tape, they are more likely to say that they enjoyed the novel than that they did not enjoy it.

(D) Many novels that are available in text versions are not available in audio versions.

(E) The novel in question, unlike most novels, included dialogue in many different dialects that are more understandable when heard than when read.

GO ON TO THE NEXT PAGE.

8. To qualify as a medical specialist, one must usually graduate from a university, then complete approximately four years of medical school, followed by a residency of two to six years in one's specialty. Finally, a physician who desires to become a recognized specialist must complete an evaluation program directed by a medical specialty board. Therefore, anyone who has qualified as a recognized medical specialist is competent to practice in his or her specialty.

    Which one of the following is an assumption on which the argument depends?

    (A) People who are not highly motivated will not complete the demanding course of study and examination required to become qualified as a recognized medical specialist.

    (B) Only the most talented people will successfully complete the rigorous course of study necessary for qualification as a recognized medical specialist.

    (C) No one incompetent to practice a particular specialty completes the evaluation program for that specialty.

    (D) Usually, six to ten years of medical training beyond a university degree is sufficient to render someone competent to practice in his or her medical specialty.

    (E) Usually, six to ten years of medical training beyond a university degree is necessary to render someone competent to practice in his or her medical specialty.

9. Archaeologists are currently analyzing plant remains found at a site that was last occupied more than 10,000 years ago. If the plants were cultivated, then the people who occupied the site discovered agriculture thousands of years before any other people are known to have done so. On the other hand, if the plants were wild—that is, uncultivated—then the people who occupied the site ate a wider variety of wild plants than did any other people at the time.

    The statements above, if true, most strongly support which one of the following?

    (A) The archaeologists analyzing the plant remains at the site will be able to determine whether the plants were cultivated or were wild.

    (B) The people who occupied the site used some plants in ways that no other people did at that time.

    (C) If the people who occupied the site had reached a more advanced stage in the use of wild plants than any other people at the time, then the plants found at the site were uncultivated.

    (D) If the people who occupied the site discovered agriculture thousands of years before people anywhere else are known to have done so, then there are remains of cultivated plants at the site.

    (E) It is more likely that the people who occupied the site discovered agriculture thousands of years before people anywhere else did than it is that they ate a wider variety of wild plants than any other people at the time.

GO ON TO THE NEXT PAGE.

10. In a test of fuel efficiency, car X and car Y yielded the same average fuel mileage, even though car X was driven in a less fuel-efficient manner than car Y was. Thus, car X is more fuel efficient than car Y.

Which one of the following arguments is most similar in its reasoning to the argument above?

(A) In an experiment, subject X consistently gave lower pain ratings in response to pinpricks than subject Y did. Therefore, it is reasonable to conclude that subjects X and Y experience pain differently.

(B) Our hamster gained the same amount of weight as our neighbors' hamster, even though our hamster ate more than theirs. So it must be that our hamster burned more calories than theirs did.

(C) When on his bicycle, Roland makes better time coasting down a hill than pedaling on a horizontal path. So he would make even better time on the hills if he were to pedal rather than coast.

(D) When asked to judge the value of various pieces of antique furniture, I gave lower estimates on average than you did. So in those cases where we both gave the same estimate, I must have overestimated the piece's value.

(E) Jean demonstrates a high level of visual acuity when she wears prescription glasses. Thus, it must be that without those prescription glasses, she would demonstrate a lower level of visual acuity.

11. Plumb-Ace advertises that its plumbers are more qualified than plumbers at any other major plumbing firm in the region because Plumb-Ace plumbers must complete a very difficult certification process. Plumb-Ace plumbers may or may not be more qualified, but clearly the certification process is not very difficult, because nearly everyone who takes the written portion of the certification exam passes it very easily.

The reasoning in the argument is flawed in that it

(A) treats something that is necessary to make a certification process very difficult as if it were sufficient by itself to make the process very difficult

(B) takes for granted that plumbers are not qualified unless they complete some certification process

(C) overlooks the possibility that plumbers at other firms in the region complete certification processes that are even easier than that completed by Plumb-Ace's plumbers

(D) infers that a claim is false on the grounds that an inadequate argument has been given for that claim

(E) presumes that since one part of a whole lacks a certain characteristic, the whole must lack that characteristic as well

12. Historian: The early Egyptian pharaohs spent as much wealth on largely ceremonial and hugely impressive architecture as they did on roads and irrigation systems. This was not mere frivolousness, however, for if people under a pharaoh's rule could be made to realize the extent of their ruler's mastery of the physical world, their loyalty could be maintained without military coercion.

The claim that early Egyptian expenditure on largely ceremonial architecture was not frivolous plays which one of the following roles in the historian's argument?

(A) It is a conclusion purportedly justified by the argument's appeal to the psychological effects of these structures on the Egyptian population.

(B) It is offered in support of the claim that Egyptian pharaohs spent as much on ceremonial architecture as they did on roads and irrigation systems.

(C) It is a premise given in support of the claim that the loyalty of people under a pharaoh's rule was maintained over time without reliance on military force.

(D) It is offered as an illustration of the principle that social and political stability do not depend ultimately on force.

(E) It is a premise used to justify the pharaohs' policy of spending scarce resources on structures that have only military utility.

13. The proposed change to the patent system is bound to have a chilling effect on scientific research. Under current rules, researchers have one full year after the initial publication of a new discovery to patent the discovery. This allows research results to be shared widely prior to the patent application. The proposed change would have the application precede initial publication, which would delay the communication of discoveries.

The conclusion drawn above follows logically if which one of the following is assumed?

(A) The proposed change will encourage more patent applications to be filed.

(B) Dramatic advances in scientific research have occurred while the current patent system has been in place.

(C) Delays in the communication of discoveries will have a chilling effect on scientific research.

(D) Most researchers oppose the proposed change to the patent system.

(E) The current rules for patent applications facilitate progress in scientific research by rewarding the communication of discoveries.

GO ON TO THE NEXT PAGE.

14. Every time people get what they want they feel pleasure. Pleasure is a natural result of getting what one wants. We can conclude that no one fundamentally desires anything except pleasure.

Which one of the following uses questionable reasoning most similar to that used in the argument above?

(A) I sure am enjoying the party even though I was sure I would not, so I guess I wanted to come after all.

(B) I have never been skiing, but just thinking about it terrifies me, so I guess I must not want to learn how.

(C) Every time I eat pizza I get a stomachache, so I suppose the reason I eat pizza in the first place is so that I can have a stomachache.

(D) Every time I have gone to a party with Julio I have enjoyed myself, so I expect I will enjoy myself if Julio and I go to a party tonight.

(E) I never enjoy a soccer game without eating hot dogs, so I guess I would not enjoy going to a basketball game if I could not eat hot dogs at the game.

15. Linguist: You philosophers say that we linguists do not have a deep understanding of language, but you have provided no evidence.

Philosopher: Well, you have said that you believe that "Joan and Ivan are siblings" is identical in meaning to "Ivan and Joan are siblings." But this cannot be the case, for the sentences are physically different; yet for two things to be identical, they must have all the same attributes.

Of the following, which one is the strongest logical counter that the linguist can make to the philosopher?

(A) Two things can have a few minor differences and still be identical.

(B) Two sentences can be identical physically, and yet, depending on the context in which they are uttered, not be identical in meaning.

(C) It is necessarily true that Joan is Ivan's sibling if Ivan is Joan's sibling.

(D) The issue is not whether the two sentences are completely identical, but whether they mean the same thing.

(E) A linguist has more experience with language than a philosopher, and so is in a better position to answer such questions.

16. Salespeople always steer customers toward products from which they make their highest commissions, and all salespeople in major health stores work on commission. Hence, when you buy vitamin supplements in a major health store, you can be sure that the claims the salespeople make about the quality of the products are inaccurate.

The reasoning in the argument is flawed in that the argument

(A) offers as a premise a claim that merely paraphrases the conclusion and for which no support is provided

(B) infers that some claims are inaccurate solely on the basis of the source of those claims

(C) infers that just because a group of people has a certain property, each member of the group has that property

(D) takes a condition that is sufficient for the conclusion to be true as one that is necessary for the conclusion to be true

(E) relies on the claims of an authority on a topic outside that authority's area of expertise

17. Because no other theory has been able to predict it so simply and accurately, the advance of the perihelion of Mercury is sometimes cited as evidence in support of Einstein's theory of general relativity. However, this phenomenon was already well known when Einstein developed his theory, and he quite probably adjusted his equations to generate the correct numbers for the perihelion advance. Therefore, accounting for this advance should not be counted as evidence in support of Einstein's theory.

Which one of the following principles, if valid, most helps to justify the argument above?

(A) Unless a phenomenon predicted by a scientific theory is unknown at the time the theory is developed, the theory should not be credited with the discovery of that phenomenon.

(B) A phenomenon that is predicted by a scientific theory should not count as evidence in favor of that theory unless the theory was developed with that phenomenon in mind.

(C) Unless a theory can accurately account for all relevant phenomena that are already well known at the time of its development, it cannot be regarded as well supported.

(D) If a theory is adjusted specifically to account for some particular phenomenon, a match between that theory and that phenomenon should not count as evidence in favor of the theory.

(E) If a theory is adjusted to generate the correct predictions for some phenomenon that is already known to the scientist developing the theory, the theory should not be counted as predicting that phenomenon.

GO ON TO THE NEXT PAGE.

18. Computer store manager: Last year we made an average of 13 percent profit on the high-end computer models—those priced over $1,000—that we sold, while low-end models—those priced below $1,000—typically returned at least 25 percent profit. Since there is a limit to how many models we can display and sell, we should sell only low-end models. This would maximize our profits, since we would probably sell as many low-end models if that is all we sold as we would sell both kinds combined if we continued to sell both.

The reasoning in the manager's argument is vulnerable to criticism on which one of the following grounds?

(A) The argument fails to consider the possibility that the money earned on each high-end computer is significantly higher than the money earned on each low-end computer.

(B) The argument fails to address the possibility that, despite the price differential, the store sold as many high-end models as low-end models last year.

(C) The argument ignores the possibility that some customers who come into a computer store expecting to purchase a low-end model end up purchasing a high-end model.

(D) The argument presumes, without providing justification, that the sole objective in managing the computer store should be maximizing profits.

(E) The argument fails to recognize that future sales of low-end computers may not be the same as past sales.

19. Professor: Economists argue that buying lottery tickets is an unwise use of resources, because the average payoff for the tickets sold in a lottery is much lower than the cost of a ticket. But this reasoning is faulty. The average amount paid out on individual insurance policies is much lower than the average cost of a policy, yet nobody would argue that purchasing insurance is an unwise use of resources.

Which one of the following, if true, most weakens the professor's argument?

(A) Individuals spend, on average, much more on insurance than on lottery tickets.

(B) Insurance companies generally retain a higher proportion of total revenue than do organizations that sponsor lotteries.

(C) Taking small financial risks can often greatly increase one's chances of obtaining much larger benefits.

(D) In general, the odds of winning the grand prize in a lottery are significantly lower than the odds of collecting a settlement from a typical insurance policy.

(E) The protection against loss that insurance provides is more important to one's well-being than is the possibility of a windfall gain.

20. Unusually large and intense forest fires swept the tropics in 1997. The tropics were quite susceptible to fire at that time because of the widespread drought caused by an unusually strong El Niño, an occasional global weather phenomenon. Many scientists believe the strength of the El Niño was enhanced by the global warming caused by air pollution.

Which one of the following can be properly inferred from the information above?

(A) Air pollution was largely responsible for the size and intensity of the forest fires that swept the tropics in 1997.

(B) If the El Niño in 1997 had not been unusually strong, few if any large and intense forest fires would have swept the tropics in that year.

(C) Forest fires in the tropics are generally larger and more intense than usual during a strong El Niño.

(D) At least some scientists believe that air pollution was responsible for the size and intensity of the forest fires that swept the tropics in 1997.

(E) If air pollution enhanced the strength of the El Niño in 1997, then it also contributed to the widespread drought in that year.

GO ON TO THE NEXT PAGE.

21. If Skiff's book is published this year, Professor Nguyen vows she will urge the dean to promote Skiff. Thus, if Skiff's book is as important and as well written as Skiff claims, he will be promoted, for Nguyen will certainly keep her promise, and the dean will surely promote Skiff if Nguyen recommends it.

The argument's conclusion can be properly inferred if which one of the following is assumed?

(A)   Skiff's book will be published this year if it is as important as he claims it is.
(B)   Skiff needs to publish a book before he can be promoted.
(C)   Professor Nguyen believes that Skiff's book is well written.
(D)   Skiff's book will not be published unless it is as important and as well written as he claims it is.
(E)   Skiff will not be promoted unless Professor Nguyen urges the dean to do so.

22. If the magazine's circulation continues to rise as it has over the last ten years, in another ten years it will be the largest-selling martial arts magazine in the world. Unfortunately, it has now become clear that the magazine's publisher will not allow the managing editor to make the changes she has proposed, and without these changes, the magazine's circulation will not rise as quickly over the next ten years as it has over the last ten. So the magazine will not be the largest-selling martial arts magazine ten years from now.

The argument's reasoning is flawed because the argument

(A)   identifies some changes required for the magazine's circulation to continue its rapid increase and concludes from this that no other changes are needed
(B)   equates a reduction in the rate at which the magazine's circulation is increasing with a decline in the magazine's circulation
(C)   draws a conclusion that simply restates a claim that is presented in support of that conclusion
(D)   takes a single fact that is incompatible with a general claim as enough to show that claim to be false
(E)   treats an occurrence that will ensure a certain outcome as something that is required for that outcome

23. Botanist: In an experiment, scientists raised domesticated radishes in a field with wild radishes, which are considered weeds. Within several generations, the wild radishes began to show the same flower color as the domesticated ones. This suggests that resistance to pesticides, which is often a genetically engineered trait, would also be passed from domesticated crop plants to their relatives that are considered weeds.

Which one of the following, if true, most strengthens the botanist's argument?

(A)   It is much easier in principle for genetic traits to be passed from wild plants to their domesticated relatives than it is for such traits to be passed from the domesticated plant to the wild relative.
(B)   When the ratio of domesticated radishes to wild radishes in the field increased, the speed with which the flower color passed to the wild radishes also increased.
(C)   Radishes are not representative of crop plants in general with respect to the ease with which various traits are passed among members of closely related species.
(D)   The flower color of the domesticated radishes had not been introduced into them via genetic engineering.
(E)   It is more difficult for flower color to be transferred between domesticated and wild radishes than it is for almost any other trait to be passed between any two similarly related plant species.

GO ON TO THE NEXT PAGE.

24. Parents who consistently laud their children for every attempt to accomplish something, whether successful or not, actually erode the youngsters' sense of self-esteem. Children require commendation for their achievements, but if uniformly praised for both what they have accomplished and what they have merely attempted, they will eventually discount all words of commendation. In effect, such children never hear any praise at all.

Which one of the following most accurately expresses the overall conclusion of the argument?

(A)   Parents should praise their children for their achievements.

(B)   Children whose actions are praised undeservedly eventually learn to discount all words of praise.

(C)   Parents need to distinguish between their own expectations for their children and what their children are actually capable of accomplishing.

(D)   Children's self-esteem will suffer if their parents uniformly praise their attempts to accomplish things regardless of their success or failure.

(E)   Children will develop low self-esteem if their parents do not praise them when they succeed.

25. Pauline: Some environmentalists claim that for the salmon to be saved, the hydroelectric dams on the river must be breached. But if the dams are breached, given the region's growing population and booming industry, electrical costs will skyrocket.

Roger: The dams are already producing electricity at optimal capacity. So regardless of whether they are breached, we will have to find additional energy sources for the region.

The dialogue provides the most support for the claim that Pauline and Roger agree that

(A)   production from other energy sources cannot be increased in the near future to compensate for electricity production lost by breaching the dams

(B)   there will be no significant decrease in demand for electricity in the region in the near future

(C)   if the dams remain in service but do not operate at optimal capacity, electrical costs in the region will rise

(D)   some environmentalists who advocate saving the salmon believe that that goal overrides concerns about electrical costs

(E)   finding additional energy sources will not decrease the electrical costs in the region

STOP

IF YOU FINISH BEFORE TIME IS CALLED, YOU MAY CHECK YOUR WORK ON THIS SECTION ONLY.
DO NOT WORK ON ANY OTHER SECTION IN THE TEST.

Acknowledgment is made to the following sources from which material has been adapted for use in this test:

Marc D. Hauser, "Thinking Like an Animal" in *Defenders*. ©2001 by Defenders of Wildlife.

Jorge Huerta, "When Sleeping Giants Awaken: Chicano Theatre in the 1960s." ©2002 by The American Society for Theatre Research, Inc.

Wolfgang H. Kirchner and William F. Towne, "The Sensory Basis of the Honeybee's Dance Language" in *Scientific American*. ©2001 by Scientific American, a Division of Nature America, Inc.

Timothy B. Lee, "Vonage Is the Latest Victim of Patent Abuse." ©2007 by The American.

Jeff Minerd, "Impacts of Sprawl." ©2000 by World Future Society.

David Quammen, *The Song of the Dodo: Island Biography in an Age of Extinctions*. ©1996 by David Quammen.

Red Hat, Inc., "Statement of Position and Our Promise on Software Patents." ©2007 by Red Hat, Inc.

Lyle Rexer, "Photographers Move Forward into the Past." ©1998 by The New York Times Company.

GiGi Visscher, "Contingency Fees in Western Australia." ©2000 by eLaw Journal: Murdoch University Electronic Journal of Law. http://www.murdoch.edu.au/elaw/issues/v7n1/visscher71.html.

Booker T. Whatley, *How to Make $100,000 Farming 25 Acres*. ©1987 by the Regenerative Agriculture Association.

Computing Your Score

Directions:

1. Use the Answer Key on the next page to check your answers.

2. Use the Scoring Worksheet below to compute your raw score.

3. Use the Score Conversion Chart to convert your raw score into the 120–180 scale.*

Scoring Worksheet

1. Enter the number of questions you answered correctly in each section.

	Number Correct
SECTION I	_____
SECTION II	Unscored
SECTION III	_____
SECTION IV	_____

2. Enter the sum here: _____
   This is your Raw Score.

*Scores are reported on a 120–180 score scale, with 120 being the lowest possible score and 180 being the highest possible score.

Score Conversion Chart

Use the table below to convert your raw score to the corresponding 120–180 scaled score for PrepTest 139.

Raw Score	Scaled Score	Raw Score	Scaled Score
77	180	38	147
76	180	37	146
75	179	36	145
74	178	35	144
73	176	34	144
72	175	33	143
71	173	32	142
70	172	31	141
69	171	30	141
68	170	29	140
67	169	28	139
66	168	27	138
65	167	26	137
64	166	25	137
63	165	24	136
62	164	23	135
61	163	22	134
60	162	21	133
59	162	20	132
58	161	19	131
57	160	18	130
56	159	17	128
55	159	16	127
54	158	15	126
53	157	14	124
52	156	13	123
51	156	12	122
50	155	11	121
49	154	10	120
48	154	9	120
47	153	8	120
46	152	7	120
45	151	6	120
44	151	5	120
43	150	4	120
42	149	3	120
41	149	2	120
40	148	1	120
39	147	0	120

Answer Key

Question	Section I	Section II*	Section III	Section IV
1	B	D	A	E
2	A	C	B	D
3	D	D	C	B
4	D	B	A	B
5	C	D	D	E
6	A	E	D	D
7	B	A	B	E
8	C	C	A	C
9	A	A	B	B
10	D	D	E	B
11	E	D	C	E
12	E	C	D	A
13	B	C	B	C
14	A	E	A	C
15	C	A	C	D
16	D	D	B	B
17	C	D	E	D
18	E	C	B	A
19	E	C	A	E
20	B	B	D	E
21	C	B	D	A
22	B	A	B	E
23	A	E	A	E
24	C	C	D	D
25	B	B	A	B
26		D	E	
27		B	C	

*Section II is unscored. The number of items answered correctly in Section II should not be added to the raw score.

LSAC LawHub®

What You Need for Your Journey, from Prelaw Through Practice

At LSAC, we believe everyone should have the support they need to succeed on their journey to law school and beyond.

Tens of thousands of law school candidates already **rely on LawHub** and its growing portfolio of information and resources to support that journey from prelaw to practice. From LSAT preparation in the authentic test interface to education programs designed to prepare you for the modern law practice, discover what LawHub has to offer to help you develop the confidence and skills needed to achieve your academic and professional goals.

Sign up today at **LSAC.org**.

Connect with Us

 @LawSchoolAdmissionCouncil

 @LSAC_Official

 @official_lsac

 Law School Admission Council

 Law School Admission Council

General Directions for the LSAT Answer Sheet

This test consists of four multiple-choice sections. The proctor will tell you when to begin and end each section. If you finish a section before time is called, you may check your work on that section **only**; do not turn to any other section of the test book and do not work on any other section either in the test book or on the answer sheet.

Answer spaces for each question are lettered to correspond with the letters of the potential answers to each question in the test book. After you have decided which of the answers is correct, mark the corresponding letter on the answer sheet. Give only one answer to each question. If you change an answer, be sure that all previous marks are **erased completely**. Incomplete erasures may be interpreted as intended answers. **All your answers must be marked on the answer sheet unless you have been specifically approved by Accommodated Testing to mark your answers in your test book.**

There may be more question numbers on the answer sheet than there are questions in a section. Do not be concerned, but be certain that the section and number of the question you are answering matches the answer sheet section and question number. Additional answer spaces in any answer sheet section should be left blank. Begin your next section in the number one answer space for that section.

MARKING INSTRUCTIONS

MARK ONE AND ONLY ONE ANSWER CHOICE TO EACH QUESTION. BE SURE TO FILL IN COMPLETELY THE SPACE FOR YOUR INTENDED ANSWER CHOICE USING A NO. 2 OR HB PENCIL. FAILURE TO DO SO INCREASES THE POSSIBILITY OF INACCURATE MACHINE SCORING. IF YOU ERASE, DO SO COMPLETELY. MAKE NO STRAY MARKS. EXAMPLES OF VALID AND INVALID MARKS ARE GIVEN BELOW.

VALID MARK	Ⓐ Ⓑ ● Ⓓ Ⓔ	**STRAY MARKS**	● Ⓑ Ⓒ Ⓓ Ⓔ
TOO LIGHT	Ⓐ Ⓑ Ⓒ Ⓓ Ⓔ	**MULTIPLE MARKS**	Ⓐ Ⓑ ● ● Ⓔ
INCOMPLETE	Ⓐ Ⓑ ◓ ◑ Ⓔ		

YOU MAY FIND MORE ANSWER SPACES THAN YOU NEED; LEAVE THE EXTRA SPACES BLANK.

LSAT Answer Sheet

Instructions for completing these items are at the back of your LSAT test book.

1. Name (Print)

Last   First   MI

2. LSAC Account Number   L ☐☐☐☐☐☐☐

Section 1	Section 2	Section 3	Section 4
1 Ⓐ Ⓑ Ⓒ Ⓓ Ⓔ	1 Ⓐ Ⓑ Ⓒ Ⓓ Ⓔ	1 Ⓐ Ⓑ Ⓒ Ⓓ Ⓔ	1 Ⓐ Ⓑ Ⓒ Ⓓ Ⓔ
2 Ⓐ Ⓑ Ⓒ Ⓓ Ⓔ	2 Ⓐ Ⓑ Ⓒ Ⓓ Ⓔ	2 Ⓐ Ⓑ Ⓒ Ⓓ Ⓔ	2 Ⓐ Ⓑ Ⓒ Ⓓ Ⓔ
3 Ⓐ Ⓑ Ⓒ Ⓓ Ⓔ	3 Ⓐ Ⓑ Ⓒ Ⓓ Ⓔ	3 Ⓐ Ⓑ Ⓒ Ⓓ Ⓔ	3 Ⓐ Ⓑ Ⓒ Ⓓ Ⓔ
4 Ⓐ Ⓑ Ⓒ Ⓓ Ⓔ	4 Ⓐ Ⓑ Ⓒ Ⓓ Ⓔ	4 Ⓐ Ⓑ Ⓒ Ⓓ Ⓔ	4 Ⓐ Ⓑ Ⓒ Ⓓ Ⓔ
5 Ⓐ Ⓑ Ⓒ Ⓓ Ⓔ	5 Ⓐ Ⓑ Ⓒ Ⓓ Ⓔ	5 Ⓐ Ⓑ Ⓒ Ⓓ Ⓔ	5 Ⓐ Ⓑ Ⓒ Ⓓ Ⓔ
6 Ⓐ Ⓑ Ⓒ Ⓓ Ⓔ	6 Ⓐ Ⓑ Ⓒ Ⓓ Ⓔ	6 Ⓐ Ⓑ Ⓒ Ⓓ Ⓔ	6 Ⓐ Ⓑ Ⓒ Ⓓ Ⓔ
7 Ⓐ Ⓑ Ⓒ Ⓓ Ⓔ	7 Ⓐ Ⓑ Ⓒ Ⓓ Ⓔ	7 Ⓐ Ⓑ Ⓒ Ⓓ Ⓔ	7 Ⓐ Ⓑ Ⓒ Ⓓ Ⓔ
8 Ⓐ Ⓑ Ⓒ Ⓓ Ⓔ	8 Ⓐ Ⓑ Ⓒ Ⓓ Ⓔ	8 Ⓐ Ⓑ Ⓒ Ⓓ Ⓔ	8 Ⓐ Ⓑ Ⓒ Ⓓ Ⓔ
9 Ⓐ Ⓑ Ⓒ Ⓓ Ⓔ	9 Ⓐ Ⓑ Ⓒ Ⓓ Ⓔ	9 Ⓐ Ⓑ Ⓒ Ⓓ Ⓔ	9 Ⓐ Ⓑ Ⓒ Ⓓ Ⓔ
10 Ⓐ Ⓑ Ⓒ Ⓓ Ⓔ	10 Ⓐ Ⓑ Ⓒ Ⓓ Ⓔ	10 Ⓐ Ⓑ Ⓒ Ⓓ Ⓔ	10 Ⓐ Ⓑ Ⓒ Ⓓ Ⓔ
11 Ⓐ Ⓑ Ⓒ Ⓓ Ⓔ	11 Ⓐ Ⓑ Ⓒ Ⓓ Ⓔ	11 Ⓐ Ⓑ Ⓒ Ⓓ Ⓔ	11 Ⓐ Ⓑ Ⓒ Ⓓ Ⓔ
12 Ⓐ Ⓑ Ⓒ Ⓓ Ⓔ	12 Ⓐ Ⓑ Ⓒ Ⓓ Ⓔ	12 Ⓐ Ⓑ Ⓒ Ⓓ Ⓔ	12 Ⓐ Ⓑ Ⓒ Ⓓ Ⓔ
13 Ⓐ Ⓑ Ⓒ Ⓓ Ⓔ	13 Ⓐ Ⓑ Ⓒ Ⓓ Ⓔ	13 Ⓐ Ⓑ Ⓒ Ⓓ Ⓔ	13 Ⓐ Ⓑ Ⓒ Ⓓ Ⓔ
14 Ⓐ Ⓑ Ⓒ Ⓓ Ⓔ	14 Ⓐ Ⓑ Ⓒ Ⓓ Ⓔ	14 Ⓐ Ⓑ Ⓒ Ⓓ Ⓔ	14 Ⓐ Ⓑ Ⓒ Ⓓ Ⓔ
15 Ⓐ Ⓑ Ⓒ Ⓓ Ⓔ	15 Ⓐ Ⓑ Ⓒ Ⓓ Ⓔ	15 Ⓐ Ⓑ Ⓒ Ⓓ Ⓔ	15 Ⓐ Ⓑ Ⓒ Ⓓ Ⓔ
16 Ⓐ Ⓑ Ⓒ Ⓓ Ⓔ	16 Ⓐ Ⓑ Ⓒ Ⓓ Ⓔ	16 Ⓐ Ⓑ Ⓒ Ⓓ Ⓔ	16 Ⓐ Ⓑ Ⓒ Ⓓ Ⓔ
17 Ⓐ Ⓑ Ⓒ Ⓓ Ⓔ	17 Ⓐ Ⓑ Ⓒ Ⓓ Ⓔ	17 Ⓐ Ⓑ Ⓒ Ⓓ Ⓔ	17 Ⓐ Ⓑ Ⓒ Ⓓ Ⓔ
18 Ⓐ Ⓑ Ⓒ Ⓓ Ⓔ	18 Ⓐ Ⓑ Ⓒ Ⓓ Ⓔ	18 Ⓐ Ⓑ Ⓒ Ⓓ Ⓔ	18 Ⓐ Ⓑ Ⓒ Ⓓ Ⓔ
19 Ⓐ Ⓑ Ⓒ Ⓓ Ⓔ	19 Ⓐ Ⓑ Ⓒ Ⓓ Ⓔ	19 Ⓐ Ⓑ Ⓒ Ⓓ Ⓔ	19 Ⓐ Ⓑ Ⓒ Ⓓ Ⓔ
20 Ⓐ Ⓑ Ⓒ Ⓓ Ⓔ	20 Ⓐ Ⓑ Ⓒ Ⓓ Ⓔ	20 Ⓐ Ⓑ Ⓒ Ⓓ Ⓔ	20 Ⓐ Ⓑ Ⓒ Ⓓ Ⓔ
21 Ⓐ Ⓑ Ⓒ Ⓓ Ⓔ	21 Ⓐ Ⓑ Ⓒ Ⓓ Ⓔ	21 Ⓐ Ⓑ Ⓒ Ⓓ Ⓔ	21 Ⓐ Ⓑ Ⓒ Ⓓ Ⓔ
22 Ⓐ Ⓑ Ⓒ Ⓓ Ⓔ	22 Ⓐ Ⓑ Ⓒ Ⓓ Ⓔ	22 Ⓐ Ⓑ Ⓒ Ⓓ Ⓔ	22 Ⓐ Ⓑ Ⓒ Ⓓ Ⓔ
23 Ⓐ Ⓑ Ⓒ Ⓓ Ⓔ	23 Ⓐ Ⓑ Ⓒ Ⓓ Ⓔ	23 Ⓐ Ⓑ Ⓒ Ⓓ Ⓔ	23 Ⓐ Ⓑ Ⓒ Ⓓ Ⓔ
24 Ⓐ Ⓑ Ⓒ Ⓓ Ⓔ	24 Ⓐ Ⓑ Ⓒ Ⓓ Ⓔ	24 Ⓐ Ⓑ Ⓒ Ⓓ Ⓔ	24 Ⓐ Ⓑ Ⓒ Ⓓ Ⓔ
25 Ⓐ Ⓑ Ⓒ Ⓓ Ⓔ	25 Ⓐ Ⓑ Ⓒ Ⓓ Ⓔ	25 Ⓐ Ⓑ Ⓒ Ⓓ Ⓔ	25 Ⓐ Ⓑ Ⓒ Ⓓ Ⓔ
26 Ⓐ Ⓑ Ⓒ Ⓓ Ⓔ	26 Ⓐ Ⓑ Ⓒ Ⓓ Ⓔ	26 Ⓐ Ⓑ Ⓒ Ⓓ Ⓔ	26 Ⓐ Ⓑ Ⓒ Ⓓ Ⓔ
27 Ⓐ Ⓑ Ⓒ Ⓓ Ⓔ	27 Ⓐ Ⓑ Ⓒ Ⓓ Ⓔ	27 Ⓐ Ⓑ Ⓒ Ⓓ Ⓔ	27 Ⓐ Ⓑ Ⓒ Ⓓ Ⓔ
28 Ⓐ Ⓑ Ⓒ Ⓓ Ⓔ	28 Ⓐ Ⓑ Ⓒ Ⓓ Ⓔ	28 Ⓐ Ⓑ Ⓒ Ⓓ Ⓔ	28 Ⓐ Ⓑ Ⓒ Ⓓ Ⓔ
29 Ⓐ Ⓑ Ⓒ Ⓓ Ⓔ	29 Ⓐ Ⓑ Ⓒ Ⓓ Ⓔ	29 Ⓐ Ⓑ Ⓒ Ⓓ Ⓔ	29 Ⓐ Ⓑ Ⓒ Ⓓ Ⓔ
30 Ⓐ Ⓑ Ⓒ Ⓓ Ⓔ	30 Ⓐ Ⓑ Ⓒ Ⓓ Ⓔ	30 Ⓐ Ⓑ Ⓒ Ⓓ Ⓔ	30 Ⓐ Ⓑ Ⓒ Ⓓ Ⓔ

LSAT Answer Sheet

Instructions for completing these items are at the back of your LSAT test book.

1. Name (Print)

Last   First   MI

2. LSAC Account Number L

Section 1	Section 2	Section 3	Section 4
1 Ⓐ Ⓑ Ⓒ Ⓓ Ⓔ	1 Ⓐ Ⓑ Ⓒ Ⓓ Ⓔ	1 Ⓐ Ⓑ Ⓒ Ⓓ Ⓔ	1 Ⓐ Ⓑ Ⓒ Ⓓ Ⓔ
2 Ⓐ Ⓑ Ⓒ Ⓓ Ⓔ	2 Ⓐ Ⓑ Ⓒ Ⓓ Ⓔ	2 Ⓐ Ⓑ Ⓒ Ⓓ Ⓔ	2 Ⓐ Ⓑ Ⓒ Ⓓ Ⓔ
3 Ⓐ Ⓑ Ⓒ Ⓓ Ⓔ	3 Ⓐ Ⓑ Ⓒ Ⓓ Ⓔ	3 Ⓐ Ⓑ Ⓒ Ⓓ Ⓔ	3 Ⓐ Ⓑ Ⓒ Ⓓ Ⓔ
4 Ⓐ Ⓑ Ⓒ Ⓓ Ⓔ	4 Ⓐ Ⓑ Ⓒ Ⓓ Ⓔ	4 Ⓐ Ⓑ Ⓒ Ⓓ Ⓔ	4 Ⓐ Ⓑ Ⓒ Ⓓ Ⓔ
5 Ⓐ Ⓑ Ⓒ Ⓓ Ⓔ	5 Ⓐ Ⓑ Ⓒ Ⓓ Ⓔ	5 Ⓐ Ⓑ Ⓒ Ⓓ Ⓔ	5 Ⓐ Ⓑ Ⓒ Ⓓ Ⓔ
6 Ⓐ Ⓑ Ⓒ Ⓓ Ⓔ	6 Ⓐ Ⓑ Ⓒ Ⓓ Ⓔ	6 Ⓐ Ⓑ Ⓒ Ⓓ Ⓔ	6 Ⓐ Ⓑ Ⓒ Ⓓ Ⓔ
7 Ⓐ Ⓑ Ⓒ Ⓓ Ⓔ	7 Ⓐ Ⓑ Ⓒ Ⓓ Ⓔ	7 Ⓐ Ⓑ Ⓒ Ⓓ Ⓔ	7 Ⓐ Ⓑ Ⓒ Ⓓ Ⓔ
8 Ⓐ Ⓑ Ⓒ Ⓓ Ⓔ	8 Ⓐ Ⓑ Ⓒ Ⓓ Ⓔ	8 Ⓐ Ⓑ Ⓒ Ⓓ Ⓔ	8 Ⓐ Ⓑ Ⓒ Ⓓ Ⓔ
9 Ⓐ Ⓑ Ⓒ Ⓓ Ⓔ	9 Ⓐ Ⓑ Ⓒ Ⓓ Ⓔ	9 Ⓐ Ⓑ Ⓒ Ⓓ Ⓔ	9 Ⓐ Ⓑ Ⓒ Ⓓ Ⓔ
10 Ⓐ Ⓑ Ⓒ Ⓓ Ⓔ	10 Ⓐ Ⓑ Ⓒ Ⓓ Ⓔ	10 Ⓐ Ⓑ Ⓒ Ⓓ Ⓔ	10 Ⓐ Ⓑ Ⓒ Ⓓ Ⓔ
11 Ⓐ Ⓑ Ⓒ Ⓓ Ⓔ	11 Ⓐ Ⓑ Ⓒ Ⓓ Ⓔ	11 Ⓐ Ⓑ Ⓒ Ⓓ Ⓔ	11 Ⓐ Ⓑ Ⓒ Ⓓ Ⓔ
12 Ⓐ Ⓑ Ⓒ Ⓓ Ⓔ	12 Ⓐ Ⓑ Ⓒ Ⓓ Ⓔ	12 Ⓐ Ⓑ Ⓒ Ⓓ Ⓔ	12 Ⓐ Ⓑ Ⓒ Ⓓ Ⓔ
13 Ⓐ Ⓑ Ⓒ Ⓓ Ⓔ	13 Ⓐ Ⓑ Ⓒ Ⓓ Ⓔ	13 Ⓐ Ⓑ Ⓒ Ⓓ Ⓔ	13 Ⓐ Ⓑ Ⓒ Ⓓ Ⓔ
14 Ⓐ Ⓑ Ⓒ Ⓓ Ⓔ	14 Ⓐ Ⓑ Ⓒ Ⓓ Ⓔ	14 Ⓐ Ⓑ Ⓒ Ⓓ Ⓔ	14 Ⓐ Ⓑ Ⓒ Ⓓ Ⓔ
15 Ⓐ Ⓑ Ⓒ Ⓓ Ⓔ	15 Ⓐ Ⓑ Ⓒ Ⓓ Ⓔ	15 Ⓐ Ⓑ Ⓒ Ⓓ Ⓔ	15 Ⓐ Ⓑ Ⓒ Ⓓ Ⓔ
16 Ⓐ Ⓑ Ⓒ Ⓓ Ⓔ	16 Ⓐ Ⓑ Ⓒ Ⓓ Ⓔ	16 Ⓐ Ⓑ Ⓒ Ⓓ Ⓔ	16 Ⓐ Ⓑ Ⓒ Ⓓ Ⓔ
17 Ⓐ Ⓑ Ⓒ Ⓓ Ⓔ	17 Ⓐ Ⓑ Ⓒ Ⓓ Ⓔ	17 Ⓐ Ⓑ Ⓒ Ⓓ Ⓔ	17 Ⓐ Ⓑ Ⓒ Ⓓ Ⓔ
18 Ⓐ Ⓑ Ⓒ Ⓓ Ⓔ	18 Ⓐ Ⓑ Ⓒ Ⓓ Ⓔ	18 Ⓐ Ⓑ Ⓒ Ⓓ Ⓔ	18 Ⓐ Ⓑ Ⓒ Ⓓ Ⓔ
19 Ⓐ Ⓑ Ⓒ Ⓓ Ⓔ	19 Ⓐ Ⓑ Ⓒ Ⓓ Ⓔ	19 Ⓐ Ⓑ Ⓒ Ⓓ Ⓔ	19 Ⓐ Ⓑ Ⓒ Ⓓ Ⓔ
20 Ⓐ Ⓑ Ⓒ Ⓓ Ⓔ	20 Ⓐ Ⓑ Ⓒ Ⓓ Ⓔ	20 Ⓐ Ⓑ Ⓒ Ⓓ Ⓔ	20 Ⓐ Ⓑ Ⓒ Ⓓ Ⓔ
21 Ⓐ Ⓑ Ⓒ Ⓓ Ⓔ	21 Ⓐ Ⓑ Ⓒ Ⓓ Ⓔ	21 Ⓐ Ⓑ Ⓒ Ⓓ Ⓔ	21 Ⓐ Ⓑ Ⓒ Ⓓ Ⓔ
22 Ⓐ Ⓑ Ⓒ Ⓓ Ⓔ	22 Ⓐ Ⓑ Ⓒ Ⓓ Ⓔ	22 Ⓐ Ⓑ Ⓒ Ⓓ Ⓔ	22 Ⓐ Ⓑ Ⓒ Ⓓ Ⓔ
23 Ⓐ Ⓑ Ⓒ Ⓓ Ⓔ	23 Ⓐ Ⓑ Ⓒ Ⓓ Ⓔ	23 Ⓐ Ⓑ Ⓒ Ⓓ Ⓔ	23 Ⓐ Ⓑ Ⓒ Ⓓ Ⓔ
24 Ⓐ Ⓑ Ⓒ Ⓓ Ⓔ	24 Ⓐ Ⓑ Ⓒ Ⓓ Ⓔ	24 Ⓐ Ⓑ Ⓒ Ⓓ Ⓔ	24 Ⓐ Ⓑ Ⓒ Ⓓ Ⓔ
25 Ⓐ Ⓑ Ⓒ Ⓓ Ⓔ	25 Ⓐ Ⓑ Ⓒ Ⓓ Ⓔ	25 Ⓐ Ⓑ Ⓒ Ⓓ Ⓔ	25 Ⓐ Ⓑ Ⓒ Ⓓ Ⓔ
26 Ⓐ Ⓑ Ⓒ Ⓓ Ⓔ	26 Ⓐ Ⓑ Ⓒ Ⓓ Ⓔ	26 Ⓐ Ⓑ Ⓒ Ⓓ Ⓔ	26 Ⓐ Ⓑ Ⓒ Ⓓ Ⓔ
27 Ⓐ Ⓑ Ⓒ Ⓓ Ⓔ	27 Ⓐ Ⓑ Ⓒ Ⓓ Ⓔ	27 Ⓐ Ⓑ Ⓒ Ⓓ Ⓔ	27 Ⓐ Ⓑ Ⓒ Ⓓ Ⓔ
28 Ⓐ Ⓑ Ⓒ Ⓓ Ⓔ	28 Ⓐ Ⓑ Ⓒ Ⓓ Ⓔ	28 Ⓐ Ⓑ Ⓒ Ⓓ Ⓔ	28 Ⓐ Ⓑ Ⓒ Ⓓ Ⓔ
29 Ⓐ Ⓑ Ⓒ Ⓓ Ⓔ	29 Ⓐ Ⓑ Ⓒ Ⓓ Ⓔ	29 Ⓐ Ⓑ Ⓒ Ⓓ Ⓔ	29 Ⓐ Ⓑ Ⓒ Ⓓ Ⓔ
30 Ⓐ Ⓑ Ⓒ Ⓓ Ⓔ	30 Ⓐ Ⓑ Ⓒ Ⓓ Ⓔ	30 Ⓐ Ⓑ Ⓒ Ⓓ Ⓔ	30 Ⓐ Ⓑ Ⓒ Ⓓ Ⓔ

LSAT Answer Sheet

Instructions for completing these items are at the back of your LSAT test book.

1. Name (Print)

Last   First   MI

2. LSAC Account Number L ☐☐☐☐☐☐☐

Section 1	Section 2	Section 3	Section 4
1 Ⓐ Ⓑ Ⓒ Ⓓ Ⓔ	1 Ⓐ Ⓑ Ⓒ Ⓓ Ⓔ	1 Ⓐ Ⓑ Ⓒ Ⓓ Ⓔ	1 Ⓐ Ⓑ Ⓒ Ⓓ Ⓔ
2 Ⓐ Ⓑ Ⓒ Ⓓ Ⓔ	2 Ⓐ Ⓑ Ⓒ Ⓓ Ⓔ	2 Ⓐ Ⓑ Ⓒ Ⓓ Ⓔ	2 Ⓐ Ⓑ Ⓒ Ⓓ Ⓔ
3 Ⓐ Ⓑ Ⓒ Ⓓ Ⓔ	3 Ⓐ Ⓑ Ⓒ Ⓓ Ⓔ	3 Ⓐ Ⓑ Ⓒ Ⓓ Ⓔ	3 Ⓐ Ⓑ Ⓒ Ⓓ Ⓔ
4 Ⓐ Ⓑ Ⓒ Ⓓ Ⓔ	4 Ⓐ Ⓑ Ⓒ Ⓓ Ⓔ	4 Ⓐ Ⓑ Ⓒ Ⓓ Ⓔ	4 Ⓐ Ⓑ Ⓒ Ⓓ Ⓔ
5 Ⓐ Ⓑ Ⓒ Ⓓ Ⓔ	5 Ⓐ Ⓑ Ⓒ Ⓓ Ⓔ	5 Ⓐ Ⓑ Ⓒ Ⓓ Ⓔ	5 Ⓐ Ⓑ Ⓒ Ⓓ Ⓔ
6 Ⓐ Ⓑ Ⓒ Ⓓ Ⓔ	6 Ⓐ Ⓑ Ⓒ Ⓓ Ⓔ	6 Ⓐ Ⓑ Ⓒ Ⓓ Ⓔ	6 Ⓐ Ⓑ Ⓒ Ⓓ Ⓔ
7 Ⓐ Ⓑ Ⓒ Ⓓ Ⓔ	7 Ⓐ Ⓑ Ⓒ Ⓓ Ⓔ	7 Ⓐ Ⓑ Ⓒ Ⓓ Ⓔ	7 Ⓐ Ⓑ Ⓒ Ⓓ Ⓔ
8 Ⓐ Ⓑ Ⓒ Ⓓ Ⓔ	8 Ⓐ Ⓑ Ⓒ Ⓓ Ⓔ	8 Ⓐ Ⓑ Ⓒ Ⓓ Ⓔ	8 Ⓐ Ⓑ Ⓒ Ⓓ Ⓔ
9 Ⓐ Ⓑ Ⓒ Ⓓ Ⓔ	9 Ⓐ Ⓑ Ⓒ Ⓓ Ⓔ	9 Ⓐ Ⓑ Ⓒ Ⓓ Ⓔ	9 Ⓐ Ⓑ Ⓒ Ⓓ Ⓔ
10 Ⓐ Ⓑ Ⓒ Ⓓ Ⓔ	10 Ⓐ Ⓑ Ⓒ Ⓓ Ⓔ	10 Ⓐ Ⓑ Ⓒ Ⓓ Ⓔ	10 Ⓐ Ⓑ Ⓒ Ⓓ Ⓔ
11 Ⓐ Ⓑ Ⓒ Ⓓ Ⓔ	11 Ⓐ Ⓑ Ⓒ Ⓓ Ⓔ	11 Ⓐ Ⓑ Ⓒ Ⓓ Ⓔ	11 Ⓐ Ⓑ Ⓒ Ⓓ Ⓔ
12 Ⓐ Ⓑ Ⓒ Ⓓ Ⓔ	12 Ⓐ Ⓑ Ⓒ Ⓓ Ⓔ	12 Ⓐ Ⓑ Ⓒ Ⓓ Ⓔ	12 Ⓐ Ⓑ Ⓒ Ⓓ Ⓔ
13 Ⓐ Ⓑ Ⓒ Ⓓ Ⓔ	13 Ⓐ Ⓑ Ⓒ Ⓓ Ⓔ	13 Ⓐ Ⓑ Ⓒ Ⓓ Ⓔ	13 Ⓐ Ⓑ Ⓒ Ⓓ Ⓔ
14 Ⓐ Ⓑ Ⓒ Ⓓ Ⓔ	14 Ⓐ Ⓑ Ⓒ Ⓓ Ⓔ	14 Ⓐ Ⓑ Ⓒ Ⓓ Ⓔ	14 Ⓐ Ⓑ Ⓒ Ⓓ Ⓔ
15 Ⓐ Ⓑ Ⓒ Ⓓ Ⓔ	15 Ⓐ Ⓑ Ⓒ Ⓓ Ⓔ	15 Ⓐ Ⓑ Ⓒ Ⓓ Ⓔ	15 Ⓐ Ⓑ Ⓒ Ⓓ Ⓔ
16 Ⓐ Ⓑ Ⓒ Ⓓ Ⓔ	16 Ⓐ Ⓑ Ⓒ Ⓓ Ⓔ	16 Ⓐ Ⓑ Ⓒ Ⓓ Ⓔ	16 Ⓐ Ⓑ Ⓒ Ⓓ Ⓔ
17 Ⓐ Ⓑ Ⓒ Ⓓ Ⓔ	17 Ⓐ Ⓑ Ⓒ Ⓓ Ⓔ	17 Ⓐ Ⓑ Ⓒ Ⓓ Ⓔ	17 Ⓐ Ⓑ Ⓒ Ⓓ Ⓔ
18 Ⓐ Ⓑ Ⓒ Ⓓ Ⓔ	18 Ⓐ Ⓑ Ⓒ Ⓓ Ⓔ	18 Ⓐ Ⓑ Ⓒ Ⓓ Ⓔ	18 Ⓐ Ⓑ Ⓒ Ⓓ Ⓔ
19 Ⓐ Ⓑ Ⓒ Ⓓ Ⓔ	19 Ⓐ Ⓑ Ⓒ Ⓓ Ⓔ	19 Ⓐ Ⓑ Ⓒ Ⓓ Ⓔ	19 Ⓐ Ⓑ Ⓒ Ⓓ Ⓔ
20 Ⓐ Ⓑ Ⓒ Ⓓ Ⓔ	20 Ⓐ Ⓑ Ⓒ Ⓓ Ⓔ	20 Ⓐ Ⓑ Ⓒ Ⓓ Ⓔ	20 Ⓐ Ⓑ Ⓒ Ⓓ Ⓔ
21 Ⓐ Ⓑ Ⓒ Ⓓ Ⓔ	21 Ⓐ Ⓑ Ⓒ Ⓓ Ⓔ	21 Ⓐ Ⓑ Ⓒ Ⓓ Ⓔ	21 Ⓐ Ⓑ Ⓒ Ⓓ Ⓔ
22 Ⓐ Ⓑ Ⓒ Ⓓ Ⓔ	22 Ⓐ Ⓑ Ⓒ Ⓓ Ⓔ	22 Ⓐ Ⓑ Ⓒ Ⓓ Ⓔ	22 Ⓐ Ⓑ Ⓒ Ⓓ Ⓔ
23 Ⓐ Ⓑ Ⓒ Ⓓ Ⓔ	23 Ⓐ Ⓑ Ⓒ Ⓓ Ⓔ	23 Ⓐ Ⓑ Ⓒ Ⓓ Ⓔ	23 Ⓐ Ⓑ Ⓒ Ⓓ Ⓔ
24 Ⓐ Ⓑ Ⓒ Ⓓ Ⓔ	24 Ⓐ Ⓑ Ⓒ Ⓓ Ⓔ	24 Ⓐ Ⓑ Ⓒ Ⓓ Ⓔ	24 Ⓐ Ⓑ Ⓒ Ⓓ Ⓔ
25 Ⓐ Ⓑ Ⓒ Ⓓ Ⓔ	25 Ⓐ Ⓑ Ⓒ Ⓓ Ⓔ	25 Ⓐ Ⓑ Ⓒ Ⓓ Ⓔ	25 Ⓐ Ⓑ Ⓒ Ⓓ Ⓔ
26 Ⓐ Ⓑ Ⓒ Ⓓ Ⓔ	26 Ⓐ Ⓑ Ⓒ Ⓓ Ⓔ	26 Ⓐ Ⓑ Ⓒ Ⓓ Ⓔ	26 Ⓐ Ⓑ Ⓒ Ⓓ Ⓔ
27 Ⓐ Ⓑ Ⓒ Ⓓ Ⓔ	27 Ⓐ Ⓑ Ⓒ Ⓓ Ⓔ	27 Ⓐ Ⓑ Ⓒ Ⓓ Ⓔ	27 Ⓐ Ⓑ Ⓒ Ⓓ Ⓔ
28 Ⓐ Ⓑ Ⓒ Ⓓ Ⓔ	28 Ⓐ Ⓑ Ⓒ Ⓓ Ⓔ	28 Ⓐ Ⓑ Ⓒ Ⓓ Ⓔ	28 Ⓐ Ⓑ Ⓒ Ⓓ Ⓔ
29 Ⓐ Ⓑ Ⓒ Ⓓ Ⓔ	29 Ⓐ Ⓑ Ⓒ Ⓓ Ⓔ	29 Ⓐ Ⓑ Ⓒ Ⓓ Ⓔ	29 Ⓐ Ⓑ Ⓒ Ⓓ Ⓔ
30 Ⓐ Ⓑ Ⓒ Ⓓ Ⓔ	30 Ⓐ Ⓑ Ⓒ Ⓓ Ⓔ	30 Ⓐ Ⓑ Ⓒ Ⓓ Ⓔ	30 Ⓐ Ⓑ Ⓒ Ⓓ Ⓔ

LSAT Answer Sheet

Instructions for completing these items are at the back of your LSAT test book.

1. Name (Print)

Last   First   MI

2. LSAC Account Number L

Section 1

#	A	B	C	D	E
1	Ⓐ	Ⓑ	Ⓒ	Ⓓ	Ⓔ
2	Ⓐ	Ⓑ	Ⓒ	Ⓓ	Ⓔ
3	Ⓐ	Ⓑ	Ⓒ	Ⓓ	Ⓔ
4	Ⓐ	Ⓑ	Ⓒ	Ⓓ	Ⓔ
5	Ⓐ	Ⓑ	Ⓒ	Ⓓ	Ⓔ
6	Ⓐ	Ⓑ	Ⓒ	Ⓓ	Ⓔ
7	Ⓐ	Ⓑ	Ⓒ	Ⓓ	Ⓔ
8	Ⓐ	Ⓑ	Ⓒ	Ⓓ	Ⓔ
9	Ⓐ	Ⓑ	Ⓒ	Ⓓ	Ⓔ
10	Ⓐ	Ⓑ	Ⓒ	Ⓓ	Ⓔ
11	Ⓐ	Ⓑ	Ⓒ	Ⓓ	Ⓔ
12	Ⓐ	Ⓑ	Ⓒ	Ⓓ	Ⓔ
13	Ⓐ	Ⓑ	Ⓒ	Ⓓ	Ⓔ
14	Ⓐ	Ⓑ	Ⓒ	Ⓓ	Ⓔ
15	Ⓐ	Ⓑ	Ⓒ	Ⓓ	Ⓔ
16	Ⓐ	Ⓑ	Ⓒ	Ⓓ	Ⓔ
17	Ⓐ	Ⓑ	Ⓒ	Ⓓ	Ⓔ
18	Ⓐ	Ⓑ	Ⓒ	Ⓓ	Ⓔ
19	Ⓐ	Ⓑ	Ⓒ	Ⓓ	Ⓔ
20	Ⓐ	Ⓑ	Ⓒ	Ⓓ	Ⓔ
21	Ⓐ	Ⓑ	Ⓒ	Ⓓ	Ⓔ
22	Ⓐ	Ⓑ	Ⓒ	Ⓓ	Ⓔ
23	Ⓐ	Ⓑ	Ⓒ	Ⓓ	Ⓔ
24	Ⓐ	Ⓑ	Ⓒ	Ⓓ	Ⓔ
25	Ⓐ	Ⓑ	Ⓒ	Ⓓ	Ⓔ
26	Ⓐ	Ⓑ	Ⓒ	Ⓓ	Ⓔ
27	Ⓐ	Ⓑ	Ⓒ	Ⓓ	Ⓔ
28	Ⓐ	Ⓑ	Ⓒ	Ⓓ	Ⓔ
29	Ⓐ	Ⓑ	Ⓒ	Ⓓ	Ⓔ
30	Ⓐ	Ⓑ	Ⓒ	Ⓓ	Ⓔ

Section 2

#	A	B	C	D	E
1	Ⓐ	Ⓑ	Ⓒ	Ⓓ	Ⓔ
2	Ⓐ	Ⓑ	Ⓒ	Ⓓ	Ⓔ
3	Ⓐ	Ⓑ	Ⓒ	Ⓓ	Ⓔ
4	Ⓐ	Ⓑ	Ⓒ	Ⓓ	Ⓔ
5	Ⓐ	Ⓑ	Ⓒ	Ⓓ	Ⓔ
6	Ⓐ	Ⓑ	Ⓒ	Ⓓ	Ⓔ
7	Ⓐ	Ⓑ	Ⓒ	Ⓓ	Ⓔ
8	Ⓐ	Ⓑ	Ⓒ	Ⓓ	Ⓔ
9	Ⓐ	Ⓑ	Ⓒ	Ⓓ	Ⓔ
10	Ⓐ	Ⓑ	Ⓒ	Ⓓ	Ⓔ
11	Ⓐ	Ⓑ	Ⓒ	Ⓓ	Ⓔ
12	Ⓐ	Ⓑ	Ⓒ	Ⓓ	Ⓔ
13	Ⓐ	Ⓑ	Ⓒ	Ⓓ	Ⓔ
14	Ⓐ	Ⓑ	Ⓒ	Ⓓ	Ⓔ
15	Ⓐ	Ⓑ	Ⓒ	Ⓓ	Ⓔ
16	Ⓐ	Ⓑ	Ⓒ	Ⓓ	Ⓔ
17	Ⓐ	Ⓑ	Ⓒ	Ⓓ	Ⓔ
18	Ⓐ	Ⓑ	Ⓒ	Ⓓ	Ⓔ
19	Ⓐ	Ⓑ	Ⓒ	Ⓓ	Ⓔ
20	Ⓐ	Ⓑ	Ⓒ	Ⓓ	Ⓔ
21	Ⓐ	Ⓑ	Ⓒ	Ⓓ	Ⓔ
22	Ⓐ	Ⓑ	Ⓒ	Ⓓ	Ⓔ
23	Ⓐ	Ⓑ	Ⓒ	Ⓓ	Ⓔ
24	Ⓐ	Ⓑ	Ⓒ	Ⓓ	Ⓔ
25	Ⓐ	Ⓑ	Ⓒ	Ⓓ	Ⓔ
26	Ⓐ	Ⓑ	Ⓒ	Ⓓ	Ⓔ
27	Ⓐ	Ⓑ	Ⓒ	Ⓓ	Ⓔ
28	Ⓐ	Ⓑ	Ⓒ	Ⓓ	Ⓔ
29	Ⓐ	Ⓑ	Ⓒ	Ⓓ	Ⓔ
30	Ⓐ	Ⓑ	Ⓒ	Ⓓ	Ⓔ

Section 3

#	A	B	C	D	E
1	Ⓐ	Ⓑ	Ⓒ	Ⓓ	Ⓔ
2	Ⓐ	Ⓑ	Ⓒ	Ⓓ	Ⓔ
3	Ⓐ	Ⓑ	Ⓒ	Ⓓ	Ⓔ
4	Ⓐ	Ⓑ	Ⓒ	Ⓓ	Ⓔ
5	Ⓐ	Ⓑ	Ⓒ	Ⓓ	Ⓔ
6	Ⓐ	Ⓑ	Ⓒ	Ⓓ	Ⓔ
7	Ⓐ	Ⓑ	Ⓒ	Ⓓ	Ⓔ
8	Ⓐ	Ⓑ	Ⓒ	Ⓓ	Ⓔ
9	Ⓐ	Ⓑ	Ⓒ	Ⓓ	Ⓔ
10	Ⓐ	Ⓑ	Ⓒ	Ⓓ	Ⓔ
11	Ⓐ	Ⓑ	Ⓒ	Ⓓ	Ⓔ
12	Ⓐ	Ⓑ	Ⓒ	Ⓓ	Ⓔ
13	Ⓐ	Ⓑ	Ⓒ	Ⓓ	Ⓔ
14	Ⓐ	Ⓑ	Ⓒ	Ⓓ	Ⓔ
15	Ⓐ	Ⓑ	Ⓒ	Ⓓ	Ⓔ
16	Ⓐ	Ⓑ	Ⓒ	Ⓓ	Ⓔ
17	Ⓐ	Ⓑ	Ⓒ	Ⓓ	Ⓔ
18	Ⓐ	Ⓑ	Ⓒ	Ⓓ	Ⓔ
19	Ⓐ	Ⓑ	Ⓒ	Ⓓ	Ⓔ
20	Ⓐ	Ⓑ	Ⓒ	Ⓓ	Ⓔ
21	Ⓐ	Ⓑ	Ⓒ	Ⓓ	Ⓔ
22	Ⓐ	Ⓑ	Ⓒ	Ⓓ	Ⓔ
23	Ⓐ	Ⓑ	Ⓒ	Ⓓ	Ⓔ
24	Ⓐ	Ⓑ	Ⓒ	Ⓓ	Ⓔ
25	Ⓐ	Ⓑ	Ⓒ	Ⓓ	Ⓔ
26	Ⓐ	Ⓑ	Ⓒ	Ⓓ	Ⓔ
27	Ⓐ	Ⓑ	Ⓒ	Ⓓ	Ⓔ
28	Ⓐ	Ⓑ	Ⓒ	Ⓓ	Ⓔ
29	Ⓐ	Ⓑ	Ⓒ	Ⓓ	Ⓔ
30	Ⓐ	Ⓑ	Ⓒ	Ⓓ	Ⓔ

Section 4

#	A	B	C	D	E
1	Ⓐ	Ⓑ	Ⓒ	Ⓓ	Ⓔ
2	Ⓐ	Ⓑ	Ⓒ	Ⓓ	Ⓔ
3	Ⓐ	Ⓑ	Ⓒ	Ⓓ	Ⓔ
4	Ⓐ	Ⓑ	Ⓒ	Ⓓ	Ⓔ
5	Ⓐ	Ⓑ	Ⓒ	Ⓓ	Ⓔ
6	Ⓐ	Ⓑ	Ⓒ	Ⓓ	Ⓔ
7	Ⓐ	Ⓑ	Ⓒ	Ⓓ	Ⓔ
8	Ⓐ	Ⓑ	Ⓒ	Ⓓ	Ⓔ
9	Ⓐ	Ⓑ	Ⓒ	Ⓓ	Ⓔ
10	Ⓐ	Ⓑ	Ⓒ	Ⓓ	Ⓔ
11	Ⓐ	Ⓑ	Ⓒ	Ⓓ	Ⓔ
12	Ⓐ	Ⓑ	Ⓒ	Ⓓ	Ⓔ
13	Ⓐ	Ⓑ	Ⓒ	Ⓓ	Ⓔ
14	Ⓐ	Ⓑ	Ⓒ	Ⓓ	Ⓔ
15	Ⓐ	Ⓑ	Ⓒ	Ⓓ	Ⓔ
16	Ⓐ	Ⓑ	Ⓒ	Ⓓ	Ⓔ
17	Ⓐ	Ⓑ	Ⓒ	Ⓓ	Ⓔ
18	Ⓐ	Ⓑ	Ⓒ	Ⓓ	Ⓔ
19	Ⓐ	Ⓑ	Ⓒ	Ⓓ	Ⓔ
20	Ⓐ	Ⓑ	Ⓒ	Ⓓ	Ⓔ
21	Ⓐ	Ⓑ	Ⓒ	Ⓓ	Ⓔ
22	Ⓐ	Ⓑ	Ⓒ	Ⓓ	Ⓔ
23	Ⓐ	Ⓑ	Ⓒ	Ⓓ	Ⓔ
24	Ⓐ	Ⓑ	Ⓒ	Ⓓ	Ⓔ
25	Ⓐ	Ⓑ	Ⓒ	Ⓓ	Ⓔ
26	Ⓐ	Ⓑ	Ⓒ	Ⓓ	Ⓔ
27	Ⓐ	Ⓑ	Ⓒ	Ⓓ	Ⓔ
28	Ⓐ	Ⓑ	Ⓒ	Ⓓ	Ⓔ
29	Ⓐ	Ⓑ	Ⓒ	Ⓓ	Ⓔ
30	Ⓐ	Ⓑ	Ⓒ	Ⓓ	Ⓔ

LSAT Answer Sheet

Instructions for completing these items are at the back of your LSAT test book.

1. Name (Print)

Last   First   MI

2. LSAC Account Number L ☐☐☐☐☐☐☐☐

Section 1	Section 2	Section 3	Section 4
1 Ⓐ Ⓑ Ⓒ Ⓓ Ⓔ	1 Ⓐ Ⓑ Ⓒ Ⓓ Ⓔ	1 Ⓐ Ⓑ Ⓒ Ⓓ Ⓔ	1 Ⓐ Ⓑ Ⓒ Ⓓ Ⓔ
2 Ⓐ Ⓑ Ⓒ Ⓓ Ⓔ	2 Ⓐ Ⓑ Ⓒ Ⓓ Ⓔ	2 Ⓐ Ⓑ Ⓒ Ⓓ Ⓔ	2 Ⓐ Ⓑ Ⓒ Ⓓ Ⓔ
3 Ⓐ Ⓑ Ⓒ Ⓓ Ⓔ	3 Ⓐ Ⓑ Ⓒ Ⓓ Ⓔ	3 Ⓐ Ⓑ Ⓒ Ⓓ Ⓔ	3 Ⓐ Ⓑ Ⓒ Ⓓ Ⓔ
4 Ⓐ Ⓑ Ⓒ Ⓓ Ⓔ	4 Ⓐ Ⓑ Ⓒ Ⓓ Ⓔ	4 Ⓐ Ⓑ Ⓒ Ⓓ Ⓔ	4 Ⓐ Ⓑ Ⓒ Ⓓ Ⓔ
5 Ⓐ Ⓑ Ⓒ Ⓓ Ⓔ	5 Ⓐ Ⓑ Ⓒ Ⓓ Ⓔ	5 Ⓐ Ⓑ Ⓒ Ⓓ Ⓔ	5 Ⓐ Ⓑ Ⓒ Ⓓ Ⓔ
6 Ⓐ Ⓑ Ⓒ Ⓓ Ⓔ	6 Ⓐ Ⓑ Ⓒ Ⓓ Ⓔ	6 Ⓐ Ⓑ Ⓒ Ⓓ Ⓔ	6 Ⓐ Ⓑ Ⓒ Ⓓ Ⓔ
7 Ⓐ Ⓑ Ⓒ Ⓓ Ⓔ	7 Ⓐ Ⓑ Ⓒ Ⓓ Ⓔ	7 Ⓐ Ⓑ Ⓒ Ⓓ Ⓔ	7 Ⓐ Ⓑ Ⓒ Ⓓ Ⓔ
8 Ⓐ Ⓑ Ⓒ Ⓓ Ⓔ	8 Ⓐ Ⓑ Ⓒ Ⓓ Ⓔ	8 Ⓐ Ⓑ Ⓒ Ⓓ Ⓔ	8 Ⓐ Ⓑ Ⓒ Ⓓ Ⓔ
9 Ⓐ Ⓑ Ⓒ Ⓓ Ⓔ	9 Ⓐ Ⓑ Ⓒ Ⓓ Ⓔ	9 Ⓐ Ⓑ Ⓒ Ⓓ Ⓔ	9 Ⓐ Ⓑ Ⓒ Ⓓ Ⓔ
10 Ⓐ Ⓑ Ⓒ Ⓓ Ⓔ	10 Ⓐ Ⓑ Ⓒ Ⓓ Ⓔ	10 Ⓐ Ⓑ Ⓒ Ⓓ Ⓔ	10 Ⓐ Ⓑ Ⓒ Ⓓ Ⓔ
11 Ⓐ Ⓑ Ⓒ Ⓓ Ⓔ	11 Ⓐ Ⓑ Ⓒ Ⓓ Ⓔ	11 Ⓐ Ⓑ Ⓒ Ⓓ Ⓔ	11 Ⓐ Ⓑ Ⓒ Ⓓ Ⓔ
12 Ⓐ Ⓑ Ⓒ Ⓓ Ⓔ	12 Ⓐ Ⓑ Ⓒ Ⓓ Ⓔ	12 Ⓐ Ⓑ Ⓒ Ⓓ Ⓔ	12 Ⓐ Ⓑ Ⓒ Ⓓ Ⓔ
13 Ⓐ Ⓑ Ⓒ Ⓓ Ⓔ	13 Ⓐ Ⓑ Ⓒ Ⓓ Ⓔ	13 Ⓐ Ⓑ Ⓒ Ⓓ Ⓔ	13 Ⓐ Ⓑ Ⓒ Ⓓ Ⓔ
14 Ⓐ Ⓑ Ⓒ Ⓓ Ⓔ	14 Ⓐ Ⓑ Ⓒ Ⓓ Ⓔ	14 Ⓐ Ⓑ Ⓒ Ⓓ Ⓔ	14 Ⓐ Ⓑ Ⓒ Ⓓ Ⓔ
15 Ⓐ Ⓑ Ⓒ Ⓓ Ⓔ	15 Ⓐ Ⓑ Ⓒ Ⓓ Ⓔ	15 Ⓐ Ⓑ Ⓒ Ⓓ Ⓔ	15 Ⓐ Ⓑ Ⓒ Ⓓ Ⓔ
16 Ⓐ Ⓑ Ⓒ Ⓓ Ⓔ	16 Ⓐ Ⓑ Ⓒ Ⓓ Ⓔ	16 Ⓐ Ⓑ Ⓒ Ⓓ Ⓔ	16 Ⓐ Ⓑ Ⓒ Ⓓ Ⓔ
17 Ⓐ Ⓑ Ⓒ Ⓓ Ⓔ	17 Ⓐ Ⓑ Ⓒ Ⓓ Ⓔ	17 Ⓐ Ⓑ Ⓒ Ⓓ Ⓔ	17 Ⓐ Ⓑ Ⓒ Ⓓ Ⓔ
18 Ⓐ Ⓑ Ⓒ Ⓓ Ⓔ	18 Ⓐ Ⓑ Ⓒ Ⓓ Ⓔ	18 Ⓐ Ⓑ Ⓒ Ⓓ Ⓔ	18 Ⓐ Ⓑ Ⓒ Ⓓ Ⓔ
19 Ⓐ Ⓑ Ⓒ Ⓓ Ⓔ	19 Ⓐ Ⓑ Ⓒ Ⓓ Ⓔ	19 Ⓐ Ⓑ Ⓒ Ⓓ Ⓔ	19 Ⓐ Ⓑ Ⓒ Ⓓ Ⓔ
20 Ⓐ Ⓑ Ⓒ Ⓓ Ⓔ	20 Ⓐ Ⓑ Ⓒ Ⓓ Ⓔ	20 Ⓐ Ⓑ Ⓒ Ⓓ Ⓔ	20 Ⓐ Ⓑ Ⓒ Ⓓ Ⓔ
21 Ⓐ Ⓑ Ⓒ Ⓓ Ⓔ	21 Ⓐ Ⓑ Ⓒ Ⓓ Ⓔ	21 Ⓐ Ⓑ Ⓒ Ⓓ Ⓔ	21 Ⓐ Ⓑ Ⓒ Ⓓ Ⓔ
22 Ⓐ Ⓑ Ⓒ Ⓓ Ⓔ	22 Ⓐ Ⓑ Ⓒ Ⓓ Ⓔ	22 Ⓐ Ⓑ Ⓒ Ⓓ Ⓔ	22 Ⓐ Ⓑ Ⓒ Ⓓ Ⓔ
23 Ⓐ Ⓑ Ⓒ Ⓓ Ⓔ	23 Ⓐ Ⓑ Ⓒ Ⓓ Ⓔ	23 Ⓐ Ⓑ Ⓒ Ⓓ Ⓔ	23 Ⓐ Ⓑ Ⓒ Ⓓ Ⓔ
24 Ⓐ Ⓑ Ⓒ Ⓓ Ⓔ	24 Ⓐ Ⓑ Ⓒ Ⓓ Ⓔ	24 Ⓐ Ⓑ Ⓒ Ⓓ Ⓔ	24 Ⓐ Ⓑ Ⓒ Ⓓ Ⓔ
25 Ⓐ Ⓑ Ⓒ Ⓓ Ⓔ	25 Ⓐ Ⓑ Ⓒ Ⓓ Ⓔ	25 Ⓐ Ⓑ Ⓒ Ⓓ Ⓔ	25 Ⓐ Ⓑ Ⓒ Ⓓ Ⓔ
26 Ⓐ Ⓑ Ⓒ Ⓓ Ⓔ	26 Ⓐ Ⓑ Ⓒ Ⓓ Ⓔ	26 Ⓐ Ⓑ Ⓒ Ⓓ Ⓔ	26 Ⓐ Ⓑ Ⓒ Ⓓ Ⓔ
27 Ⓐ Ⓑ Ⓒ Ⓓ Ⓔ	27 Ⓐ Ⓑ Ⓒ Ⓓ Ⓔ	27 Ⓐ Ⓑ Ⓒ Ⓓ Ⓔ	27 Ⓐ Ⓑ Ⓒ Ⓓ Ⓔ
28 Ⓐ Ⓑ Ⓒ Ⓓ Ⓔ	28 Ⓐ Ⓑ Ⓒ Ⓓ Ⓔ	28 Ⓐ Ⓑ Ⓒ Ⓓ Ⓔ	28 Ⓐ Ⓑ Ⓒ Ⓓ Ⓔ
29 Ⓐ Ⓑ Ⓒ Ⓓ Ⓔ	29 Ⓐ Ⓑ Ⓒ Ⓓ Ⓔ	29 Ⓐ Ⓑ Ⓒ Ⓓ Ⓔ	29 Ⓐ Ⓑ Ⓒ Ⓓ Ⓔ
30 Ⓐ Ⓑ Ⓒ Ⓓ Ⓔ	30 Ⓐ Ⓑ Ⓒ Ⓓ Ⓔ	30 Ⓐ Ⓑ Ⓒ Ⓓ Ⓔ	30 Ⓐ Ⓑ Ⓒ Ⓓ Ⓔ

LSAT Answer Sheet

Instructions for completing these items are at the back of your LSAT test book.

1. Name (Print)

Last ⬜⬜⬜⬜⬜⬜⬜⬜⬜⬜⬜⬜⬜⬜⬜⬜

First ⬜⬜⬜⬜⬜⬜⬜⬜⬜⬜⬜⬜⬜⬜⬜⬜⬜

MI ⬜

2. LSAC Account Number L ⬜⬜⬜⬜⬜⬜⬜⬜

Section 1	Section 2	Section 3	Section 4
1 Ⓐ Ⓑ Ⓒ Ⓓ Ⓔ	1 Ⓐ Ⓑ Ⓒ Ⓓ Ⓔ	1 Ⓐ Ⓑ Ⓒ Ⓓ Ⓔ	1 Ⓐ Ⓑ Ⓒ Ⓓ Ⓔ
2 Ⓐ Ⓑ Ⓒ Ⓓ Ⓔ	2 Ⓐ Ⓑ Ⓒ Ⓓ Ⓔ	2 Ⓐ Ⓑ Ⓒ Ⓓ Ⓔ	2 Ⓐ Ⓑ Ⓒ Ⓓ Ⓔ
3 Ⓐ Ⓑ Ⓒ Ⓓ Ⓔ	3 Ⓐ Ⓑ Ⓒ Ⓓ Ⓔ	3 Ⓐ Ⓑ Ⓒ Ⓓ Ⓔ	3 Ⓐ Ⓑ Ⓒ Ⓓ Ⓔ
4 Ⓐ Ⓑ Ⓒ Ⓓ Ⓔ	4 Ⓐ Ⓑ Ⓒ Ⓓ Ⓔ	4 Ⓐ Ⓑ Ⓒ Ⓓ Ⓔ	4 Ⓐ Ⓑ Ⓒ Ⓓ Ⓔ
5 Ⓐ Ⓑ Ⓒ Ⓓ Ⓔ	5 Ⓐ Ⓑ Ⓒ Ⓓ Ⓔ	5 Ⓐ Ⓑ Ⓒ Ⓓ Ⓔ	5 Ⓐ Ⓑ Ⓒ Ⓓ Ⓔ
6 Ⓐ Ⓑ Ⓒ Ⓓ Ⓔ	6 Ⓐ Ⓑ Ⓒ Ⓓ Ⓔ	6 Ⓐ Ⓑ Ⓒ Ⓓ Ⓔ	6 Ⓐ Ⓑ Ⓒ Ⓓ Ⓔ
7 Ⓐ Ⓑ Ⓒ Ⓓ Ⓔ	7 Ⓐ Ⓑ Ⓒ Ⓓ Ⓔ	7 Ⓐ Ⓑ Ⓒ Ⓓ Ⓔ	7 Ⓐ Ⓑ Ⓒ Ⓓ Ⓔ
8 Ⓐ Ⓑ Ⓒ Ⓓ Ⓔ	8 Ⓐ Ⓑ Ⓒ Ⓓ Ⓔ	8 Ⓐ Ⓑ Ⓒ Ⓓ Ⓔ	8 Ⓐ Ⓑ Ⓒ Ⓓ Ⓔ
9 Ⓐ Ⓑ Ⓒ Ⓓ Ⓔ	9 Ⓐ Ⓑ Ⓒ Ⓓ Ⓔ	9 Ⓐ Ⓑ Ⓒ Ⓓ Ⓔ	9 Ⓐ Ⓑ Ⓒ Ⓓ Ⓔ
10 Ⓐ Ⓑ Ⓒ Ⓓ Ⓔ	10 Ⓐ Ⓑ Ⓒ Ⓓ Ⓔ	10 Ⓐ Ⓑ Ⓒ Ⓓ Ⓔ	10 Ⓐ Ⓑ Ⓒ Ⓓ Ⓔ
11 Ⓐ Ⓑ Ⓒ Ⓓ Ⓔ	11 Ⓐ Ⓑ Ⓒ Ⓓ Ⓔ	11 Ⓐ Ⓑ Ⓒ Ⓓ Ⓔ	11 Ⓐ Ⓑ Ⓒ Ⓓ Ⓔ
12 Ⓐ Ⓑ Ⓒ Ⓓ Ⓔ	12 Ⓐ Ⓑ Ⓒ Ⓓ Ⓔ	12 Ⓐ Ⓑ Ⓒ Ⓓ Ⓔ	12 Ⓐ Ⓑ Ⓒ Ⓓ Ⓔ
13 Ⓐ Ⓑ Ⓒ Ⓓ Ⓔ	13 Ⓐ Ⓑ Ⓒ Ⓓ Ⓔ	13 Ⓐ Ⓑ Ⓒ Ⓓ Ⓔ	13 Ⓐ Ⓑ Ⓒ Ⓓ Ⓔ
14 Ⓐ Ⓑ Ⓒ Ⓓ Ⓔ	14 Ⓐ Ⓑ Ⓒ Ⓓ Ⓔ	14 Ⓐ Ⓑ Ⓒ Ⓓ Ⓔ	14 Ⓐ Ⓑ Ⓒ Ⓓ Ⓔ
15 Ⓐ Ⓑ Ⓒ Ⓓ Ⓔ	15 Ⓐ Ⓑ Ⓒ Ⓓ Ⓔ	15 Ⓐ Ⓑ Ⓒ Ⓓ Ⓔ	15 Ⓐ Ⓑ Ⓒ Ⓓ Ⓔ
16 Ⓐ Ⓑ Ⓒ Ⓓ Ⓔ	16 Ⓐ Ⓑ Ⓒ Ⓓ Ⓔ	16 Ⓐ Ⓑ Ⓒ Ⓓ Ⓔ	16 Ⓐ Ⓑ Ⓒ Ⓓ Ⓔ
17 Ⓐ Ⓑ Ⓒ Ⓓ Ⓔ	17 Ⓐ Ⓑ Ⓒ Ⓓ Ⓔ	17 Ⓐ Ⓑ Ⓒ Ⓓ Ⓔ	17 Ⓐ Ⓑ Ⓒ Ⓓ Ⓔ
18 Ⓐ Ⓑ Ⓒ Ⓓ Ⓔ	18 Ⓐ Ⓑ Ⓒ Ⓓ Ⓔ	18 Ⓐ Ⓑ Ⓒ Ⓓ Ⓔ	18 Ⓐ Ⓑ Ⓒ Ⓓ Ⓔ
19 Ⓐ Ⓑ Ⓒ Ⓓ Ⓔ	19 Ⓐ Ⓑ Ⓒ Ⓓ Ⓔ	19 Ⓐ Ⓑ Ⓒ Ⓓ Ⓔ	19 Ⓐ Ⓑ Ⓒ Ⓓ Ⓔ
20 Ⓐ Ⓑ Ⓒ Ⓓ Ⓔ	20 Ⓐ Ⓑ Ⓒ Ⓓ Ⓔ	20 Ⓐ Ⓑ Ⓒ Ⓓ Ⓔ	20 Ⓐ Ⓑ Ⓒ Ⓓ Ⓔ
21 Ⓐ Ⓑ Ⓒ Ⓓ Ⓔ	21 Ⓐ Ⓑ Ⓒ Ⓓ Ⓔ	21 Ⓐ Ⓑ Ⓒ Ⓓ Ⓔ	21 Ⓐ Ⓑ Ⓒ Ⓓ Ⓔ
22 Ⓐ Ⓑ Ⓒ Ⓓ Ⓔ	22 Ⓐ Ⓑ Ⓒ Ⓓ Ⓔ	22 Ⓐ Ⓑ Ⓒ Ⓓ Ⓔ	22 Ⓐ Ⓑ Ⓒ Ⓓ Ⓔ
23 Ⓐ Ⓑ Ⓒ Ⓓ Ⓔ	23 Ⓐ Ⓑ Ⓒ Ⓓ Ⓔ	23 Ⓐ Ⓑ Ⓒ Ⓓ Ⓔ	23 Ⓐ Ⓑ Ⓒ Ⓓ Ⓔ
24 Ⓐ Ⓑ Ⓒ Ⓓ Ⓔ	24 Ⓐ Ⓑ Ⓒ Ⓓ Ⓔ	24 Ⓐ Ⓑ Ⓒ Ⓓ Ⓔ	24 Ⓐ Ⓑ Ⓒ Ⓓ Ⓔ
25 Ⓐ Ⓑ Ⓒ Ⓓ Ⓔ	25 Ⓐ Ⓑ Ⓒ Ⓓ Ⓔ	25 Ⓐ Ⓑ Ⓒ Ⓓ Ⓔ	25 Ⓐ Ⓑ Ⓒ Ⓓ Ⓔ
26 Ⓐ Ⓑ Ⓒ Ⓓ Ⓔ	26 Ⓐ Ⓑ Ⓒ Ⓓ Ⓔ	26 Ⓐ Ⓑ Ⓒ Ⓓ Ⓔ	26 Ⓐ Ⓑ Ⓒ Ⓓ Ⓔ
27 Ⓐ Ⓑ Ⓒ Ⓓ Ⓔ	27 Ⓐ Ⓑ Ⓒ Ⓓ Ⓔ	27 Ⓐ Ⓑ Ⓒ Ⓓ Ⓔ	27 Ⓐ Ⓑ Ⓒ Ⓓ Ⓔ
28 Ⓐ Ⓑ Ⓒ Ⓓ Ⓔ	28 Ⓐ Ⓑ Ⓒ Ⓓ Ⓔ	28 Ⓐ Ⓑ Ⓒ Ⓓ Ⓔ	28 Ⓐ Ⓑ Ⓒ Ⓓ Ⓔ
29 Ⓐ Ⓑ Ⓒ Ⓓ Ⓔ	29 Ⓐ Ⓑ Ⓒ Ⓓ Ⓔ	29 Ⓐ Ⓑ Ⓒ Ⓓ Ⓔ	29 Ⓐ Ⓑ Ⓒ Ⓓ Ⓔ
30 Ⓐ Ⓑ Ⓒ Ⓓ Ⓔ	30 Ⓐ Ⓑ Ⓒ Ⓓ Ⓔ	30 Ⓐ Ⓑ Ⓒ Ⓓ Ⓔ	30 Ⓐ Ⓑ Ⓒ Ⓓ Ⓔ